# Training Systems Using Python Statistical Modeling

Explore popular techniques for modeling your data in Python

**Curtis Miller**

**BIRMINGHAM - MUMBAI**

# Training Systems Using Python Statistical Modeling

**Commissioning Editor:** Sunith Shetty
**Acquisition Editor:** Devika Battike
**Content Development Editor:** Athikho Sapuni Rishana
**Technical Editor:** Joseph Sunil
**Copy Editor:** Safis Editing
**Project Coordinator:** Kirti Pisat
**Proofreader:** Safis Editing
**Indexer:** Rekha Nair
**Graphics:** Jisha Chirayil
**Production Coordinator:** Nilesh Mohite

First published: May 2019

Production reference: 1150519

Published by Packt Publishing Ltd.
Livery Place
35 Livery Street
Birmingham
B3 2PB, UK.

ISBN 978-1-83882-373-3

www.packtpub.com

`mapt.io`

Mapt is an online digital library that gives you full access to over 5,000 books and videos, as well as industry leading tools to help you plan your personal development and advance your career. For more information, please visit our website.

# Why subscribe?

- Spend less time learning and more time coding with practical eBooks and Videos from over 4,000 industry professionals

- Improve your learning with Skill Plans built especially for you

- Get a free eBook or video every month

- Mapt is fully searchable

- Copy and paste, print, and bookmark content

# Packt.com

Did you know that Packt offers eBook versions of every book published, with PDF and ePub files available? You can upgrade to the eBook version at `www.packt.com` and as a print book customer, you are entitled to a discount on the eBook copy. Get in touch with us at `customercare@packtpub.com` for more details.

At `www.packt.com`, you can also read a collection of free technical articles, sign up for a range of free newsletters, and receive exclusive discounts and offers on Packt books and eBooks.

# Contributors

## About the author

**Curtis Miller** is a doctoral candidate at the University of Utah studying mathematical statistics. He writes software for both research and personal interest, including the R package (CPAT) available on the Comprehensive R Archive Network (CRAN). Among Curtis Miller's publications are academic papers along with books and video courses all published by Packt Publishing. Curtis Miller's video courses include Unpacking NumPy and Pandas, Data Acquisition and Manipulation with Python, Training Your Systems with Python Statistical Modelling, and Applications of Statistical Learning with Python. His books include Hands-On Data Analysis with NumPy and Pandas.

## Packt is searching for authors like you

If you're interested in becoming an author for Packt, please visit `authors.packtpub.com` and apply today. We have worked with thousands of developers and tech professionals, just like you, to help them share their insight with the global tech community. You can make a general application, apply for a specific hot topic that we are recruiting an author for, or submit your own idea.

# Table of Contents

# Preface

Python, a multi-paradigm programming language, has become the language of choice for data scientists for data analysis, visualization, and machine learning. *Training Systems Using Python Statistical Modeling* takes you through various different concepts that get you acquainted and working with the different aspects of machine learning.

You will get acquainted and work with the different aspects of machine learning and statistical analysis. You will start with classical statistical analysis. You will explore the principles of machine learning and train different machine learning models, and work with binary prediction models, decision trees, and random forests. You will implement different types of regression, work on neural networks, and train them. You will also learn how to evaluate cluster model results. By the end of this book, you will be confident in using various machine learning models, training them, evaluating model results, and implementing various dimensionality reduction techniques.

## Who this book is for

If you are a statistician or a data analyst and want to learn how to build statistical modeling systems using Python tools and packages, then this is the perfect book for you. You will dive into various different aspects of statistical modeling and training, and will learn how to employ those concepts using the Python programming language.

## What this book covers

Chapter 1, *Classical Statistical Analysis*, helps you apply your knowledge of Python and machine learning to create data models and perform statistical analysis. You will learn about various statistical learning techniques and learn how to apply them in data analysis.

Chapter 2, *Introduction to Supervised Learning*, discusses what's involved in machine learning and what it is all about. We start by discussing the principles involved in machine learning, with a particular focus on binary classification. Then, we will look at various techniques used when training models. Finally, we will look at some common metrics that people use to judge how well an algorithm is performing.

Chapter 3, *Binary Prediction Models*, looks at various methods for classifying data, focusing on binary data. We will see how we can extend algorithms for binary classification to algorithms that are capable of multiclass classification.

Chapter 4, *Regression Analysis and How to Use It*, covers a different variant of supervised learning. It focuses on different modes of linear regression and how to apply them for various purposes.

Chapter 5, *Neural Networks*, talks about classification and regression using neural networks. We will learn about perceptrons. We will also discuss the idea behind neural networks, including the different types of perceptrons, and what a multilayer perceptron is. You will also learn how to train a neural network for various purposes.

Chapter 6, *Clustering Techniques*, goes into detail about unsupervised learning. You'll learn about clustering and various approaches to clustering. You'll also learn how to implement those approaches for various purposes, such as image compression.

Chapter 7, *Dimensionality Reduction*, focuses on dimensionality reduction techniques. You will learn about various techniques, such as PCA, SVD, and MDS.

# To get the most out of this book

You will need Anaconda and Jupyter Notebook. You also need to be familiar with Python, and various machine learning libraries such as NumPy and pandas.

# Download the example code files

You can download the example code files for this book from your account at www.packt.com. If you purchased this book elsewhere, you can visit www.packt.com/support and register to have the files emailed directly to you.

You can download the code files by following these steps:

1. Log in or register at www.packt.com.
2. Select the **SUPPORT** tab.
3. Click on **Code Downloads & Errata**.
4. Enter the name of the book in the **Search** box and follow the onscreen instructions.

Once the file is downloaded, please make sure that you unzip or extract the folder using the latest version of:

- WinRAR/7-Zip for Windows
- Zipeg/iZip/UnRarX for Mac
- 7-Zip/PeaZip for Linux

The code bundle for the book is also hosted on GitHub at `https://github.com/PacktPublishing/Training-Your-Systems-with-Python-Statistical-Modeling`. In case there's an update to the code, it will be updated on the existing GitHub repository.

We also have other code bundles from our rich catalog of books and videos available at `https://github.com/PacktPublishing/`. Check them out!

# Download the color images

We also provide a PDF file that has color images of the screenshots/diagrams used in this book. You can download it here: `http://www.packtpub.com/sites/default/files/downloads/9781838823733_ColorImages.pdf`.

# Conventions used

There are a number of text conventions used throughout this book.

`CodeInText`: Indicates code words in text, database table names, folder names, filenames, file extensions, pathnames, dummy URLs, user input, and Twitter handles. Here is an example: "As seen here, the `iris` dataset comes with `sepal length`, `sepal width`, `petal length`, and `petal width`."

Any command-line input or output is written as follows:

```
$ jupyter notebook
```

 Warnings or important notes appear like this.

 Tips and tricks appear like this.

# Get in touch

Feedback from our readers is always welcome.

**General feedback**: If you have questions about any aspect of this book, mention the book title in the subject of your message and email us at customercare@packtpub.com.

**Errata**: Although we have taken every care to ensure the accuracy of our content, mistakes do happen. If you have found a mistake in this book, we would be grateful if you would report this to us. Please visit www.packt.com/submit-errata, selecting your book, clicking on the Errata Submission Form link, and entering the details.

**Piracy**: If you come across any illegal copies of our works in any form on the Internet, we would be grateful if you would provide us with the location address or website name. Please contact us at copyright@packt.com with a link to the material.

**If you are interested in becoming an author**: If there is a topic that you have expertise in and you are interested in either writing or contributing to a book, please visit authors.packtpub.com.

# Reviews

Please leave a review. Once you have read and used this book, why not leave a review on the site that you purchased it from? Potential readers can then see and use your unbiased opinion to make purchase decisions, we at Packt can understand what you think about our products, and our authors can see your feedback on their book. Thank you!

For more information about Packt, please visit packt.com.

# Classical Statistical Analysis

**1**

Welcome to the first chapter of our book! In this book, we will use our knowledge of Python and machine learning to create data models and perform statistical analysis on different data schemas. We will learn about various techniques pertaining to statistical learning and how to apply them in data analysis. By the end of this book, you will be confident in using various machine learning models, training them, and learning how to evaluate model results and implement various dimensionality reduction techniques. So, without further ado, let's dive right in! In this chapter, we will look at the following topics:

- Computing descriptive statistics
- Classical inference for proportions
- Classical inference for means
- Diving into Bayesian analysis
- Bayesian analysis for proportions
- Bayesian analysis for means
- Finding correlations

# Technical requirements

The following is required to get the most out of this book:

- A Windows or Linux system with internet access
- A basic understanding of Python
- A basic understanding of the various libraries in Python, such as NumPy, pandas, and matplotlib
- A basic understanding of Anaconda and Jupyter Notebook

Before starting on this book, the first thing you need to do is to install Anaconda on your system, if you haven't done so already. The installation process is pretty straightforward, as shown in the following steps:

1. Go to the Anaconda website at `https://www.anaconda.com/distribution/#download-section`. You will be greeted by the following download section:

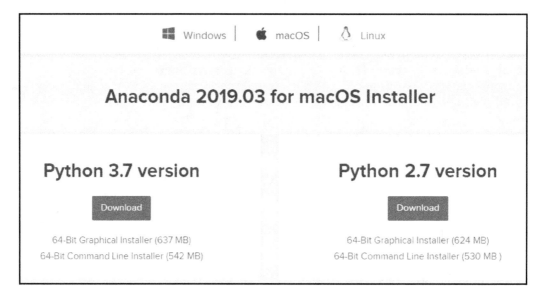

2. Here, you need to select the appropriate installer for your system and download it. Once the download is done, the installation wizard should take you through the whole process easily.
3. Once the installation is completed, to access the Jupyter Notebook, you should open the Anaconda command line or Terminal and enter the following command:

```
jupyter notebook
```

This results in the following screen:

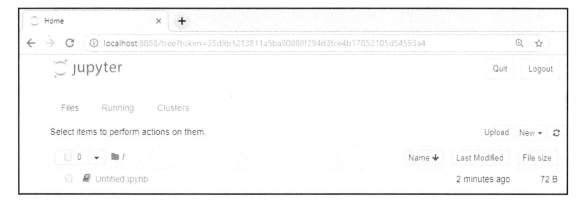

You are now ready to start working!

# Computing descriptive statistics

In this section, we will review methods for obtaining descriptive statistics from data that is stored in a `pandas` DataFrame. We will use the `pandas` library to compute statistics from the data. So, let's jump right in!

DataFrames come equipped with many methods for computing common descriptive statistics for the data they contain. This is one of the advantages of storing data in DataFrames—working with data stored this way is easy. Getting common descriptive statistics, such as the mean, the median, the standard deviation, and more, is easy for data that is present in DataFrames. There are methods that can be called in order to quickly compute each of these. We will review several of these methods now.

If you want a basic set of descriptive statistics, just to get a sense of the contents of the DataFrame, consider using the `describe()` method. It includes the mean, standard deviation, an account of how much data there is, and the five-number summary built in.

Sometimes, the statistic that you want isn't a built-in DataFrame method. In this case, you will write a function that works for a `pandas` series, and then apply that function to each column using the `apply()` method.

# Preprocessing the data

Now let's open up the Jupyter Notebook and get started on our first program, using the methods that we discussed in the previous section:

1. The first thing we need to do is load the various libraries that we need. We will also load the `iris` dataset from the `scikit-learn` library, using the following code:

```
In [1]:  import pandas as pd
         from pandas import DataFrame
         from sklearn.datasets import load_iris
```

2. After importing all the required libraries and the dataset, we will go ahead and create an object called `iris_obj`, which loads the `iris` dataset into an object. Then, we will go ahead and use the `data` method to preview the dataset; and this results in the following output:

```
In [4]:  iris_obj = load_iris()
         iris_obj.data

Out[4]:  array([[5.1, 3.5, 1.4, 0.2],
                [4.9, 3. , 1.4, 0.2],
                [4.7, 3.2, 1.3, 0.2],
                [4.6, 3.1, 1.5, 0.2],
                [5. , 3.6, 1.4, 0.2],
                [5.4, 3.9, 1.7, 0.4],
                [4.6, 3.4, 1.4, 0.3],
                [5. , 3.4, 1.5, 0.2],
                [4.4, 2.9, 1.4, 0.2],
```

Notice that it's a NumPy array. This contains a lot of the data that we want, and each of these columns corresponds to a feature.

3. We will now see what those feature names are in the following output:

```
In [5]:  iris_obj.feature_names

Out[5]:  ['sepal length (cm)',
          'sepal width (cm)',
          'petal length (cm)',
          'petal width (cm)']
```

As you can see here, the first column shows the sepal length, the next column shows the sepal width, the third column shows the petal length, and the final column shows the petal width.

4. Now, there is a fifth column that is not displayed here—it's referred to as the target column. This is stored in a separate array; we will now look at this column as follows:

```
In [6]:  iris_obj.target

Out[6]:  array([0, 0, 0, 0, 0, 0, 0, 0, 0, 0, 0, 0, 0, 0, 0, 0, 0, 0, 0, 0, 0, 0,
                0, 0, 0, 0, 0, 0, 0, 0, 0, 0, 0, 0, 0, 0, 0, 0, 0, 0, 0, 0, 0, 0,
                0, 0, 0, 0, 0, 0, 1, 1, 1, 1, 1, 1, 1, 1, 1, 1, 1, 1, 1, 1, 1, 1,
                1, 1, 1, 1, 1, 1, 1, 1, 1, 1, 1, 1, 1, 1, 1, 1, 1, 1, 1, 1, 1, 1,
                1, 1, 1, 1, 1, 1, 1, 1, 1, 1, 1, 1, 2, 2, 2, 2, 2, 2, 2, 2, 2, 2,
                2, 2, 2, 2, 2, 2, 2, 2, 2, 2, 2, 2, 2, 2, 2, 2, 2, 2, 2, 2, 2, 2,
                2, 2, 2, 2, 2, 2, 2, 2, 2, 2, 2, 2, 2, 2, 2, 2, 2, 2])
```

This displays the target column in an array.

5. Now, if you want to see the labels of the array header, we can use the following code:

```
In [8]:  iris_obj.target_names

Out[8]:  array(['setosa', 'versicolor', 'virginica'], dtype='<U10')
```

As you can see, the target column consists of data with three different labels. The flowers come from either the setosa, the versicolor, or the virginica species.

6. Our next step is to take this dataset and turn it into a `pandas` DataFrame, using the following code:

```
In [7]:  iris = DataFrame(iris_obj.data, columns=iris_obj.feature_names,
                   index=pd.Index([i for i in range(iris_obj.data.shape[0])])).\
              join(DataFrame(iris_obj.target, columns=pd.Index(["species"]),
                   index=pd.Index([i for i in range(iris_obj.target.shape[0])])))
         iris
```

This results in the following output:

| | sepal length (cm) | sepal width (cm) | petal length (cm) | petal width (cm) | species |
|---|---|---|---|---|---|
| 0 | 5.1 | 3.5 | 1.4 | 0.2 | 0 |
| 1 | 4.9 | 3.0 | 1.4 | 0.2 | 0 |
| 2 | 4.7 | 3.2 | 1.3 | 0.2 | 0 |
| 3 | 4.6 | 3.1 | 1.5 | 0.2 | 0 |
| 4 | 5.0 | 3.6 | 1.4 | 0.2 | 0 |
| 5 | 5.4 | 3.9 | 1.7 | 0.4 | 0 |
| 6 | 4.6 | 3.4 | 1.4 | 0.3 | 0 |
| 7 | 5.0 | 3.4 | 1.5 | 0.2 | 0 |
| 8 | 4.4 | 2.9 | 1.4 | 0.2 | 0 |
| 9 | 4.9 | 3.1 | 1.5 | 0.1 | 0 |
| 10 | 5.4 | 3.7 | 1.5 | 0.2 | 0 |
| 11 | 4.8 | 3.4 | 1.6 | 0.2 | 0 |
| 12 | 4.8 | 3.0 | 1.4 | 0.1 | 0 |
| 13 | 4.3 | 3.0 | 1.1 | 0.1 | 0 |

As you can see, we have successfully loaded the data into a DataFrame.

7. We can see that the `species` column still shows the various species using numeric values. So, we will replace the final column, which indicates the various species, with strings that indicate the values, rather than numbers, using the following code block:

```
In [7]:  iris.species.replace({0: 'setosa', 1: 'versicolor', 2: 'virginica'}, inplace=True)
         iris
```

The following screenshot shows the result:

|    | sepal length (cm) | sepal width (cm) | petal length (cm) | petal width (cm) | species |
|----|-------------------|------------------|-------------------|------------------|---------|
| 0  | 5.1 | 3.5 | 1.4 | 0.2 | setosa |
| 1  | 4.9 | 3.0 | 1.4 | 0.2 | setosa |
| 2  | 4.7 | 3.2 | 1.3 | 0.2 | setosa |
| 3  | 4.6 | 3.1 | 1.5 | 0.2 | setosa |
| 4  | 5.0 | 3.6 | 1.4 | 0.2 | setosa |
| 5  | 5.4 | 3.9 | 1.7 | 0.4 | setosa |
| 6  | 4.6 | 3.4 | 1.4 | 0.3 | setosa |
| 7  | 5.0 | 3.4 | 1.5 | 0.2 | setosa |
| 8  | 4.4 | 2.9 | 1.4 | 0.2 | setosa |
| 9  | 4.9 | 3.1 | 1.5 | 0.1 | setosa |
| 10 | 5.4 | 3.7 | 1.5 | 0.2 | setosa |
| 11 | 4.8 | 3.4 | 1.6 | 0.2 | setosa |
| 12 | 4.8 | 3.0 | 1.4 | 0.1 | setosa |
| 13 | 4.3 | 3.0 | 1.1 | 0.1 | setosa |
| 14 | 5.8 | 4.0 | 1.2 | 0.2 | setosa |

As you can see, the `species` column now has the actual species names—this makes it much easier to work with the data.

Now, for this dataset, the fact that each flower comes from a different species suggests that we may want to actually group the data when we're doing statistical summaries—therefore, we can try grouping by species.

8. So, we will now group the dataset values using the `species` column as the anchor, and then print out the details of each group to make sure that everything is working. We will use the following lines of code to do so:

```
In [8]:  iris_grps = iris.groupby("species")

         for name, data in iris_grps:
             print(name)
             print("---------------------\n\n")
             print(data.iloc[:, 0:4])
             print("\n\n\n")
```

This results in the following output:

```
setosa
- - - - - - - - - - - - - - - - - - - - - - - -


     sepal length (cm)  sepal width (cm)  petal length (cm)  petal width (cm)
0                  5.1               3.5                1.4               0.2
1                  4.9               3.0                1.4               0.2
2                  4.7               3.2                1.3               0.2
3                  4.6               3.1                1.5               0.2
4                  5.0               3.6                1.4               0.2
5                  5.4               3.9                1.7               0.4
6                  4.6               3.4                1.4               0.3
7                  5.0               3.4                1.5               0.2
8                  4.4               2.9                1.4               0.2
9                  4.9               3.1                1.5               0.1
10                 5.4               3.7                1.5               0.2
```

Now that the data has been loaded and set up, we will use it to perform some basic statistical operations in the next section.

# Computing basic statistics

Now we can use the DataFrame that we created to get some basic numbers; we will use the following steps to do so:

1. We can count how much data there is through the `count ()` method, as shown in the following screenshot:

```
In [13]:  iris.count()

Out[13]:  sepal length (cm)    150
          sepal width (cm)     150
          petal length (cm)    150
          petal width (cm)     150
          species              150
          dtype: int64
```

We can see that there are 150 observations. Note that this excludes NA values (that is, missing values), so it is possible that not all of these observations will be 150.

2. We can also compute the sample mean, which is the arithmetic average of all the numbers in the dataset, by simply calling the mean() method, as shown in the following screenshot:

```
In [14]:  iris.mean()

Out[14]:  sepal length (cm)    5.843333
          sepal width (cm)     3.054000
          petal length (cm)    3.758667
          petal width (cm)     1.198667
          dtype: float64
```

Here, we can see the arithmetic means for the numeric columns. The sample mean can also be calculated arithmetically, using the following formula:

$$\overline{x} = \frac{1}{n} \sum_{i=1}^{n} x_i$$

3. Next, we can compute the sample median using the median() method:

```
In [11]:  iris.median()

Out[11]:  sepal length (cm)    5.80
          sepal width (cm)     3.00
          petal length (cm)    4.35
          petal width (cm)     1.30
          dtype: float64
```

Here, we can see the median values; the sample median is the middle data point, which we get after ordering the dataset. It can be computed arithmetically by using the following formula:

$$\tilde{x} = \begin{cases} x_{(\frac{n+1}{2})} & \text{if } n \text{ is odd} \\ \frac{1}{2}\left(x_{(\frac{n}{2})} + x_{(\frac{n}{2}+1)}\right) & \text{if } n \text{ is even} \end{cases}$$

Here, $x_{(n)}$ represents ordered data.

4. We can compute the variance as follows:

```
In [12]:  iris.var()

Out[12]:  sepal length (cm)    0.685694
          sepal width (cm)     0.189979
          petal length (cm)    3.116278
          petal width (cm)     0.581006
          dtype: float64
```

The sample variance is a measure of dispersion and is roughly the average squared distance of a data point from the mean. It can be calculated arithmetically, as follows:

$$s^2 = \frac{1}{n-1} \sum_{i=1}^{n} (x_i - \bar{x})^2$$

5. The most interesting quantity is the sample standard deviation, which is the square root of the variance. It is computed as follows:

```
In [13]:  iris.std()

Out[13]:  sepal length (cm)    0.828066
          sepal width (cm)     0.435866
          petal length (cm)    1.765298
          petal width (cm)     0.762238
          dtype: float64
```

The standard deviation is the square root of the variance and is interpreted as the average distance that a data point is from the mean. It can be represented arithmetically, as follows:

$$s = \sqrt{s^2}$$

6. We can also compute percentiles; we do that by defining the value of the percentile that you want to see using the following command:

```
iris.quantile(.p)
```

So, here, roughly $p\%$ of the data is less than that percentile.

7. Let's find out the 1st, 3rd, 10th, and 95th percentiles as an example, as follows:

```
In [15]:  iris.quantile(.95)

Out[15]:  sepal length (cm)    7.255
          sepal width (cm)     3.800
          petal length (cm)    6.100
          petal width (cm)     2.300
          dtype: float64

In [16]:  iris.quantile(.75)

Out[16]:  sepal length (cm)    6.4
          sepal width (cm)     3.3
          petal length (cm)    5.1
          petal width (cm)     1.8
          dtype: float64
```

8. Now, we will compute the **interquartile range** (**IQR**) between the 3rd and 1st quantile using the following function:

```
In [18]:
          iris.quantile(.75) - iris.quantile(.25)

Out[18]:  sepal length (cm)    1.3
          sepal width (cm)     0.5
          petal length (cm)    3.5
          petal width (cm)     1.5
          dtype: float64
```

9. Other interesting quantities include the maximum value of the dataset, and the minimum value of the dataset. Both of these values can be computed as follows:

```
In [19]:  iris.max()

Out[19]:  sepal length (cm)           7.9
          sepal width (cm)            4.4
          petal length (cm)           6.9
          petal width (cm)            2.5
          species               virginica
          dtype: object


In [20]:  iris.min()

Out[20]:  sepal length (cm)           4.3
          sepal width (cm)              2
          petal length (cm)             1
          petal width (cm)            0.1
          species                  setosa
          dtype: object
```

Most of the methods mentioned here also work with grouped data. As an exercise, try summarizing the data that we grouped in the previous section, using the previous methods.

10. Another useful method includes the describe() method. This method can be useful if all you want is just a basic statistical summary of the dataset:

```
In [25]:  iris.describe()

Out[25]:
```

|  | sepal length (cm) | sepal width (cm) | petal length (cm) | petal width (cm) |
|---|---|---|---|---|
| count | 150.000000 | 150.000000 | 150.000000 | 150.000000 |
| mean | 5.843333 | 3.057333 | 3.758000 | 1.199333 |
| std | 0.828066 | 0.435866 | 1.765298 | 0.762238 |
| min | 4.300000 | 2.000000 | 1.000000 | 0.100000 |
| 25% | 5.100000 | 2.800000 | 1.600000 | 0.300000 |
| 50% | 5.800000 | 3.000000 | 4.350000 | 1.300000 |
| 75% | 6.400000 | 3.300000 | 5.100000 | 1.800000 |
| max | 7.900000 | 4.400000 | 6.900000 | 2.500000 |

Note that this method includes the count, mean, standard deviations, the five-number summary—from the minimum to the maximum, and the quantiles in between. This will also work for grouped data. As an exercise, why don't you try finding the summary of the grouped data?

11. Now, if we want a custom numerical summary, then we can write a function that will work for a `pandas` series, and then apply that to the columns of a DataFrame. For example, there isn't a function that computes the range of a dataset, which is the difference between the maximum and the minimum of the dataset. So, we will define a function that can compute the range if it were given a `pandas` series; here, you can see that by sending it to `apply()`, you get the ranges that you want:

```
In [27]:  # Compute the range of a dataset
          def range_stat(s):
              return s.max() - s.min()

          iris.iloc[:, 0:4].apply(range_stat)

Out[27]:  sepal length (cm)    3.6
          sepal width (cm)     2.4
          petal length (cm)    5.9
          petal width (cm)     2.4
          dtype: float64
```

Notice that I was more selective in choosing columns in terms of which columns to work with. Previously, a lot of the methods were able to weed out columns that weren't numeric; however, to use `apply()`, you need to specifically select the columns that are numeric, otherwise, you may end up with an error.

12. We can't directly use the preceding code if we want to filter for grouped data. Instead, we can use the `.aggregate()` method, as follows:

```
In [28]: # Use aggregate() for groups
         iris_grps.aggregate(range_stat)
Out[28]:
```

| species | sepal length (cm) | sepal width (cm) | petal length (cm) | petal width (cm) |
|---|---|---|---|---|
| setosa | 1.5 | 2.1 | 0.9 | 0.5 |
| versicolor | 2.1 | 1.4 | 2.1 | 0.8 |
| virginica | 3.0 | 1.6 | 2.4 | 1.1 |

Thus, we have learned all about computing various statistics using the methods present in pandas. In the next section, we will look at classical statistical inference, specifically with inference for a population proportion.

# Classical inference for proportions

In classical statistical inference, we often answer questions about a population, which is a hypothetical group of all possible values and data (including future ones). A sample, on the other hand, is a subset of the population that we use to observe values. In classical statistical inference, we often seek to answer questions about a fixed, non-random, unknown population parameter.

Confidence intervals are computed from data, and are expected to contain $\theta$. We may refer to, say, a 95% confidence interval—that is, an interval that we are 95% confident contains $\theta$, in the sense that there is a 95% chance that when we compute such an interval, we capture $\theta$ in it.

This section focuses on binary variables, where the variable is either a success or a failure, and successes occur with a proportion or probability of $p$.

An example situation of this is tracking whether a visitor to a website clicked on an ad during their visit. Often, these variables are encoded numerically, with 1 for success, and 0 for a failure.

In classical statistics, we assume that our data is a random sample drawn from a population with a fixed, yet unknown, proportion, $p$. We can construct a confidence interval based on the sample proportion, which gives us an idea of the proportion of the population. A 95% confidence interval captures the proportion of the population approximately 95% of the time. We can construct confidence intervals using the `proportion_confint()` function, which is found in the `statsmodel` package, which allows the easy computation of confidence intervals. Let's now see this in action!

# Computing confidence intervals for proportions

The sample proportion is computed by counting the number of successes and dividing this by the total sample size. This can be better explained using the following formula:

$$\hat{p} = \frac{M}{N}$$

Here, $N$ is the sample size and $M$ is the number of success variables; this gives you the sample proportion of successes.

Now, we want to be able to make a statement about the population proportion, which is a fixed, yet unknown, quantity. We will construct a confidence interval for this proportion, using the following formula:

$$\hat{p} \pm z_{1-\frac{a}{2}} \sqrt{\hat{p}^{(1-\hat{p})}} \equiv \left( \hat{p} - z_{1-\frac{a}{2}} \sqrt{\hat{p}^{(1-\hat{p})}}, \hat{p} + z_{1-\frac{a}{2}} \sqrt{\hat{p}^{(1-\hat{p})}} \right)$$

Here, $z_p$ is the *$100 \times p^{th}$* percentile of the normal distribution.

Now, let's suppose that, on a certain website, out of 1,126 visitors, 310 clicked on a certain ad. Let's construct a confidence interval for the population proportion of visitors who clicked on the ad. This will allow us to predict future clicks. We will use the following steps to do so:

1. Let's first load the data in the `statsmodels` package and actually compute the sample proportion, which, in this case, is 310 out of 1,126:

```
In [1]:  import statsmodels.api as sm

In [2]:  310 / 1126

Out[2]:  0.2753108348134991
```

You can see that appropriately 28% of the visitors to the website clicked on the ad on that day.

2. Our next step is to actually construct a confidence interval using the `proportion_confint ()` function. We assign the number of successes in the `count` variable, the number of trials in the `nobs` variable, and the confidence in the `alpha` variable, as shown in the following code snippet:

```
In [3]:  from statsmodels.stats.proportion import proportion_confint
         proportion_confint(count=310,
                            nobs=1126,
                            alpha=(1 - 0.95))

Out[3]:  (0.24922129423231776, 0.30140037539468045)
```

As you can see here, with 95% confidence, the proportion is between approximately 25% and 30%.

3. If we wanted a larger confidence interval, that is, a 99% confidence interval, then we could specify a different alpha, as follows:

```
In [4]:  proportion_confint(310, 1126, alpha=(1 - 0.99))

Out[4]:  (0.24102336643386685, 0.30959830319313136)
```

# Hypothesis testing for proportions

With hypothesis testing, we attempt to decide between two competing hypotheses that are statements about the value of the population proportion. These hypotheses are referred to as the null or alternative hypotheses; this idea is better illustrated in the following diagram:

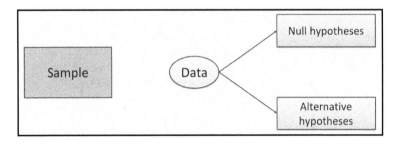

If the sample is unlikely to be seen at the null hypothesis for true, then we reject the null hypothesis and assume that the alternative hypothesis must be true. We measure how unlikely a sample is by computing a $p$ value, using a test statistic. $p$ values represent the probability of observing a test statistic that is, at least, as contradictory to the null hypothesis as the one computed. Small $p$ values indicate stronger evidence against the null hypothesis. Statisticians often introduce a cutoff and say that if the $p$ value is less than, say, 0.05, then we should reject the null hypothesis in favor of the alternative. We can choose any cutoff we want, depending on how strong we want the evidence against the null hypothesis to be before rejecting it. I don't recommend making your cutoff greater than 0.05. So, let's examine this in action.

Let's say that the website's administrator claims that 30% of visitors to the website clicked on the advertisement—is this true? Well, the sample proportion will never exactly match this number, but we can still decide whether the sample proportion is evidence against this number. So, we're going to test the null hypothesis that $p = 0.3$, which is what the website administrator claims, against the alternative hypothesis that $p \neq 0.3$. So, now let's go ahead and compute the $p$ value.

First, we're going to import the `proportions_ztest()` function. We give it how many successes there were in the data, the total number of observations, the value of $p$ under the null hypothesis, and, additionally, we tell it what type of alternative hypothesis we're using:

```
In [5]:  from statsmodels.stats.proportion import proportions_ztest

         res = proportions_ztest(count=310,
                                 nobs=1126,
                                 value=0.3,
                                 alternative='two-sided')

         res

Out[5]:  (-1.8547614674673856, 0.06363029677684083)
```

We can see the result here; the first value is the test statistic and the second one is the $p$ value. In this case, the $p$ value is 0.0636, which is greater than 0.05. Since this is greater than our cutoff, we conclude that there is not enough statistical evidence to disagree with the website administrator.

# Testing for common proportions

Now, let's move on to comparing the proportions between two samples. We want to know whether the samples were drawn from populations with the same proportion or not. This could show up in the context, such as A/B testing, where a website wants to determine which of two types of ads generates more clicks.

We can still use the `statsmodels` function, `proportions_ztest()`, but we now pass NumPy arrays to the `count` and `nobs` arguments, which contain the relevant data for the two samples.

So, our website wants to conduct an experiment. The website will show some of its visitors different versions of an advertisement created by a sponsor. Users are randomly assigned by the server to either Version A or Version B. The website will track how often Version A was clicked on and how often Version B was clicked on by its users. On a particular day, 516 visitors saw Version A and 510 saw Version B. 108 of those who saw Version A clicked on it, and 144 who saw Version B clicked on it. So, we want to know which ad generated more clicks.

We're going to be testing the following hypotheses:

$$H_0 : p_A = p_B$$
$$H_A : p_A \neq p_B$$

Let's go ahead and import the `numpy` library. When we import NumPy, we're going to use NumPy arrays to contain our data, as follows:

```
In [6]:  import numpy as np

In [7]:  np.array([108, 144])

Out[7]:  array([108, 144])
```

We will then assign the arrays and define the alternative as `two-sided`, as follows:

```
In [8]:  proportions_ztest(count=np.array([108, 144]),
                           nobs=np.array([516, 510]),
                           alternative='two-sided')

Out[8]:  (-2.7179204953199174, 0.0065693621488401655)
```

We end up with a *p* value of around 0.0066, which is small in our case, so we reject the null hypothesis. It appears that the two ads do not have the same proportion of clicks. We have looked at hypothesis testing for proportions. We will now look at applying everything that we have learned to mean values.

# Classical inference for means

We'll continue along a similar line to the previous section, in discussing classical statistical methods, but now in a new context. This section focuses on the mean of data that is quantitative, and not necessarily binary. We will demonstrate how to construct confidence intervals for the population mean, as well as several statistical tests that we can perform. Bear in mind throughout this section that we want to infer from a sample mean properties about a theoretical, unseen, yet fixed, population mean. We also want to compare the means of multiple populations, so as to determine whether they are the same or not.

When we assume that the population is a normal distribution, otherwise known as a **classic bell curve**, then we may use confidence intervals constructed using the t-distribution. These confidence intervals assume a normal distribution but tend to work well for large sample sizes even if the data is not normally distributed. In other words, these intervals tend to be robust. Unfortunately, statsmodels does not have a stable function with an easy user interface for competing these confidence intervals; however, there is a function, called _tconfint_generic(), that can compute them. You need to supply a lot of what this function needs to compute the confidence interval yourself. This means supplying the sample mean, the standard error of the mean, and the degrees of freedom, as shown in the following diagram:

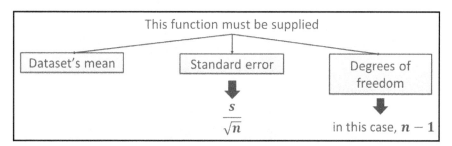

As this looks like an unstable function, this procedure could change in future versions of statsmodels.

# Computing confidence intervals for means

Consider the following scenario—you are employed by a company that fabricates chips and other electronic components. The company wants you to investigate the resistors that it uses in producing its components. In particular, while the resistors used by the company are labeled with a particular resistance, the company wants to ensure that the manufacturer of the resistors produces high-quality products. In particular, when they label a resistor as having 1,000 Ω, they want to know that resistors of that type do, in fact, have 1,000 Ω, on average:

1. Let's first import NumPy, and then define our dataset in an array, as follows:

```
In [2]: res = np.array([ 0.984,  0.988,  0.984,  0.987,  0.976,  0.997,  0.993,  0.985,
                         1.002,  0.987,  1.005,  0.993,  0.987,  0.992,  0.976,  0.998,
                         1.011,  0.971,  0.981,  1.008,  0.963,  0.992,  0.995,  0.99 ,
                         0.996,  0.99 ,  0.985,  0.997,  0.983,  0.981,  0.988,  0.991,
                         0.971,  0.982,  0.979,  1.008,  1.006,  1.006,  1.001,  0.999,
                         0.98 ,  0.996,  0.979,  1.009,  0.99 ,  0.996,  1.001,  0.981,
                         0.99 ,  0.987,  0.97 ,  0.992,  0.982,  0.983,  0.974,  0.999,
                         0.987,  1.002,  0.971,  0.982,  0.989,  0.985,  1.014,  0.991,
                         0.984,  0.992,  1.003,  0.985,  0.987,  0.985,  1.  ,  0.978,
                         0.99 ,  0.99 ,  0.985,  0.983,  0.981,  0.993,  0.993,  0.973,
                         1.  ,  0.982,  0.987,  0.988,  0.982,  0.978,  0.989,  1.  ,
                         0.983,  1.008,  0.997,  0.974,  0.988,  1.002,  0.988,  0.994,
                         0.991,  1.  ,  0.976,  0.987,  0.991,  1.010,  0.999,  1.002])
        res.mean()
```

2. We read in this dataset, and the mean resistance is displayed as follows:

```
          res.mean()

Out[2]:  0.9897692307692308
```

Now, we want to know whether it is close to 0 or not. The following is the formula for the confidence interval:

$$\bar{x} \pm t_{n-1,1-\frac{a}{2}} \frac{s}{\sqrt{n}}$$

Here, $x$ is the sample mean, $s$ is the sample distribution, $\alpha$ is one minus the confidence level, and $t_{v,p}$ is the $p^{th}$ percentile of the t-distribution with $v$ degrees of freedom.

3. We're going to import the `_tconfint_generic()` function from `statsmodels`. The following code block contains the statement to import the function:

```
In [3]:  from statsmodels.stats.weightstats import _tconfint_generic
```

I don't believe that this function is stable, which means that this code could change in the future.

4. Our next step is to define all the parameters that we will assign to the function. We are going to assign our mean, standard deviation, degrees of freedom, the confidence limit, and the alternative, which is `two-sided`. This results in the following output:

```
In [4]:  _tconfint_generic(mean=res.mean(),
                           std_mean=res.std()/np.sqrt(len(res)),
                           dof=len(res) - 1,
                           alpha=(1 - 0.95),
                           alternative="two-sided")

Out[4]:  (0.9877736770045356, 0.9917647845339261)
```

You will notice that 1 is not in this confidence interval. This might lead you to suspect that the resistors that the supplier produces are not being properly manufactured.

# Hypothesis testing for means

We can test the null hypothesis that the population mean (often denoted by the Greek letter $\mu$) is equal to a hypothesized number (denoted by $\mu_0$) against an alternative hypothesis. The alternative will state that the population mean is either less than, greater than, or not equal to the mean we hypothesized. Again, if we assume that data was drawn from a normal distribution, we can use t-procedures—namely, the t-test. This test works well for non-normal data, when the sample size is large. Unfortunately, there is not a stable function in `statmodels` for this test; however, we can use the `_tstat_generic()` function, from version 0.8.0, for this test. We may need to hack it a little bit, but it can get us the $p$ value for this test.

So, the confidence interval that you computed earlier suggests that the resistors this manufacturer is sending your company are not being properly manufactured. In fact, you believe that their resistors have a resistance level that's less than that specified. So, you'll be testing the following hypotheses:

$$H_0 : \mu = 1k\Omega$$
$$H_A : \mu < 1k\Omega$$

The first hypothesis indicates that the company is telling the truth, so you assumed that at the outset. The alternative hypothesis says that the true mean is less than 1,000 $\Omega$. So, you are going to assume that the resistance is normally distributed, and this will be your test statistic. We will now perform the hypotheses testing using the following steps:

1. Our first step is to import the _tstat_generic() function, as follows:

```
In [5]:  from statsmodels.stats.weightstats import _tstat_generic
```

2. Then, we're going to define all the parameters that will be used in the function. This includes the mean of the dataset, the mean under the null hypothesis, the standard deviation, and so on. This results in the following output:

```
In [4]:  _tstat_generic(value1=res.mean(),
                         value2=0,
                         diff=1,
                         std_diff=res.std()/np.sqrt(len(res)),
                         dof=len(res) - 1,
                         alternative="smaller")

Out[4]:  (-10.167763027563376, 1.566340927584771e-17)
```

So, we compute the *p* value, and this *p* value is minuscule. So, clearly, the resistance of the resistors the manufacturer makes is less than 1,000$\Omega$—therefore, your company is being fleeced by this manufacturer; they're not actually producing quality parts. We can also test whether two populations have the same mean, or whether their means are different in some way.

# Testing with two samples

If we assume that our data was drawn from normal distributions, the t-test can be used. For this test, we can use the `statsmodels` function, `ttest_ind()`. This is a more stable function from the package, and uses a different interface. So, here, we're going to test for a common mean.

Let's assume that your company has decided to stop outsourcing resistor production, and they're experimenting with different methods so that they can start producing resistors in-house. So, they have process A and process B, and they want you to test whether the mean resistance for these two processes is the same, or whether they're different. Therefore, you feel safe, assuming again that the resistance level of resistors is normally distributed regardless of whatever manufacturing process is employed, and you don't assume that they have the same standard deviation. Thus, the test statistic is as follows:

$$H_0 : \mu_A = \mu_B$$
$$H_A : \mu_A \neq \mu_B$$

So, let's use this test statistic to perform your test:

Our first step is to load in the data, as follows:

```
In [7]:  res_A = np.array([ 1.002,  1.001,  1.   ,  0.999,  0.998,  1.   ,  1.001,  0.999,
                            1.002,  0.998,  1.   ,  0.998,  1.001,  1.001,  1.002,  0.997,
                            1.001,  1.   ,  1.001,  0.999,  0.998,  0.998,  1.002,  1.002,
                            0.996,  0.998,  0.997,  1.001,  1.002,  0.997,  1.   ,  1.   ,
                            0.998,  0.997])

         res_B = np.array([ 0.995,  1.022,  0.993,  1.014,  0.998,  0.99 ,  0.998,  0.998,
                            0.99 ,  1.003,  1.016,  0.992,  1.   ,  1.002,  1.003,  1.005,
                            0.979,  1.012,  0.978,  1.01 ,  1.001,  1.026,  1.011,  1.   ,
                            0.98 ,  0.993,  1.016,  0.991,  0.986,  0.987,  1.012,  0.996,
                            1.013,  1.001,  0.984,  1.011,  1.01 ,  1.   ,  1.001])
```

Our next step is to load and define the `ttest_ind` function, as follows:

```
In [8]:  from statsmodels.stats.weightstats import ttest_ind

In [9]:  ttest_ind(res_A, res_B,      # The datasets
                   alternative="two-sided",
                   usevar="unequal")

Out[9]:  (-0.4442926812820534, 0.6592217943569274, 40.062908701724936)
```

This will give us a *p* value. In this case, the *p* value is 0.659—this is a very large *p* value. It suggests that we should not reject the null hypothesis, and it appears that the two processes produce resistors with the same mean level of resistance.

# One-way analysis of variance (ANOVA)

One-way ANOVA tests whether all groups share a common mean with their own sample. The null hypothesis assumes that all populations share the same mean, while the alternative hypothesis simply states that the null hypothesis is false. One-way ANOVA assumes that data was drawn from normal distributions with a common standard deviation. While normality can be relaxed for larger sample sizes, the assumption of common standard deviation is, in practice, more critical.

Before performing this test, let's consider doing a visual check to see whether the data has a common spread. For example, you could create side-by-side box and whisker plots. If the data does not appear to have a common standard deviation, you should not perform this test.

The `f_oneway()` function from SciPy can perform this test; so, let's start performing one-way ANOVA.

Your company now has multiple processes. Therefore, before you were able to return your report for the other two, you were given data for processes C, D, and E. Your company wants to test whether all of these processes have the same mean level of resistance or whether this is not true—in other words, whether one of these processes has a different mean level of resistance. So, let's get into it:

1.  We will first define the data for these other processes, as follows:

```
In [10]:  res_C = np.array([ 1.005,  1.012,  1.003,  0.993,  0.998,  1.002,  1.002,  0.996,
                             0.999,  1.004,  1.006,  1.007,  0.991,  1.011,  1.   ,  1.   ,
                             1.005,  1.   ,  0.995,  0.995,  1.002,  1.002,  0.991,  1.003,
                             0.997,  0.994,  0.995,  1.   ,  1.001,  1.005,  0.992,  0.999,
                             0.999,  1.002,  1.   ,  0.994,  1.001,  1.007,  1.003,  0.993])

          res_D = np.array([ 1.006,  0.996,  0.986,  1.004,  1.004,  1.   ,  1.   ,  0.993,
                             0.991,  0.992,  0.989,  0.996,  1.   ,  0.996,  1.001,  0.989,
                             1.   ,  1.004,  0.997,  0.99 ,  0.998,  0.994,  0.991,  0.995,
                             1.002,  0.997,  0.998,  0.99 ,  0.996,  0.994,  0.988,  0.996,
                             0.998])

          res_E = np.array([ 1.009,  0.999,  0.995,  1.008,  0.998,  1.001,  1.001,  1.001,
                             0.993,  0.992,  1.007,  1.005,  0.997,  1.   ,  1.   ,  1.   ,
                             0.996,  1.005,  0.997,  1.013,  1.002,  1.006,  1.004,  1.002,
                             1.001,  0.999,  1.001,  1.004,  0.994,  0.999,  0.997,  1.004,
                             0.996])
```

2. We're going to use the `f_oneway()` function from SciPy to perform this test, and we can simply pass the data from each of these samples to this function, as follows:

```
In [11]:  from scipy.stats import f_oneway

In [12]:  f_oneway(res_A, res_B, res_C, res_D, res_E)
```

3. This will give us the *p* value, which, in this case, is 0.03:

```
In [12]:  f_oneway(res_A, res_B, res_C, res_D, res_E)

Out[12]:  F_onewayResult(statistic=2.6539731195650056, pvalue=0.03473143851921515)
```

This appears to be small, so we're going to reject the null hypothesis that all processes yield resistors with the same level of resistance. It appears at least one of them has a different mean level of resistance.

This concludes our discussion of classical statistical methods for now. We will now move on to discussing Bayesian statistics.

# Diving into Bayesian analysis

Welcome to the first section on Bayesian analysis. This section discusses the basic concepts used in Bayesian statistics. This branch of statistics often involves classical statistics and requires more knowledge of mathematics and probability, but it seems to be popular in computer science. This section will get you up to speed with what you need to know to understand and perform Bayesian statistics.

All Bayesian statistics are based on Bayes' theorem; in Bayesian statistics, we consider an event or parameter as a random variable. For example, suppose that we're talking about a parameter; we give a prior distribution to the parameter, and a likelihood of observing a certain outcome given the value of the parameter. Bayes' theorem lets us compute the posterior distribution of the parameter, which we can use to reach conclusions about it. The following formula shows Bayes' theorem:

$$p(\theta|D) = \frac{p(D|\theta)p(\theta)}{p(D)} \propto p(D|\theta)p(\theta)$$

All Bayesian statistics are an exercise in applying this theorem. The $\alpha$ symbol means proportional to, that is, that the two sides differ by a multiplicative factor.

# How Bayesian analysis works

I assume that we are interested in the value of a parameter, such as the mean or proportion. We start by giving this parameter a prior distribution quantifying our beliefs about where the parameter is located, based on what we believe about it before collecting data. There are lots of ways to pick the prior; for example, we could pick an uninformative prior that says little about a parameter's value. Alternatively, we could use a prior that gives beliefs based on, say, previous studies, therefore biasing the value of the parameter to these values.

Then, we collect data and use it to compute the posterior distribution of the parameter, which is our updated belief about its location after seeing new evidence. This posterior distribution is then used to answer all our questions about the parameter's location. Note that the posterior distribution will answer all questions with probabilities. This means that we don't say whether the parameter is in a particular region or not, but the probability that it is located in that region instead. In general, the posterior distribution is difficult to compute. Often, we need to rely on computationally intensive methods such as Monte Carlo simulation to estimate posterior quantities. So, let's examine a very simple example of Bayesian analysis.

# Using Bayesian analysis to solve a hit-and-run

In this case, we're going to be solving a hit-and-run. In a certain city, 95% of cabs are owned by the Yellow Cab Company, and 5% are owned by Green Cab, Inc. Recently, a cab was involved in a hit-and-run accident, injuring a pedestrian. A witness saw the accident and claimed that the cab that hit the pedestrian was a green cab. Tests by investigators revealed that, under similar circumstances, this witness is correctly able to identify a green cab 90% of the time and correctly identify a yellow cab 85% of the time. This means that they incorrectly call a yellow cab a green cab 15% of the time, and incorrectly call a green cab a yellow cab 10% of the time. So, the question is, *should we pursue Green Cab, Inc.?*

The following formula shows Bayes' theorem:

$$P(H|D) = \frac{P(D|H)P(H)}{P(D|H)P(H) + P(D|\ not\ H)P(not\ H)} = \frac{P(D|H)P(H)}{P(D)}$$

Here, $H$ represents the event that a green cab hit the pedestrian, while $G$ represents the event that the witness claims to have seen a green cab.

So, let's encode these probabilities, as follows:

```
In [1]:  d_h = 0.9
         h = 0.05
         d_nh = 0.1
         nh = 0.95

         h

Out[1]:  0.05
```

Now that we have these probabilities, we can use Bayes' theorem to compute the posterior probability, which is given as follows:

```
In [2]:  h_d = (d_h * h)/(d_h * h + d_nh * nh)
         h_d

Out[2]:  0.32142857142857145
```

So, the result is that the prior probability that the cab was actually green was 0.05, which was very low. The posterior probability, that is, the probability that the cab that hit the pedestrian was green, given that the witness said the cab was green, is now 32%, which is higher than that number, but it is still less than 50%.

Additionally, considering that this city consists only of yellow cabs and green cabs, this indicates that even though the witness saw a green cab or claimed to have seen a green cab, there are too few green cabs and the witness is not accurate enough to override how few green cabs there are. This means that it's still more likely that the pedestrian was hit by a yellow cab and that the witness made a mistake.

Now, let's take a look at some useful applications of Bayesian analysis. We will go through topics similar to those seen previously, but from the Bayesian perspective.

# Bayesian analysis for proportions

In this section, we'll revisit inference for proportions, but from a Bayesian perspective. We will look at Bayesian methods for analyzing proportions of success in a group. This includes talking about computing credible intervals, and the Bayesian version of hypothesis testing for both one and two samples.

Conjugate priors are a class of prior probability distributions common in Bayesian statistics. A conjugate prior is a prior distribution such that the posterior distribution belongs to the same family of probability distributions as the prior. For binary data, the beta distribution is a conjugate prior. This is a distribution defined where only values in the *(0, 1)* interval have a chance of appearing. They are specified by two parameters. In a trial, if there are $M$ successes out of $N$ trials, then the posterior distribution is the prior distribution when we add $M$ to the first parameter of the prior, and $N$ - $M$ to the second parameter of the prior. This concentrates the distribution to the observed population proportion.

# Conjugate priors for proportions

So, let's see this in action. For data that takes values of either 0 or 1, we're going to use the beta distribution as our conjugate prior. The notation that is used to refer to the beta distribution is $B(\alpha, \beta)$.

$\alpha$ - *1* can be interpreted as imaginary prior successes, and $\beta$ - *1* can be interpreted as imaginary prior failures. That's if you have added the data to your dataset—imaginary successes and imaginary failures.

If $\alpha = \beta = 1$, then we interpret this as being no prior successes or failures; therefore, every probability of success, $\theta$, is equally likely in some sense. This is referred to as an **uninformative prior**. Let's now implement this using the following steps:

1. First, we're going to import the `beta` function from `scipy.stats`; this is the `beta` distribution. In addition to this, we will import the `numpy` library and the `matplotlib` library, as follows:

```
In [1]:  from scipy.stats import beta
         import numpy as np
         import matplotlib.pyplot as plt
         %matplotlib inline
```

2. We're then going to plot the function and see how it looks, using the following code:

```
In [2]:  x = np.linspace(0, 1, num=1000)
         plt.plot(x, beta.pdf(x, a=1, b=1))
         plt.show()
```

This results in the following output:

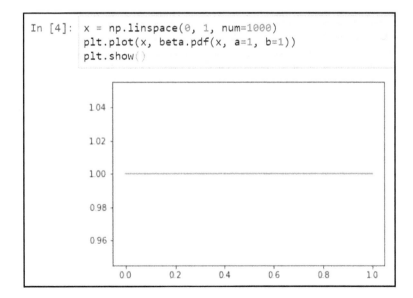

So, if we plot $\beta$ when $\alpha=1$ and $\beta=1$, we end up with a uniform distribution. In some sense, each $p$ is equally likely.

3. Now, we will use `a=3` and `b=3`, to indicate two imaginary successes and two imaginary failures, which gives us the following output:

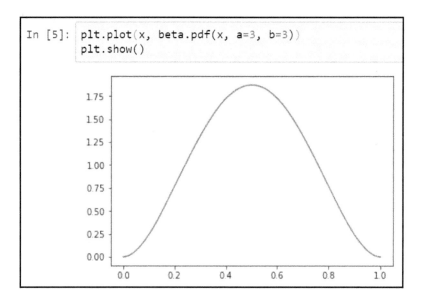

```
In [5]: plt.plot(x, beta.pdf(x, a=3, b=3))
        plt.show()
```

Now, our prior distribution biases our data toward `0.5`—in other words, it is equally likely to succeed as it is to fail.

Given a sample size of $N$, if there are $M$ successes, then the posterior distribution when the prior is $\beta$, with the parameters $(\alpha, \beta)$, will be $B(\alpha + M, \beta + N - M)$. So, let's reconsider an earlier example; we have a website with 1,126 visitors. 310 clicked on an ad purchased by a sponsor, and we want to know what proportion of individuals will click on the ad in general.

4. So, we're going to use our prior distribution beta (3, 3). This means that the posterior distribution will be given by the beta distribution, with the first parameter, 313, and the second parameter, 819. This is what the prior distribution and posterior distribution looks like when plotted against each other:

```
In [6]:  plt.plot(x, beta.pdf(x, a=3, b=3), 'b-')
         plt.plot(x, beta.pdf(x, a=313, b=819), 'r-')
         plt.show()
```

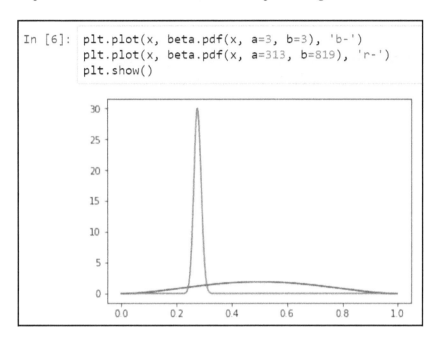

The blue represents the prior distribution, and red represents the posterior distribution.

# Credible intervals for proportions

Bayesian statistics doesn't use confidence intervals but credible intervals instead. We specify a probability, and that will be the probability that the parameter of interest lies in the credible interval. For example, there's a 95% chance that $\theta$ lies in its 95% credible interval. We compute credible intervals by computing the quantiles from the posterior distribution of the parameter, so that the chosen proportion of the posterior distribution lies between these two quantiles.

So, I've already gone ahead and written a function that will compute credible intervals for you. You give this function the number of successes, the total sample size, the first argument of the prior and the second argument of the prior, and the credibility (or chance of containing θ) of the interval. You can see the entire function as follows:

```
In [5]: def bernoulli_beta_credible_interval(M, N, a=1, b=1, C=.95):
            """Computes a 100C% credible interval for Bernoulli (0/1) data

            args:
                M: int; number of "successes"
                N: int; total sample size
                a: float; first argument of the prior Beta distribution
                b: float; second argument of the prior Beta distribution
                C: float; the credibility (chance of containing theta) of the interval

            return:
                tuple; first number is the lower bound, second the upper bound, of the credible interval
            """

            # Error checking
            if type(M) is not int or type(N) is not int:
                raise TypeError("M, N must both be integers")
            elif M < 0 or N < M:
                raise ValueError("M, N must be non-negative, and N >= M")
            elif a <= 0 or b <= 0:
                raise ValueError("Cannot have negative prior parameters!")
            elif type(C) is not float:
                raise TypeError("C must be numeric")
            elif C < 0 or C > 1:
                raise ValueError("C must be interpretable as a probability")

            post = (a + M, b + N - M)
            alpha = (1 - C)/2
            return (beta.ppf(alpha, post[0], post[1]), beta.ppf(1 - alpha, post[0], post[1]))
```

So, here is the function; I've already written it so that it works for you. We can use this function to compute credible intervals for our data.

So, we have a 95% credible interval based on the uninformative prior, as follows:

```
In [8]: bernoulli_beta_credible_interval(310, 1126)
Out[8]: (0.2500262564237963, 0.3021454985368043)
```

Therefore, we believe that θ will be between 25% and 30%, with a 95% probability.

The next one is the same interval when we have a different prior—that is, the one that we actually used before and is the one that we plotted:

```
In [9]:  bernoulli_beta_credible_interval(310, 1126, a=3, b=3)
Out[9]:  (0.25083904055649237, 0.3029124943404833)
```

The data hasn't changed very much, but still, this is going to be our credible interval.

The last one is the credible interval when we increase the level of credibility to .99 or the probability of containing the true parameter:

```
In [10]:  bernoulli_beta_credible_interval(310, 1126, a=3, b=3, C=.99)

Out[10]:  (0.24304349518931037, 0.31144211849989634)
```

Since this probability is higher, this must be a longer interval, which is exactly what we see, although it's not that much longer.

# Bayesian hypothesis testing for proportions

Unlike classical statistics, where we say a hypothesis is either right or wrong, Bayesian statistics holds that every hypothesis is true, with some probability. We don't reject hypotheses, but simply ignore them if they are unlikely to be true. For one sample, computing the probability of a hypothesis can be done by considering what region of possible values of $\theta$ correspond to the hypothesis being true, and using the posterior distribution of $\theta$ to compute the probability that $\theta$ is in that region.

In this case, we need to use what's known as the **cumulative distribution function (CDF)** of the posterior distribution. This is the probability that a random variable is less than or equal to a quantity, $x$. So, what we want is the probability that $\theta$ is greater than 0.3 when $D$ is given, that is, if we are testing the website administrator's claim that there are at least 30% of visitors to the site clicking on the ad.

So, we will use the CDF function and evaluate it at 0.3. This is going to correspond to the administrator's claim. This will give us the probability that more than 30% of visitors clicked on the ad. The following screenshot shows how we define the CDF function:

```
In [11]:  1 - beta.cdf(.3,
                        a=3 + 310,
                        b=3 + 1126 - 310)

Out[11]:  0.040212562023420606
```

What we end up with is a very small probability, therefore, it's likely that the administrator is incorrect.

Now, while there's a small probability, I would like to point out that this is not the same thing as a *p* value. A *p* value says something completely different; a *p* value should not be interpreted as the probability that the null hypothesis is true, whereas, in this case, this can be interpreted as a probability that the hypothesis we asked is true. This is the probability that data is greater than 0.3, given the data that we saw.

# Comparing two proportions

Sometimes, we may want to compare two proportions from two populations. Crucially, we will assume that they are independent of each other. It's difficult to analytically compute the probability that one proportion is less than another, so we often rely on Monte Carlo methods, otherwise known as simulation or random sampling.

We randomly generate the two proportions from their respective posterior distributions, and then track how often one is less than the other. We use the frequency we observed in our simulation to estimate the desired probability.

So, let's see this in action; we have two parameters: $\theta_A$ and $\theta_B$. These correspond to the proportion of individuals who click on an ad from format A or format B. Users are randomly assigned to one format or the other, and the website tracks how many viewers click on the ad in the different formats.

516 visitors saw format A and 108 of them clicked it. 510 visitors saw format B and 144 of them clicked it. We use the same prior for both $\theta_A$ and $\theta_B$, which is beta (3, 3). Additionally, the posterior distribution for $\theta_A$ will be B (111, 411) and for $\theta_B$, it will be B (147, 369). This results in the following output:

```
In [12]:  plt.plot(x, beta.pdf(x, 111, 411), 'b-')
          plt.plot(x, beta.pdf(x, 147, 369), 'r-')
          plt.show()
```

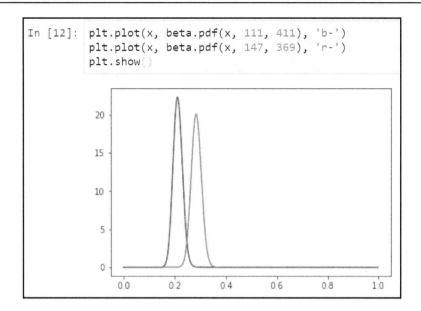

We now want to know the probability of $\theta_A$ being less than $\theta_B$—this is difficult to compute analytically. We can randomly simulate $\theta_A$ and $\theta_B$, and then use that to estimate this probability. So, let's randomly simulate one $\theta_A$, as follows:

```
In [13]:  # Demonstration: A random theta_A
          beta.rvs(111, 411)

Out[13]:  0.18723205991775277
```

Then, randomly simulate one $\theta_B$, as follows:

```
In [14]:  # A random theta_B
          beta.rvs(147, 369)

Out[14]:  0.3056753061529484
```

Finally, we're going to do 1,000 simulations by computing 1,000 $\theta_A$ values and 1,000 $\theta_B$ values, as follows:

```
In [21]:  N = 1000     # Number of simulations
          random_A = beta.rvs(111, 411, size=N)
          random_B = beta.rvs(147, 369, size=N)

In [22]:  random_A[0:10]

Out[22]:  array([0.20950737, 0.22630491, 0.23450796, 0.1902491 , 0.2148456 ,
                 0.21113803, 0.21252551, 0.20073223, 0.20307526, 0.17935545])

In [23]:  random_B[0:10]

Out[23]:  array([0.28768977, 0.26004605, 0.28018574, 0.30517745, 0.24939164,
                 0.27596163, 0.29543451, 0.26138163, 0.28330481, 0.29226554])

In [24]:  random_A[0:10] < random_B[0:10]

Out[24]:  array([ True,   True,   True,   True,   True,   True,   True,   True,   True,
                  True])

In [25]:  trial = random_A < random_B
          trial.sum()     # Number of times theta_A < theta_B

Out[25]:  996

In [26]:  trial.mean()    # Estimated probability theta_A < theta_B

Out[26]:  0.996
```

This is what we end up with; here, we can see how often $\theta_A$ is less than $\theta_B$, that is, $\theta_A$ was 996 times less than $\theta_B$. So, what's the average of this? Well, it is 0.996; this is the probability that $\theta_A$ is less than $\theta_B$, or an estimate of that probability. Given this, it seems highly likely that more people clicked on the ad for format B than people who clicked on the ad for format A.

That's it for proportions. Next up, we will look at Bayesian methods for analyzing the means of quantitative data.

# Bayesian analysis for means

Now we'll move on to discussing Bayesian methods for analyzing the means of quantitative data. This section is similar to the previous one on Bayesian methods for analyzing proportions, but it focuses on the means of quantitative data. Here, we look at constructing credible intervals and performing hypothesis testing.

Suppose that we assume that our data was drawn from a normal distribution with an unknown mean, μ, and an unknown variance, σ². The conjugate prior, in this case, will be the **normal inverse gamma** (**NIG**) distribution. This is a two-dimensional distribution, and gives a posterior distribution for both the unknown mean and the unknown variance.

In this section, we only care about what the unknown mean is. We can get a marginal distribution for the mean from the posterior distribution, which depends only on the mean. The variance no longer appears in the marginal distribution. We can use this distribution for our analysis.

So, we say that the mean and the standard deviation, both of these things being unknown, were drawn from a NIG distribution with the parameters of μ₀, μ, α, and β. This can be represented using the following formula:

$$(\mu, \sigma^2) \sim NIG(\mu_0, \nu, \alpha, \beta)$$

The posterior distribution after you have collected data can be represented as follows:

$$NIG\left(\frac{\nu\mu_0 + n\bar{x}}{\nu + n}, \nu + n, \alpha + \frac{n}{2}, \beta + \frac{1}{2}\sum_{i=1}^{n}(x_i - \bar{x})^2 + \frac{\nu n}{\nu + n}\frac{(\bar{x} - \mu_0)^2}{2}\right)$$

In this case, I'm interested in the marginal distribution of the mean, μ, under the posterior distribution. The prior marginal distribution of μ is t(2α), which means that it follows a t-distribution with two alpha degrees of freedom; this is the posterior marginal distribution of the following formula:

$$\sqrt{\frac{(n + \nu)(\alpha + \frac{n}{2})}{\beta + \frac{1}{2}\sum_{i=1}^{n}(x_i - \bar{x})^2 + \frac{\nu n}{\nu + n}\frac{(\bar{x} - \mu_0)^2}{2}}}(\mu - \nu\mu_0 + n\bar{x}\nu + n)$$

Here, it is *t(2α + n)*.

This is all very complicated, so I've written five helper functions, which are as follows:

- Compute the **probability density function** (**PDF**) of $(\mu, \sigma^2)$, which is useful for plotting.
- Compute the parameters of the posterior distribution of $(\mu, \sigma^2)$.
- Compute the PDF and CDF of the marginal distribution of $\mu$ (for either the prior or posterior distribution).
- Compute the inverse CDF of the marginal distribution of $\mu$ (for either the prior or posterior distribution).
- Simulate a draw from the marginal distribution of $\mu$ (for either the prior or posterior distribution).

We will apply these functions using the following steps:

1. So, first, we're going to need these libraries:

```
In [1]:  import numpy as np
         from scipy.special import gamma
         from scipy.stats import t
         import matplotlib.pyplot as plt
         %matplotlib inline
```

2. Then, the `dnig()` function computes the density of the normal inverse gamma distribution—this is helpful for plotting, as follows:

```
In [2]:  def dnig(x, s, mu, nu, alpha, beta):
             """Computes the PDF of the NIG(mu, nu, alpha, beta) distribution

             args:
                 x: float; The x coordinate of the PDF
                 s: float; The s coordinate of the PDF (corresponds to sigma^2)
                 mu: float; The mu parameter of NIG(mu, nu, alpha, beta)
                 nu: float; The nu parameter of NIG(mu, nu, alpha, beta)
                 alpha: float; The alpha parameter of NIG(mu, nu, alpha, beta)
                 beta: float; The beta parameter of NIG(mu, nu, alpha, beta)

             return:
                 float; The value of the PDF
             """

             if nu < 0 or alpha < 0 or beta < 0:
                 raise ValueError("Cannot have negative nu, alpha, beta")

             return np.sqrt(nu / (np.abs(s) * 2 * np.pi)) * beta ** alpha / gamma(alpha) *\
                 s**(-(alpha + 1)) * np.exp(-(2*beta + nu * (x - mu)**2)/(2*s)) * np.maximum(s, 0)
```

3. The `get_posterior_nig()` function will get the parameters of the posterior distribution, where x is our data; and these four parameters specify the parameters of the prior distribution, but will be returned as a tuple that contains the parameters of the posterior distribution:

```
In [3]:  def get_posterior_nig(x, mu, nu, alpha, beta):
             """Computes the parameters of the posterior NIG distribution

             args:
                 x: array-like; The data set
                 mu: float; prior parameter mu
                 nu: float; prior parameter nu
                 alpha: foat; prior parameter alpha
                 beta: float; prior parameter beta

             return:
                 tuple: Of the form (mu, nu, alpha, beta)
             """

             if nu < 0 or alpha < 0 or beta < 0:
                 raise ValueError("Cannot have negative nu, alpha, beta")

             xbar = x.mean()
             n = len(x)

             p_mu = (nu * mu + n * xbar)/(nu + n)
             p_nu = nu + n
             p_alpha = alpha + n/2
             p_beta = beta + ((x - xbar)**2).sum()/2 + n * nu / (n + nu) * (xbar - mu)**2/2

             return (p_mu, p_nu, p_alpha, p_beta)
```

4. The `dnig_mu_marg()` function is the density function of the marginal distribution for μ. It will be given a floating-point number that you want to evaluate the PDF on. This will be useful if you want to plot the marginal distribution of μ:

```
In [4]:  def dnig_mu_marg(x, mu, nu, alpha, beta):
             """Computes the PDF of the marginal distribution of mu from a NIG distribution

             args:
                 x: float; The value at which the PDF is being evaluated
                 mu: float; The mu parameter of NIG(mu, nu, alpha, beta)
                 nu: float; The nu parameter of NIG(mu, nu, alpha, beta)
                 alpha: float; The alpha parameter of NIG(mu, nu, alpha, beta)
                 beta: float; The beta parameter of NIG(mu, nu, alpha, beta)

             return:
                 float; The value of the PDF at x
             """

             if nu < 0 or alpha < 0 or beta < 0:
                 raise ValueError("Cannot have negative nu, alpha, beta")

             y = np.sqrt(alpha * nu / beta) * (x - mu)

             return t.pdf(y, df = 2*alpha) * np.sqrt(alpha * nu / beta)
```

5. The `pnig_mu_marg()` function computes the CDF of the marginal distribution; that is, the probability of getting a value less than or equal to your value of *x*, which you pass to the function. This'll be useful if you want to do things such as hypothesis testing or computing the probability that a hypothesis is true under the posterior distribution:

```
In [5]:  def pnig_mu_marg(x, mu, nu, alpha, beta):
             """Computes the CDF of the marginal distribution of mu from a NIG distributio

             args:
                 x: float; The value at which the CDF is being evaluated
                 mu: float; The mu parameter of NIG(mu, nu, alpha, beta)
                 nu: float; The nu parameter of NIG(mu, nu, alpha, beta)
                 alpha: float; The alpha parameter of NIG(mu, nu, alpha, beta)
                 beta: float; The beta parameter of NIG(mu, nu, alpha, beta)

             return:
                 float; The value of the CDF at x
             """

             if nu < 0 or alpha < 0 or beta < 0:
                 raise ValueError("Cannot have negative nu, alpha, beta")

             y = np.sqrt(alpha * nu / beta) * (x - mu)

             return t.cdf(y, df = 2*alpha)
```

6. The `qunig_mu_marg()` function will be the inverse CDF, however, you give it a probability, and it will give you the quantile associated with that probability. This is a function that's going to be useful if you want to construct, say, credible intervals:

```
In [6]:  def qnig_mu_marg(p, mu, nu, alpha, beta):
             """Computes the inverse CDF (quantile) of the marginal distribution of mu from a NIG distribution

             args:
                 p: float; The value at which the inverse CDF is being evaluated
                 mu: float; The mu parameter of NIG(mu, nu, alpha, beta)
                 nu: float; The nu parameter of NIG(mu, nu, alpha, beta)
                 alpha: float; The alpha parameter of NIG(mu, nu, alpha, beta)
                 beta: float; The beta parameter of NIG(mu, nu, alpha, beta)

             return:
                 float; The value of the CDF at x
             """

             if nu < 0 or alpha < 0 or beta < 0:
                 raise ValueError("Cannot have negative nu, alpha, beta")

             if p < 0 or p > 1:
                 raise ValueError("p must be a value that could be interpreted as a probability")

             y = t.ppf(p, 2*alpha)
             m = np.sqrt(beta / (nu * alpha)) * y + mu

             return m
```

7. Finally, the `rnig_mu_marg()` function draws random numbers from the marginal distribution of μ from a normal inverse gamma distribution, so this'll be useful if you want to sample from the posterior distribution of μ:

```
In [7]: def rnig_mu_marg(mu, nu, alpha, beta, n=1):
            """Draw random instances from the marginal distribution of mu from a NIG distribution

            args:
                n: int; The number of random numbers to generate
                mu: float; The mu parameter of NIG(mu, nu, alpha, beta)
                nu: float; The nu parameter of NIG(mu, nu, alpha, beta)
                alpha: float; The alpha parameter of NIG(mu, nu, alpha, beta)
                beta: float; The beta parameter of NIG(mu, nu, alpha, beta)

            return:
                np.array; Random instances of mu
            """

            if nu < 0 or alpha < 0 or beta < 0:
                raise ValueError("Cannot have negative nu, alpha, beta")

            if type(n) is not int:
                raise TypeError("n must be int")
            elif n <= 0:
                raise ValueError("n must be positive")

            y = t.rvs(df=2*alpha, size=n)
            m = np.sqrt(beta / (nu * alpha)) * y + mu

            return m
```

8. Now, we will perform a short demonstration of what the `dnig()` function does, so you can get an idea of what the normal inverse gamma distribution looks like, using the following code:

```
In [8]: # Demonstrating dnig
        x = np.linspace(-3, 3)
        y = np.linspace(-0.5, 11)
        X, Y = np.meshgrid(x, y)

        plt.contour(X, Y, dnig(X, Y, 0, 1, 1/2, 1/2))
        plt.show()
```

This results in the following output:

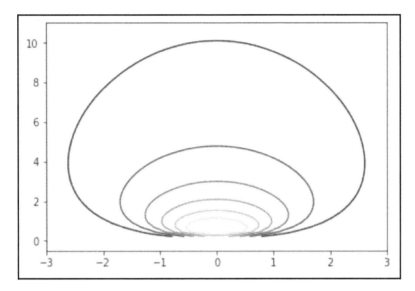

This plot gives you a sense of what the normal inverse gamma looks like. Therefore, most of the density is concentrated in this region, but it starts to spread out.

# Credible intervals for means

Getting a credible interval for the mean is the same as the one for proportions, except that we will work with the marginal distribution for just the unknown mean from the posterior distribution.

Let's repeat a context that we used in the *Computing confidence intervals for means* section of this chapter. You are employed by a company that's fabricating chips and other electronic components. The company wants you to investigate the resistors it's using to produce its components. These resistors are being manufactured by an outside company and they've been specified as having a particular resistance. They want you to ensure that the resistors being produced and sent to them are high quality products—specifically, that when they are labeled with a resistance level of 1,000 Ω, then they do in fact have a resistance of 1,000 Ω. So, let's get started, using the following steps:

1. We will use the same dataset as we did in the *Computing confidence intervals for means* section.

2. Now, we're going to use the NIG (1, 1, 1/2, 0.0005) distribution for our prior distribution. You can compute the parameters of the posterior distribution using the following code:

```
In [9]: res = np.array([ 0.984,  0.988,  0.984,  0.987,  0.976,  0.997,  0.993,  0.985,
                         1.002,  0.987,  1.005,  0.993,  0.987,  0.992,  0.976,  0.998,
                         1.011,  0.971,  0.981,  1.008,  0.963,  0.992,  0.995,  0.99 ,
                         0.996,  0.99 ,  0.985,  0.997,  0.983,  0.981,  0.988,  0.991,
                         0.971,  0.982,  0.979,  1.008,  1.006,  1.006,  1.001,  0.999,
                         0.98 ,  0.996,  0.979,  1.009,  0.99 ,  0.996,  1.001,  0.981,
                         0.99 ,  0.987,  0.97 ,  0.992,  0.982,  0.983,  0.974,  0.999,
                         0.987,  1.002,  0.971,  0.982,  0.989,  0.985,  1.014,  0.991,
                         0.984,  0.992,  1.003,  0.985,  0.987,  0.985,  1.  ,   0.978,
                         0.99 ,  0.99 ,  0.985,  0.983,  0.981,  0.993,  0.993,  0.973,
                         1.  ,   0.982,  0.987,  0.988,  0.982,  0.978,  0.989,  1.  ,
                         0.983,  1.008,  0.997,  0.974,  0.988,  1.002,  0.988,  0.994,
                         0.991,  1.  ,   0.976,  0.987,  0.991,  1.010,  0.999,  1.002])
```

When the parameters of the distribution are computed, it results in the following output:

```
In [12]: post = get_posterior_nig(res, 1, 1, 1/2, 0.0005)
         post

Out[12]: (0.9898666666666668, 105, 52.5, 0.006027066666666666)
```

It looks as if the mean has been moved; you now have 105 observations being used as your evidence.

3. Now, let's visualize the prior and posterior distribution—specifically, their marginal distributions:

```
In [13]:  # Visualizing the prior and posterior
          x1 = np.linspace(0.985, 1.015, 1000)
          plt.plot(x1, dnig_mu_marg(x1, 1, 1, 1/2, 0.0005), 'b-')
          plt.plot(x1, dnig_mu_marg(x1, *post), 'r-')
          plt.show()
```

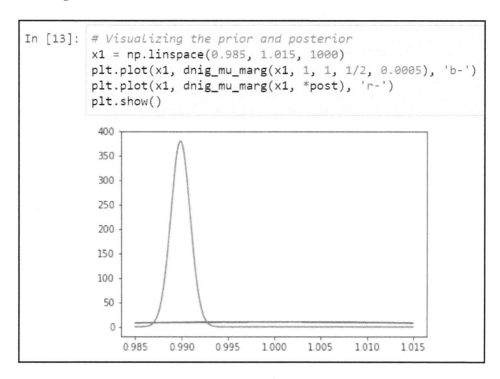

Blue represents the prior distribution, and red represents the posterior distribution. It appears that the prior distribution was largely uninformative about where the true resistance was, while the posterior distribution strongly says that the resistance is approximately 0.99.

4. Now, let's use this to compute a 95% credible interval for the mean of μ. I have written a function that will do this for you, where you feed it data and also the parameters of the prior distribution, and it will give you a credible interval with a specified level of credibility. Let's run this function as follows:

```
In [12]:  def mean_normal_nig_credible_interval(x, mu, nu, alpha, beta, C=0.95):
              """Computes a 100C% credible interval for the mean mu

              args:
                  x: array-like; The data
                  mu: float; The mu parameter of prior NIG(mu, nu, alpha, beta)
                  nu: float; The nu parameter of prior NIG(mu, nu, alpha, beta)
                  alpha: float; The alpha parameter of prior NIG(mu, nu, alpha, beta)
                  beta: float; The beta parameter of prior NIG(mu, nu, alpha, beta)
                  C: float; the credibility (chance of containing mu) of the interval

              return:
                  tuple; first number is the lower bound, second the upper bound, of the credible interval
              """

              if C < 0 or C > 1:
                  raise ValueError("C must be interpretable as a probability")

              p_mu, p_nu, p_alpha, p_beta = get_posterior_nig(x, mu, nu, alpha, beta)
              alpha = (1 - C)/2

              lower = qnig_mu_marg(alpha, p_mu, p_nu, p_alpha, p_beta)
              upper = qnig_mu_marg(1 - alpha, p_mu, p_nu, p_alpha, p_beta)

              return (lower, upper)
```

5. Now, let's compute the credible interval:

```
In [15]:  mean_normal_nig_credible_interval(res, 1, 1, 1/2, 0.0005)

Out[15]:  (0.987793372374521, 0.9919399609588125)
```

Here, what we notice is that 1 is not in this credible interval, so there's a 95% chance that the true resistance level is between $0.9877$ and $0.9919$.

# Bayesian hypothesis testing for means

Hypothesis testing is similar, in principle, to what we have done previously; only now, we are using the marginal distribution of the mean from the posterior distribution. We compute the probability that the mean lies in the region corresponding to the hypothesis being true.

So, now, you want to test whether the true mean is less than 1,000 $\Omega$. To do this, we get the parameters of the posterior distribution, and then feed these to the `pnig_mu_marg()` function:

```
In [16]: p_mu, p_nu, p_alpha, p_beta = get_posterior_nig(res, 1, 1, 1/2, 0.0005)

         pnig_mu_marg(1, p_mu, p_nu, p_alpha, p_beta)

Out[16]: 0.9999999999999998
```

We end up with a probability that is almost 1. It is all but certain that the resistors are not properly calibrated.

# Testing with two samples

Suppose that we want to compare the means of two populations. We start by assuming that the parameters of the two populations are independent and compute their posterior distributions, including the marginal distributions of the means. Then, we use Monte Carlo methods, similar to those used previously, to estimate the probability that one mean is less than the other. So, let's now take a look at two-sample testing.

Your company has decided that it no longer wants to stick with this manufacturer. They want to start producing resistors in-house, and they're looking at different methods for producing these resistors. Right now, they have two manufacturing processes known as process A and process B, and you want to know whether the mean for process A is less than the mean for process B. So, what we'll do is use Monte Carlo methods, as follows:

1. Collect data from both processes and compute the posterior distributions for both $\mu_A$ and $\mu_B$.
2. Simulate random draws of $\mu_A$ and $\mu_B$ from the posterior distributions.
3. Compute how often $\mu_A$ is less than $\mu_B$ to estimate the probability that $\mu_A > \mu_B$.

So, first, let's get the dataset for the two processes:

```
In [15]:  res_A = np.array([ 1.002,  1.001,  1.   ,  0.999,  0.998,  1.   ,  1.001,  0.999,
                             1.002,  0.998,  1.   ,  0.998,  1.001,  1.001,  1.002,  0.997,
                             1.001,  1.   ,  1.001,  0.999,  0.998,  0.998,  1.002,  1.002,
                             0.996,  0.998,  0.997,  1.001,  1.002,  0.997,  1.   ,  1.   ,
                             0.998,  0.997])

          res_B = np.array([ 0.995,  1.022,  0.993,  1.014,  0.998,  0.99 ,  0.998,  0.998,
                             0.99 ,  1.003,  1.016,  0.992,  1.   ,  1.002,  1.003,  1.005,
                             0.979,  1.012,  0.978,  1.01 ,  1.001,  1.026,  1.011,  1.   ,
                             0.98 ,  0.993,  1.016,  0.991,  0.986,  0.987,  1.012,  0.996,
                             1.013,  1.001,  0.984,  1.011,  1.01 ,  1.   ,  1.001])
```

We get the posterior distributions for both processes as follows:

```
In [18]:  postA = get_posterior_nig(res_A, 1, 1, 1/2, 0.0005)
          postA

Out[18]:  (0.9995999999999999, 35, 17.5, 0.000554199999999999)

In [19]:  postB = get_posterior_nig(res_B, 1, 1, 1/2, 0.0005)
          postB

Out[19]:  (1.000425, 40, 20.0, 0.0031258874999999997)
```

Now, let's simulate 1,000 draws from the posterior distributions:

```
In [20]:  N = 1000     # Number of simulations
          simA = rnig_mu_marg(*postA, n=N)
          simB = rnig_mu_marg(*postB, n=N)
```

Here are the random $\mu_A$ values:

```
In [21]:  simA[0:10]

Out[21]:  array([0.99863742, 0.99885439, 0.99857502, 0.99928144, 1.00171531,
                 0.99937789, 0.99695746, 1.00079628, 1.00050304, 1.00051395])
```

Here are the random $\mu_B$ values:

```
In [22]:  simB[0:10]

Out[22]:  array([0.99955569, 0.99928456, 0.99819933, 1.00000192, 0.99707296,
                 1.00098577, 0.99553932, 1.00200808, 0.99845368, 1.00049533])
```

Here is when $\mu_A$ is less than $\mu_B$:

```
In [23]:  sim = simA < simB    # mu_A < mu_B
          sim[0:10]

Out[23]:  array([ True,   True, False,   True, False,   True, False,   True, False,
                 False])
```

Finally, we add these up and take the mean, as follows:

```
In [24]:  sim.sum()

Out[24]:  629

In [25]:  sim.mean()

Out[25]:  0.629
```

We can see that about 65.8% of the time $\mu_A$ is less than $\mu_B$. This is higher than 50%, which suggests that $\mu_A$ is probably less than $\mu_B$, but this is not a very actionable probability. 65.8% is not a probability high enough to strongly suggest a change needs to be made.

So, that's it for Bayesian statistics for now. We will now move on to computing correlations in datasets.

# Finding correlations

In the final section of this chapter, we will learn about computing correlations using pandas and SciPy. We will look at how to use pandas and SciPy to compute correlations in datasets, and also explore some statistical tests to detect correlation.

In this section, I have used Pearson's correlation coefficient, which quantifies how strongly two variables are linearly correlated. This is a unitless number that takes values between -1 and 1. The sign of the correlation coefficient indicates the direction of the relationship. A positive $r$ indicates that as one variable increases, the other tends to increase; while a negative $r$ indicates that as one variable increases, the other tends to decrease. The magnitude indicates the strength of the relationship. If $r$ is close to 1 or -1, then the relationship is almost a perfect linear relationship, while an $r$ that is close to 0 indicates no linear relationship. The NumPy `corrcoef()` function computes the number for two NumPy arrays.

So, here's the correlation coefficient's definition. We're going to work with what's known as the Boston housing price dataset. This is known as a toy dataset, and is often used for evaluating statistical learning methods. I'm only interested in looking at correlations between the variables in this dataset.

 Note that we will be using a slightly modified version of the dataset, which can be found in the GitHub repository for this chapter.

We will use the following steps:

1. We will first load up all the required libraries, as follows:

```
In [1]:   from sklearn.datasets import load_boston
          import pandas as pd
          from pandas import DataFrame
          import matplotlib.pyplot as plt
          %matplotlib inline
```

2. We will then load in the dataset using the following code:

```
In [3]:   boston = pd.read_csv('Boston.csv')
```

3. Then, we will print the dataset information, so that we can have a look at it, as follows:

```
In [76]:  boston.info(verbose=True)

          <class 'pandas.core.frame.DataFrame'>
          RangeIndex: 506 entries, 0 to 505
          Data columns (total 13 columns):
          CRIM       506 non-null float64
           ZN        506 non-null float64
          INDUS      506 non-null float64
          CHAS       506 non-null int64
          NOX        506 non-null float64
          RM         506 non-null float64
          AGE        506 non-null float64
          DIS        506 non-null float64
          RAD        506 non-null int64
          TAX        506 non-null int64
          PTRATIO    506 non-null float64
          LSTAT      506 non-null float64
          MEDV       506 non-null float64
          dtypes: float64(10), int64(3)
          memory usage: 51.5 KB
```

So, these attributes tell us what this dataset contains. It has a few different variables such as, for example, the crime rate by town, the proportion of residential land zones, non-retail business acres, and others. Therefore, we have a number of different attributes for you to play with.

4. We will now load the actual dataset, as follows:

```
In [50]:  boston

Out[50]:
```

|    | CRIM    | ZN   | INDUS | CHAS | NOX   | RM    | AGE   | DIS    | RAD | TAX | PTRATIO | LSTAT |
|----|---------|------|-------|------|-------|-------|-------|--------|-----|-----|---------|-------|
| 0  | 0.00632 | 18.0 | 2.31  | 0    | 0.538 | 6.575 | 65.2  | 4.0900 | 1   | 296 | 15.3    | 4.98  |
| 1  | 0.02731 | 0.0  | 7.07  | 0    | 0.469 | 6.421 | 78.9  | 4.9671 | 2   | 242 | 17.8    | 9.14  |
| 2  | 0.02729 | 0.0  | 7.07  | 0    | 0.469 | 7.185 | 61.1  | 4.9671 | 2   | 242 | 17.8    | 4.03  |
| 3  | 0.03237 | 0.0  | 2.18  | 0    | 0.458 | 6.998 | 45.8  | 6.0622 | 3   | 222 | 18.7    | 2.94  |
| 4  | 0.06905 | 0.0  | 2.18  | 0    | 0.458 | 7.147 | 54.2  | 6.0622 | 3   | 222 | 18.7    | 5.33  |
| 5  | 0.02985 | 0.0  | 2.18  | 0    | 0.458 | 6.430 | 58.7  | 6.0622 | 3   | 222 | 18.7    | 5.21  |
| 6  | 0.08829 | 12.5 | 7.87  | 0    | 0.524 | 6.012 | 66.6  | 5.5605 | 5   | 311 | 15.2    | 12.43 |
| 7  | 0.14455 | 12.5 | 7.87  | 0    | 0.524 | 6.172 | 96.1  | 5.9505 | 5   | 311 | 15.2    | 19.15 |
| 8  | 0.21124 | 12.5 | 7.87  | 0    | 0.524 | 5.631 | 100.0 | 6.0821 | 5   | 311 | 15.2    | 29.93 |
| 9  | 0.17004 | 12.5 | 7.87  | 0    | 0.524 | 6.004 | 85.9  | 6.5921 | 5   | 311 | 15.2    | 17.10 |
| 10 | 0.22489 | 12.5 | 7.87  | 0    | 0.524 | 6.377 | 94.3  | 6.3467 | 5   | 311 | 15.2    | 20.45 |
| 11 | 0.11747 | 12.5 | 7.87  | 0    | 0.524 | 6.009 | 82.9  | 6.2267 | 5   | 311 | 15.2    | 13.27 |

This is going to very useful to us. Now, let's take a look at the correlation between the two variables.

5. We're going to import the `corrcoef()` function, and we're going to look at one of the columns from this dataset as if it were a NumPy array, as follows:

```
In [55]: from numpy import corrcoef

In [56]: boston.CRIM.as_matrix()       # As a NumPy array

Out[56]: array([6.3200e-03, 2.7310e-02, 2.7290e-02, 3.2370e-02, 6.9050e-02,
                2.9850e-02, 8.8290e-02, 1.4455e-01, 2.1124e-01, 1.7004e-01,
                2.2489e-01, 1.1747e-01, 9.3780e-02, 6.2976e-01, 6.3796e-01,
                6.2739e-01, 1.05393e+00, 7.8420e-01, 8.0271e-01, 7.2580e-01,
                1.25179e+00, 8.5204e-01, 1.23247e+00, 9.8843e-01, 7.5026e-01,
                8.4054e-01, 6.7191e-01, 9.5577e-01, 7.7299e-01, 1.00245e+00,
                1.13081e+00, 1.35472e+00, 1.38799e+00, 1.15172e+00, 1.61282e+00,
                6.4170e-02, 9.7440e-02, 8.0140e-02, 1.7505e-01, 2.76300e-02,
                3.3590e-02, 1.2744e-01, 1.4150e-01, 1.5936e-01, 1.22690e-01,
                1.7142e-01, 1.8836e-01, 2.2927e-01, 2.5387e-01, 2.19770e-01,
                8.8730e-02, 4.3370e-02, 5.3600e-02, 4.9810e-02, 1.36000e-02,
                1.3110e-02, 2.0550e-02, 1.4320e-02, 1.5445e-01, 1.03280e-01,
```

It started out as a NumPy array, but it's perfectly fine to just grab a pandas series and turn it into an array.

6. Now we're going to take `corrcoef()`, and compute the correlation between the crime rate and the price:

```
In [57]: corrcoef(boston.CRIM.as_matrix(), boston.MEDV.as_matrix())

Out[57]: array([[ 1.        , -0.38830461],
                [-0.38830461,  1.        ]])
```

We can see that the numbers in the matrix are the same.

The number in the off-diagonal entries corresponds to the correlation between the two variables. Therefore, there is a negative relationship between crime rate and price, which is not surprising. As the crime rate increases, you would expect the price to decrease. But this is not a very strong correlation. We often want correlations not just for two variables, but for many combinations of two variables. We can use the `pandas` DataFrame `corr()` method to compute what's known as the **correlation matrix**. This matrix contains correlations for every combination of variables in our dataset.

7. So, let's go ahead and compute a correlation matrix for the Boston dataset, using the `corr()` function:

```
In [58]:  boston.corr()
Out[58]:
```

|  | CRIM | ZN | INDUS | CHAS | NOX | RM | AGE | DIS |
|---|---|---|---|---|---|---|---|---|
| **CRIM** | 1.000000 | -0.200469 | 0.406583 | -0.055892 | 0.420972 | -0.219247 | 0.352734 | -0.379670 |
| **ZN** | -0.200469 | 1.000000 | -0.533828 | -0.042697 | -0.516604 | 0.311991 | -0.569537 | 0.664408 |
| **INDUS** | 0.406583 | -0.533828 | 1.000000 | 0.062938 | 0.763651 | -0.391676 | 0.644779 | -0.708027 |
| **CHAS** | -0.055892 | -0.042697 | 0.062938 | 1.000000 | 0.091203 | 0.091251 | 0.086518 | -0.099176 |
| **NOX** | 0.420972 | -0.516604 | 0.763651 | 0.091203 | 1.000000 | -0.302188 | 0.731470 | -0.769230 |
| **RM** | -0.219247 | 0.311991 | -0.391676 | 0.091251 | -0.302188 | 1.000000 | -0.240265 | 0.205246 |
| **AGE** | 0.352734 | -0.569537 | 0.644779 | 0.086518 | 0.731470 | -0.240265 | 1.000000 | -0.747881 |
| **DIS** | -0.379670 | 0.664408 | -0.708027 | -0.099176 | -0.769230 | 0.205246 | -0.747881 | 1.000000 |
| **RAD** | 0.625505 | -0.311948 | 0.595129 | -0.007368 | 0.611441 | -0.209847 | 0.456022 | -0.494588 |
| **TAX** | 0.582764 | -0.314563 | 0.720760 | -0.035587 | 0.668023 | -0.292048 | 0.506456 | -0.534432 |
| **PTRATIO** | 0.289946 | -0.391679 | 0.383248 | -0.121515 | 0.188933 | -0.355501 | 0.261515 | -0.232471 |
| **LSTAT** | 0.455621 | -0.412995 | 0.603800 | -0.053929 | 0.590879 | -0.613808 | 0.602339 | -0.496996 |
| **MEDV** | -0.388305 | 0.360445 | -0.483725 | 0.175260 | -0.427321 | 0.695360 | -0.376955 | 0.249929 |

These are all correlations. Every entry off the diagonal will have a corresponding entry on the other side of the diagonal—this is a symmetric matrix. Now, while this matrix contains all the data that we might want, it is very difficult to read.

8. So, let's use a package called `seaborn`, as this is going to allow us to plot a heatmap. A heatmap has colors with differing intensities for how large or small a number tends to be. So, we compute a heatmap and plot it as follows:

```
In [64]:   import seaborn as sns    # Allows for easy plotting of heatmaps

In [72]:   plt.subplots(figsize=(12,6))
           sns.heatmap(boston.corr(), annot=True, linewidths=.8)

Out[72]:   <matplotlib.axes._subplots.AxesSubplot at 0x1ebd46a6eb8>
```

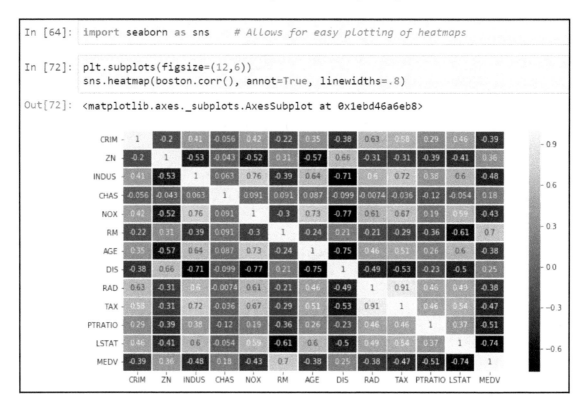

The preceding screenshot shows the resulting map. Here, black indicates correlations close to -1, and very light colors indicate correlations that are close to 1. From this heatmap, we can start to see some patterns.

# Testing for correlation

SciPy contains the `pearsonr()` function in its statistics module, which not only computes the correlation between two variables but also allows for hypothesis testing to detect correlation. Rejecting the null hypothesis will signify that the correlation between the two variables, in general, is not 0. However, be aware that rejecting the null hypothesis does not automatically signify a meaningful relationship between the two variables. It's possible that the correlation is not 0, but still too small to be meaningful. This is especially true when performing the test on large samples.

We're going to do a statistical test using the following hypotheses:

$$H_0 : \rho = 0$$
$$H_A : \rho \neq 0$$

We import the `pearsonr()` function, and we run it on crime and price to see whether these things are correlated with statistical significance:

```
In [73]:  from scipy.stats import pearsonr

In [75]:  # Test to see if crime rate and house prices are correlated
          pearsonr(boston.CRIM, boston.MEDV)

Out[75]:  (-0.38830460858681154, 1.1739870821945733e-19)
```

Here, we have a very small $p$ value, which suggests that yes, indeed, the crime rate and the price of a home appear to be correlated. If we had to take a guess, then we would say that it would be negatively correlated.

# Summary

That's all for this chapter on classical statistical methods. We learned about computing descriptive statistics for data and we learned how to implement classical inference for proportions. We also learned how to implement inference for means. We then explored Bayesian analysis and examined how to apply it to analyze proportions and means. Finally, we learned how to find correlations using pandas and SciPy.

In the next chapter, we will learn about some basic machine learning theory.

# 2
# Introduction to Supervised Learning

In this chapter, we will discuss supervised learning and what it is all about. We will start this chapter by discussing the principles involved in different types of machine learning, with a particular focus on supervised learning. Then, we will look at various techniques used when training models. Finally, we will look at some common metrics that people use to judge how well an algorithm is performing.

The following topics will be covered in this chapter:

- Principles of machine learning
- Training models
- Evaluating models

## Principles of machine learning

Without much further ado, let's start teaching machines. We will start with the principles of machine learning. This section introduces the basic framework of machine learning models, particularly for supervised learning. This includes the different types of machine learning that exist, and what the objectives of machine learning are.

Machine learning comes in a few flavors, namely the following:

- **Supervised learning**: This is machine learning for labeled data. We use data with labels or a target variable to train an algorithm and apply the algorithm to predict labels for unlabeled data. Algorithms such as **support vector machines** (**SVMs**), decision trees, and so on, engage in supervised learning. The rest of the chapter will focus on supervised learning.
- **Unsupervised learning**: This is machine learning using unlabeled data. There is no labeled data in our training set, yet the algorithm must still predict what it will be for test data. Clustering methods, such as k-means, are considered unsupervised learning.
- **Reinforcement learning**: This is a mixture of supervised and unsupervised learning, where some of the training data has labels and some does not.

We use an algorithm to approximate a function that determines the value of a **target variable**. Our target variable is the variable we are trying to predict. It could be binary (did a website visitor buy a product or not?), categorical (what color shoes did a website visitor purchase?), or continuous (how much money did a visitor spend on a website?).

Our training data includes not only the target variable for observations, but also **features**, other variables that could be used for prediction. For the examples mentioned in the preceding paragraph, features could include whether a visitor has an account with the website or not, whether the visitor has been to the website before or not, or how long the visitor's session lasted. Demographic variables, such as gender, age, geographic location, and others, could be useful features too.

# Checking the variables using the iris dataset

Handling missing data is a big topic of its own. So, let's start seeing this in action. We will use the `iris` dataset, which we worked with in Chapter 1, *Classical Statistical Analysis*. The `iris` dataset has labels corresponding to the species of flowers. Sepal length, sepal width, petal length, and petal width are features, while the species is the target. We will work on the dataset by taking the following steps:

1. Let's load in this dataset, which is available with `scikit-learn`. You've already seen how to load in `iris`; here is a quick way to get a description of what's in the dataset:

```
In [1]: from sklearn.datasets import load_iris
        import matplotlib.pyplot as plt
        import numpy as np
        %matplotlib inline


In [2]: iris_obj = load_iris()
        print(iris_obj.DESCR)

        Iris Plants Database
        ====================

        Notes
        -----
        Data Set Characteristics:
            :Number of Instances: 150 (50 in each of three classes)
            :Number of Attributes: 4 numeric, predictive attributes and the class
            :Attribute Information:
                - sepal length in cm
```

2. Now, let's have a look at the data:

```
In [3]: iris_obj.data

Out[3]: array([[ 5.1,  3.5,  1.4,  0.2],
               [ 4.9,  3. ,  1.4,  0.2],
               [ 4.7,  3.2,  1.3,  0.2],
               [ 4.6,  3.1,  1.5,  0.2],
               [ 5. ,  3.6,  1.4,  0.2],
               [ 5.4,  3.9,  1.7,  0.4],
               [ 4.6,  3.4,  1.4,  0.3],
               [ 5. ,  3.4,  1.5,  0.2],
               [ 4.4,  2.9,  1.4,  0.2],
               [ 4.9,  3.1,  1.5,  0.1],
               [ 5.4,  3.7,  1.5,  0.2],
               [ 4.8,  3.4,  1.6,  0.2],
               [ 4.8,  3. ,  1.4,  0.1],
               [ 4.3,  3. ,  1.1,  0.1],
```

3. Now, let's have a look at the names of these features, using the following screenshot:

```
In [4]:  iris_obj.feature_names

Out[4]:  ['sepal length (cm)',
          'sepal width (cm)',
          'petal length (cm)',
          'petal width (cm)']
```

As seen here, the `iris` dataset comes with `sepal length`, `sepal width`, `petal length`, and `petal width`.

4. We have a target variable, which is the species of the flowers, as shown here:

```
In [5]:  iris_obj.target

Out[5]:  array([0, 0, 0, 0, 0, 0, 0, 0, 0, 0, 0, 0, 0, 0, 0, 0, 0, 0, 0, 0, 0, 0,
                0, 0, 0, 0, 0, 0, 0, 0, 0, 0, 0, 0, 0, 0, 0, 0, 0, 0, 0, 0, 0, 0,
                0, 0, 0, 0, 1, 1, 1, 1, 1, 1, 1, 1, 1, 1, 1, 1, 1, 1, 1, 1, 1, 1,
                1, 1, 1, 1, 1, 1, 1, 1, 1, 1, 1, 1, 1, 1, 1, 1, 1, 1, 1, 1, 1, 1,
                1, 1, 1, 1, 1, 1, 1, 1, 2, 2, 2, 2, 2, 2, 2, 2, 2, 2, 2, 2, 2, 2,
                2, 2, 2, 2, 2, 2, 2, 2, 2, 2, 2, 2, 2, 2, 2, 2, 2, 2, 2, 2, 2, 2,
                2, 2, 2, 2, 2, 2, 2, 2, 2, 2, 2, 2])
```

5. We then find the target names, as follows:

```
In [6]:  iris_obj.target_names

Out[6]:  array(['setosa', 'versicolor', 'virginica'],
                dtype='<U10')
```

As seen here, the target names are `setosa`, `versicolor`, and `virginica`. So, zeros correspond to `setosa`, ones correspond to `versicolor`, and twos correspond to `virginica`.

6. Now, let's choose a random subset of this dataset, and this will simulate a training dataset. We will use the following code to do so:

```
In [7]:  # Randomly choose a subset of the iris data
         train = np.random.choice(np.arange(len(iris_obj.data)), size=100, replace=False)
         train = np.sort(train)
         train
```

This results in the following training array:

```
Out[7]: array([  1,   2,   3,   4,   5,   6,  10,  11,  13,  14,  15,  19,  20,
                22,  23,  25,  26,  27,  28,  29,  31,  33,  34,  36,  38,  39,
                40,  41,  42,  43,  44,  46,  47,  48,  52,  54,  55,  57,  58,
                61,  62,  63,  66,  67,  68,  70,  72,  73,  74,  75,  76,  77,
                78,  80,  81,  84,  85,  86,  87,  88,  90,  91,  92,  95,  96,
                97, 100, 102, 103, 104, 105, 106, 107, 110, 111, 112, 114, 117,
               119, 120, 121, 122, 123, 125, 128, 129, 130, 131, 132, 133, 134,
               136, 137, 139, 142, 144, 145, 146, 147, 149])
```

7. All remaining data will be treated as unlabeled, so we will know what the species is for the training data, but we will not know what the species is for the data. We will do so using the following code:

```
In [8]: # ALL remaining data will be treated as "unlabeled"
        test = np.setdiff1d(np.arange(len(iris_obj.data)), train)
        test
```

This results in the following test array:

```
Out[8]: array([  0,   7,   8,   9,  12,  16,  17,  18,  21,  24,  30,  32,  35,
                37,  45,  49,  50,  51,  53,  56,  59,  60,  64,  65,  69,  71,
                79,  82,  83,  89,  93,  94,  98,  99, 101, 108, 109, 113, 115,
               116, 118, 124, 126, 127, 135, 138, 140, 141, 143, 148])
```

8. We will then visualize the training dataset using the following lines of code:

```
In [9]: # Plot sepal length vs sepal width, labelling species
        marker_map = {0: 'o', 1: 's', 2: '^'}
        color_map = {0: 'blue', 1: 'green', 2: 'red'}
        var1, var2 = 0, 1    # Sepal length and sepal width variables
        for length, width, species in zip(iris_obj.data[train, var1], iris_obj.data[train, var2], iris_obj.target[train]):
            plt.scatter(x=length, y=width, marker=marker_map[species], c=color_map[species])
        plt.xlabel(iris_obj.feature_names[var1])
        plt.ylabel(iris_obj.feature_names[var2])
        plt.show()
```

This results in the following output:

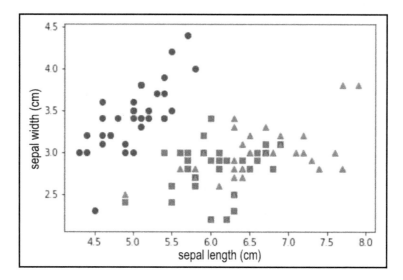

Here, blue corresponds to `setosa`, green corresponds to `versicolor`, and red to `virginica`.

9. Now, we will discover what the species is for the unlabeled data. We will visualize the test dataset using the following lines of code:

```
In [10]:  # This plot includes unlabeled data

          # Plot sepal length vs sepal width, labelling species
          marker_map = {0: 'o', 1: 's', 2: '^'}
          color_map = {0: 'blue', 1: 'green', 2: 'red'}
          var1, var2 = 0, 1    # Sepal length and sepal width variables
          for length, width, species in zip(iris_obj.data[train, var1], iris_obj.data[train, var2], iris_obj.target[train]):
              plt.scatter(x=length, y=width, marker=marker_map[species], c=color_map[species])
          # Plot unlabeled data too
          for length, width in zip(iris_obj.data[test, var1], iris_obj.data[test, var2]):
              plt.scatter(x=length, y=width, marker='o', c="black")
          plt.xlabel(iris_obj.feature_names[var1])
          plt.ylabel(iris_obj.feature_names[var2])
          plt.show()
```

This results in the following output:

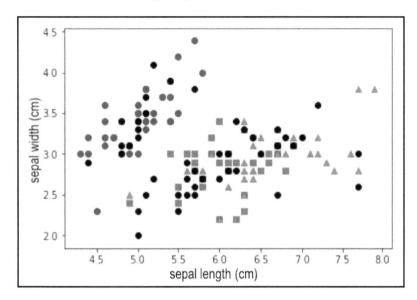

Notice that the black dots are unlabeled. We could probably guess that the blue dots correspond to the `setosa` species, although it might be uncertain as to what species the black dots belong to.

10. However, we can look at a different feature, and maybe we will see different patterns. We will use the following code to do so:

```
In [11]:  # This plot uses different variables

          # Plot petal length vs petal width, labelling species
          marker_map = {0: 'o', 1: 's', 2: '^'}
          color_map = {0: 'blue', 1: 'green', 2: 'red'}
          var1, var2 = 2, 3    # Sepal length and sepal width variables
          for length, width, species in zip(iris_obj.data[train, var1], iris_obj.data[train, var2], iris_obj.target[train]):
              plt.scatter(x=length, y=width, marker=marker_map[species], c=color_map[species])
          # Plot unlabeled data too
          for length, width in zip(iris_obj.data[test, var1], iris_obj.data[test, var2]):
              plt.scatter(x=length, y=width, marker='o', c="black")
          plt.xlabel(iris_obj.feature_names[var1])
          plt.ylabel(iris_obj.feature_names[var2])
          plt.show()
```

This results in the following output:

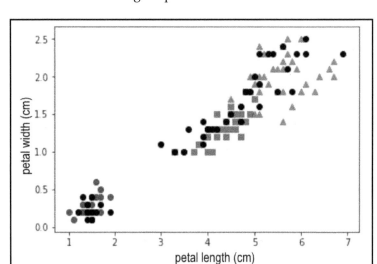

Notice that `versicolor` and `virginica` are a little bit more separated here than they were before. Perhaps this will make it easier to predict what the black dots' species is.

# The goal of supervised learning

The objective of supervised learning is to minimize errors in future prediction rates. Our algorithm trained on labeled data should be able to predict future unlabeled data well. Remember that we may never see whether our algorithm is correctly predicting future data, so it's important to do all we can to ensure that the algorithm does well on data for which we can observe the correct values of the target variable.

**Error** signifies the degree to which our algorithm does not correctly predict the target variable. For classification problems, it's how much our algorithm chooses the wrong label, and for regression problems, it may be how distant predictions are from the correct value. An ideal algorithm is one that has a small error.

In addition to error, we may have a **loss function**, which quantifies how wrong the algorithm was. This may be different than merely a count of errors or the distance from the predicted value to the actual value. Training algorithms involves choosing an algorithm that minimizes its loss function on the training data. We hope that the model will generalize to unseen data and that errors in future data are small as well.

Let's load in the `titanic.csv` dataset, which includes details about the passengers aboard the *Titanic* and who survived the disaster:

1. So, let's go ahead and import `pandas`, and let's have a look at the `titanic` dataset, using the following lines of code:

```
In [12]: import pandas as pd
         from pandas import DataFrame

In [13]: titanic = pd.read_csv("titanic.csv")
         titanic.head()
```

This results in the following data being displayed:

| Out[13]: | Survived | Pclass | Name | Sex | Age | Siblings/Spouses Aboard | Parents/Children Aboard | Fare |
|---|---|---|---|---|---|---|---|---|
| 0 | 0 | 3 | Mr. Owen Harris Braund | male | 22.0 | 1 | 0 | 7.2500 |
| 1 | 1 | 1 | Mrs. John Bradley (Florence Briggs Thayer) Cum... | female | 38.0 | 1 | 0 | 71.2833 |
| 2 | 1 | 3 | Miss. Laina Heikkinen | female | 26.0 | 0 | 0 | 7.9250 |
| 3 | 1 | 1 | Mrs. Jacques Heath (Lily May Peel) Futrelle | female | 35.0 | 1 | 0 | 53.1000 |
| 4 | 0 | 3 | Mr. William Henry Allen | male | 35.0 | 0 | 0 | 8.0500 |

Here, we see the first few rows of the `titanic` dataset.

2. Now, the variable that we would like to predict is whether an individual survived the Titanic disaster. We have their passenger class, the name of the individual, their sex, their age, how many siblings or spouses they had aboard, how many parents or children were aboard, and the fare that they paid. These will be the features that we will use to predict whether a person survived or not. We have a very simple first algorithm—predict the most common outcome of the target variable, which results in the following output:

```
In [3]:  titanic.Survived.value_counts()

Out[3]:  0    545
         1    342
         Name: Survived, dtype: int64
```

In this case, the most common outcome was *did not survive*. So, our simple algorithm will always predict that the person died. This is a dumb algorithm, yet it should be taken seriously, because, if a more sophisticated algorithm does not do better than the dumb algorithm, the sophisticated algorithm is not worth the effort that you put into it.

3. So, it's a good idea to compare your sophisticated algorithm to this dumb one. It gives you a baseline for how well an algorithm should be doing. We can say that the loss function here is the number of incorrect predictions. We're not going to say that this algorithm actually minimizes this, and we can see how well the algorithm does in the following output:

```
In [15]:  predicted = pd.Series([0] * len(titanic))
          (titanic.Survived - predicted).abs().sum()

Out[15]:  342
```

This gives an output saying that the algorithm made 342 mistakes, which is not surprising, because 342 people survived the disaster. Our objective then would be to try to find a better algorithm that would have a smaller error rate. In the next section, we will see what the process of training a machine learning model looks like.

# Training models

In this section, we will see supervised learning in action. We won't look at complicated algorithms, but we will look at how to train even a simple algorithm and machine learning best practices, such as splitting data into training and test data, and performing cross-validation.

# Issues in training supervised learning models

When a model does not predict the target variable well, it underfits. This is true for both seen and unseen future data. **Underfitting** is when an algorithm trained to predict a value does so poorly both on the training data and on future, unseen data. **Overfitting** is when a model predicts training data well, but does not generalize well, and so predicts future data poorly. Data analysts are mainly worried about overfitting, since it's easier to do, yet harder to detect.

So, let's load up the `titanic` dataset again, and we're going to re-implement our most common value algorithm, which can be done using the following code:

```
In [4]:  # Predict most common value
         if titanic.Survived.value_counts()[0] > titanic.Survived.value_counts()[1]:
             guess = 0
         else:
             guess = 1

         predicted = pd.Series([guess] * len(titanic))
         (titanic.Survived - predicted).abs().sum()     # Error count (trivial here)

Out[4]:  342
```

This displays an output stating that our algorithm made 342 mistakes.

We will then calculate the error rate, as follows:

```
In [5]:  (titanic.Survived - predicted).abs().mean()

Out[5]:  0.3855693348365276
```

It has an error rate of 39%, which means that it correctly predicted 61% of the dataset, as shown here:

```
In [6]:  1 - (titanic.Survived - predicted).abs().mean()

Out[6]:  0.6144306651634723
```

This algorithm is underfitting as much as it possibly can. It may, in fact, be a worst-case scenario for underfitting.

Overfitting occurs when an algorithm predicts training data well but does not generalize to new data; on new data, the algorithm's error rate increases unacceptably.

Underfitting is obvious when training a system, but overfitting requires more care to detect, since unseen data is not seen (obviously). There are techniques, though, for simulating unseen data.

# Splitting data

The objective of machine learning is to develop an algorithm that performs well on future data, which, by definition, is unseen. How can we simulate the behavior of feature data? We split a dataset into training and test data. Some of the dataset is held back, and we develop our algorithm using the training data.

The first technique is to split data into a training dataset and a testing dataset. We use the training data to develop our algorithm. We then see how well the algorithm generalizes by applying the trained algorithm to the test data and quantifying the error rate.

The `train_test_split()` function, from **scikit-learn (sklearn)**, makes splitting data easy, as seen in the following steps:

1. We will import this function, and we will apply it to the `titanic.csv` dataset using the following code:

```
In [7]:  from sklearn.model_selection import train_test_split
```

2. We will tell it to commit 10% of this dataset to the test set. The remainder will be training data:

```
In [8]: titanic_train, titanic_test = train_test_split(titanic,
                                                  test_size=0.1)
```

It will give out two datasets, and they will be stored in `titanic_train` and `titanic_test`.

3. We will now print out the training data as follows:

```
In [9]: titanic_train
Out[9]:
```

| | Survived | Pclass | Name | Sex | Age | Siblings/Spouses Aboard | Parents/Children Aboard | Fare |
|---|---|---|---|---|---|---|---|---|
| 784 | 1 | 3 | Master. Bertram Vere Dean | male | 1.00 | 1 | 2 | 20.5750 |
| 429 | 1 | 2 | Mrs. Charles Alexander (Alice Adelaide Slow) L... | female | 42.00 | 1 | 0 | 26.0000 |
| 671 | 0 | 2 | Mr. Ennis Hastings Watson | male | 19.00 | 0 | 0 | 0.0000 |

Here is `titanic_train`, this is all our training data. If we use the `.shape()` function, we will see that we have `798` observations in our training data.

4. We will now print out the test data as follows:

```
In [11]: titanic_test
Out[11]:
```

| | Survived | Pclass | Name | Sex | Age | Siblings/Spouses Aboard | Parents/Children Aboard | Fare |
|---|---|---|---|---|---|---|---|---|
| 390 | 0 | 3 | Mr. Johan Birger Gustafsson | male | 28.0 | 2 | 0 | 7.9250 |
| 27 | 0 | 1 | Mr. Charles Alexander Fortune | male | 19.0 | 3 | 2 | 263.0000 |
| 858 | 1 | 1 | Mrs. Frederick Joel (Margaret Welles Barron) S... | female | 48.0 | 0 | 0 | 25.9292 |
| 328 | 1 | 3 | Miss. Agnes McCoy | female | 28.0 | 2 | 0 | 23.2500 |

Here is our test set. If we use the `.shape()` function, we will see that it has 89 rows and 8 columns.

Now, let's apply a new algorithm. This is going to be a table-lookup algorithm. It does the following: looks up all individuals in the training set with the same passenger class (`Pclass`), sex (`Sex`), siblings (`Siblings/Spouses Aboard`), and parents and children aboard (`Parents/Children Aboard`). After it has done that, it will predict the most common value among those individuals.

Here is the function that performs this algorithm:

```
In [13]: def table_lookup_predictor(x, table):
             """Implements the table-lookup algorithm"""

             # Get most common label
             default = table.Survived.value_counts().argmax()
             # Get similar individuals
             similar_tab = table.loc[(table["Pclass"] == x["Pclass"]) &\
                                     (table["Sex"] == x["Sex"]) &\
                                     (table["Siblings/Spouses Aboard"] == x["Siblings/Spouses Aboard"]) &\
                                     (table["Parents/Children Aboard"] == x["Parents/Children Aboard"]), "Survived"]
             if len(similar_tab) == 0:
                 # If table is empty (no "similar" individuals), guess the most common label
                 return default
             else:
                 return similar_tab.value_counts().argmax()
```

5. We give it one observation—the first one in the dataset:

```
In [14]: titanic_train.iloc[0,:]

Out[14]: Survived                           0
         Pclass                             3
         Name                  Mr. Daniel Coxon
         Sex                             male
         Age                               59
         Siblings/Spouses Aboard            0
         Parents/Children Aboard            0
         Fare                            7.25
         Name: 93, dtype: object
```

6. We will then see what the algorithm predicts for the given value, as follows:

```
In [15]: # Demonstration 1
         table_lookup_predictor(titanic_train.iloc[0,:], titanic_train)

Out[15]: 0
```

It looks like it made a perfect prediction. It predicted that an individual like this did not survive. So far, it has made a good prediction.

7. We will then look at the predictions for all individuals in the training data:

```
In [16]:  tlu_train_predicted = titanic_train.apply(table_lookup_predictor, 1,
                                                     table=titanic_train)
          tlu_train_predicted
```

This displays the following output:

```
Out[16]:  784    0
          429    1
          671    0
          320    1
          88     0
          124    0
          318    0
          655    0
          251    0
          47     0
          364    1
          57     1
```

8. Now, let's import a function from `sklearn` called `accuracy_score()`:

```
In [17]:  from sklearn.metrics import accuracy_score
```

9. We're going to use the `accuracy_score()` function to see how accurate our algorithm was. We will apply it to the training data as follows:

```
In [18]:  accuracy_score(y_true=titanic_train.Survived,
                         y_pred=tlu_train_predicted)

Out[18]:  0.8208020050125313
```

On the training data, our algorithm has an accuracy rate of 82%, which seems pretty good.

10. Now, let's see how it does when applied to the test dataset:

```
In [19]:  tlu_test_predicted = titanic_test.apply(table_lookup_predictor, 1,
                                                  table=titanic_train)


In [20]:  accuracy_score(y_true=titanic_test.Survived,
                         y_pred=tlu_test_predicted)

Out[20]:  0.7528089887640449
```

We can see that our algorithm has an error rate of 78%, which is actually better than I thought it would be, but the accuracy has still gone down a little bit. This suggests that our algorithm is doing some overfitting, which should not come as a surprise. The moment you use the test data for anything, such as computing performance statistics, that dataset is no longer out-of-sample. You should only interact with the test set once, at the very end of the project, otherwise, you cannot trust performance metrics when the algorithm has already interacted with the test set. This is not a rule that I will hold to strictly in this book, since I'm teaching about technology and not trying to develop good algorithms, but, in practice, for real projects, the test set should never be used until the very end.

# Cross-validation

Cross-validation is a way to simulate out-of-sample unseen data when developing an algorithm, without actually touching our test set.

Many algorithms include **hyperparameters**, which are parameters that are characteristic of the algorithm itself rather than the underlying phenomenon. We need to choose the value of these parameters, and we are indifferent to their values beyond their ability to improve predictions. However, computational considerations, such as computation time, could also be a factor in deciding hyperparameter values.

Our algorithm does not account for passengers' ages when making predictions. These are unfortunately, not binary variables, but we can use them to create a binary variable by fixing an age and marking all those individuals less than that age with 1, and the rest with 0. The cut-off age behaves like a hyperparameter here.

We don't want to pick our cutoff to maximize predictive accuracy in the training set, though, and we don't want to choose it so that it improves accuracy in the test set either. Instead, we will employ **cross-validation**. The procedure works as follows:

1. Divide data into *k* folds (approximately equal-size subsets of the original dataset that together form the whole dataset).
2. For each fold, do the following:

   - Treat the fold as the **test** data and the rest of the data as **training** data.
   - For each possible value of the hyperparameter, use the **training** data to fit the model and evaluate its performance on the **test** data and track the performance.

3. Aggregate the performance of the algorithm across the different folds for each possible value of the hyperparameter.
4. Use the hyperparameter value that yielded the best performance overall.

Cross-validation can be used for purposes other than choosing hyperparameters. For example, it can be a good way to evaluate an algorithm's performance, allowing you to choose between different algorithms.

Here, I will consider six candidate cut-off ages—10, 20, 30, 40, 50, and 60. I will use 10 folds.

Now, `scikit-learn` provides multiple functions for supporting cross-validation. The `KFold` class can split a dataset up into folds as described. The `cross_val_score()` function can perform the entire cross-validation procedure and is a good choice. Here, I will do the cross-validation manually using only `KFold`:

1. So, we're going to import this function along with NumPy:

```
In [21]:  from sklearn.model_selection import KFold
          import numpy as np
```

2. We're going to split our dataset up into 10 folds:

```
In [22]:  kf = KFold(n_splits=10)
```

3. Let's have a preview of our folds:

```
In [23]:  # Preview; note that these are NumPy arrays
          for train, test in kf.split(titanic_train):
              print("Training Indices:")
              print(train)
              print("\nTest Indices")
              print(test)
              print("\n----\n")
```

This results in the following output:

```
Training Indices:
[ 80  81  82  83  84  85  86  87  88  89  90  91  92  93  94  95  96  97
  98  99 100 101 102 103 104 105 106 107 108 109 110 111 112 113 114 115
 116 117 118 119 120 121 122 123 124 125 126 127 128 129 130 131 132 133
 134 135 136 137 138 139 140 141 142 143 144 145 146 147 148 149 150 151
 152 153 154 155 156 157 158 159 160 161 162 163 164 165 166 167 168 169
 170 171 172 173 174 175 176 177 178 179 180 181 182 183 184 185 186 187
 188 189 190 191 192 193 194 195 196 197 198 199 200 201 202 203 204 205
 206 207 208 209 210 211 212 213 214 215 216 217 218 219 220 221 222 223
 224 225 226 227 228 229 230 231 232 233 234 235 236 237 238 239 240 241
 242 243 244 245 246 247 248 249 250 251 252 253 254 255 256 257 258 259
 260 261 262 263 264 265 266 267 268 269 270 271 272 273 274 275 276 277
```

These will be the training indices for one of the folds, and these will be the test indices.

So, one run through this cross-validation algorithm will have you training using the data corresponding to the indices there, and then evaluating the algorithm on the part of the dataset with these indices. You can then see all the different combinations of training and test sets that this produces.

4. Now, we're going to have a different table-lookup algorithm, where we have an age parameter that needs to be specified:

```
In [24]: def table_lookup_predictor_2(x, table, age):
             """Implements the table-lookup algorithm with ages after cufoff"""

             # Get most common Label
             default = table.Survived.value_counts().argmax()
             # Get similar individuals
             similar_tab = table.loc[(table["Pclass"] == x["Pclass"]) &\
                                     (table["Sex"] == x["Sex"]) &\
                                     (table["Siblings/Spouses Aboard"] == x["Siblings/Spouses Aboard"]) &\
                                     (table["Parents/Children Aboard"] == x["Parents/Children Aboard"]) &\
                                     ((table["Age"] < age) == (x["Age"] < age)) , "Survived"]
             if len(similar_tab) == 0:
                 # If table is empty (no "similar" individuals), guess the most common Label
                 return default
             else:
                 return similar_tab.value_counts().argmax()
```

5. So, what we're going to do is go through each of these ages and perform cross-validation, and we are going to see which `age` cutoff seems to lead to the best predictive accuracy on unseen data:

```
In [25]: ages = [10, 20, 30, 40, 50, 60]
         performance = dict()

         for age in ages:
             cv_perf = list()
             for train, test in kf.split(titanic_train):
                 # Get predicted values in "test" data using "train" data
                 predicted = titanic_train.iloc[test,:].apply(table_lookup_predictor_2, 1, table=titanic_train.iloc[train,:],
                                                              age=age)
                 actual = titanic_train.loc[:,"Survived"].iloc[test]
                 # Add performance to a list
                 cv_perf.append(accuracy_score(y_true=actual, y_pred=predicted))
             performance[age] = cv_perf
```

We're going to end up with a distribution of performance, because, for each of these ages, the algorithm is going to repeat 10 times on different training and test datasets.

6. So, let's look at the `performance` metric as if it were a `DataFrame` object:

```
In [26]:  DataFrame(performance)
Out[26]:
                10          20          30          40          50          60
   0    0.825000    0.825000    0.812500    0.812500    0.812500    0.812500
   1    0.825000    0.825000    0.812500    0.812500    0.787500    0.787500
   2    0.787500    0.787500    0.800000    0.812500    0.775000    0.775000
   3    0.850000    0.837500    0.837500    0.800000    0.812500    0.812500
   4    0.712500    0.712500    0.687500    0.675000    0.700000    0.662500
   5    0.837500    0.837500    0.812500    0.800000    0.787500    0.775000
   6    0.837500    0.812500    0.825000    0.825000    0.812500    0.812500
   7    0.775000    0.750000    0.775000    0.825000    0.787500    0.775000
   8    0.797468    0.797468    0.759494    0.772152    0.759494    0.759494
   9    0.797468    0.797468    0.797468    0.810127    0.810127    0.797468
```

So, we can see the `performance` metric when the age was 10 for each of the different splits—for 20, for 30, for 40, and so on.

7. Now, let's look at the means of each of these:

```
In [27]:  DataFrame(performance).mean()
Out[27]:  10      0.804494
          20      0.798244
          30      0.791946
          40      0.794478
          50      0.784462
          60      0.776946
          dtype: float64
```

It looks like, for an `age` cutoff of 10, we have the best performance for our algorithm. It's not a significant performance boost, but for now, we're just going to say this is good enough; and we will decide that the best choice for the `age` cutoff is 10 years.

Another important step in machine learning is evaluating an algorithm's performance. In the next section, we will look at common metrics for deciding whether an algorithm is doing a good job of making predictions.

# Evaluating models

In this section, we will look at metrics for evaluating how well a model is performing. This section focuses on metrics to use to evaluate how well a model predicts a target variable in binary classification. We will discuss how to compute accuracy, precision, recall, the F1 score, and the Bayes factor, along with how to interpret each of these metrics.

# Accuracy

**Accuracy** measures how frequently an algorithm predicted the correct label. On the surface, this looks like a good enough metric, but accuracy alone does not convey the quality of an algorithm. A problem could have an algorithm that is very accurate, but only because the learning problem is, in some sense, easy, such as predicting on any particular day whether it will rain in the Sahara Desert. More than 99% of the time, *no* would be a good prediction. Let's implement the various metrics using the following steps:

1. Let's re-import some of what we did in the previous section, where we have our titanic.csv dataset:

```
In [1]:  import pandas as pd
         from pandas import DataFrame
         from sklearn.model_selection import train_test_split
```

2.  We will split it into training and test datasets, and we're going to re-implement our second iteration of the table-lookup algorithm:

```
In [2]: titanic = pd.read_csv("titanic.csv")
        titanic_train, titanic_test = train_test_split(titanic, test_size=0.1)

        def table_lookup_predictor(x, table, age):
            """Implements the table-lookup algorithm with ages after cufoff"""

            # Get most common label
            default = table.Survived.value_counts().argmax()
            # Get similar individuals
            similar_tab = table.loc[(table["Pclass"] == x["Pclass"]) &\
                                    (table["Sex"] == x["Sex"]) &\
                                    (table["Siblings/Spouses Aboard"] == x["Siblings/Spouses Aboard"]) &\
                                    (table["Parents/Children Aboard"] == x["Parents/Children Aboard"]) &\
                                    ((table["Age"] < age) == (x["Age"] < age)) , "Survived"]
            if len(similar_tab) == 0:
                # If table is empty (no "similar" individuals), guess the most common label
                return default
            else:
                return similar_tab.value_counts().argmax()

        actual = titanic_test.Survived
        predicted = titanic_test.apply(table_lookup_predictor, 1, table=titanic_train, age=10)
```

3.  We will then display the results using the following code:

```
In [3]: DataFrame({"actual": actual, "predicted": predicted})
```

This results in the following output:

```
Out[3]:
```

|     | actual | predicted |
| --- | --- | --- |
| 548 | 0 | 0 |
| 157 | 0 | 0 |
| 596 | 1 | 0 |
| 290 | 0 | 0 |
| 115 | 0 | 0 |
| 372 | 0 | 0 |
| 305 | 1 | 1 |
| 257 | 1 | 1 |

This is the actual versus predicted result of the test set by our algorithm.

4. The first thing we're going to compute is accuracy, and we can use the `accuracy_score()` function from `sklearn` to compute this:

```
In [4]:  from sklearn.metrics import accuracy_score

In [5]:  accuracy_score(y_true=actual, y_pred=predicted)
```

We will see that the accuracy is about 77%, which is pretty decent.

Accuracy alone does not give a complete picture of how well an algorithm is doing when making predictions. It's possible that the learning problem is easy. For example, if nearly everyone on the Titanic died, always predicting did not survive would have high accuracy, yet would incorrectly predict that every survivor died.

# Precision

**Precision** describes how often a model correctly predicts a given label. For example, the table lookup algorithm would have high precision for survivors if, every time it predicts that a passenger survived, the passenger was in fact a survivor. A high score suggests that an algorithm is precise, in the sense that, when the algorithm predicts a label, that prediction is likely to be true.

So, let's compute precision by using the `precision_score()` function provided by `sklearn`:

1. We will import the function as follows:

```
In [6]:  from sklearn.metrics import precision_score
```

2. Then, we will compute the precision score for survivorship, as follows:

```
In [7]:  precision_score(y_true=actual, y_pred=predicted)
Out[7]:  0.906206896551724
```

We see that the precision score for survivorship is pretty precise. 90% of the time, when the algorithm predicts a survivor, that person was, in fact, a survivor.

3. Now, we will look at the precision for death, as follows:

```
In [8]:  precision_score(y_true=actual, y_pred=predicted, pos_label=0)

Out[8]:  0.8533333333333
```

We have a precision score of 85%.

# Recall

**Recall** is the ability of a model to correctly predict a particular outcome. In this example, recall is how many Titanic survivors were predicted by the model as being survivors. We would prefer recall to be close to one.

We can use the `recall_score()` function provided by `sklearn` to compute recall for survivors, as shown here:

```
In [9]:   from sklearn.metrics import recall_score

In [10]:  recall_score(y_true=actual, y_pred=predicted)

Out[10]:  0.6285714285714286
```

As for deaths, the recall score is shown here:

```
In [11]:  recall_score(y_true=actual, y_pred=predicted, pos_label=0)

Out[11]:  0.8703703703703703
```

So, this algorithm does not have great recall for survivors; as for those who died, it has a much better recall. In other words, it's doing a good job of predicting the people who died, because many of the people who were on the *Titanic* died.

But, as for who survived, which is the more difficult label to predict, it doesn't have great recall. So, this model seems to have a bias toward predicting that people died on the *Titanic* as opposed to people surviving.

# F1 score

Precision and recall are sometimes rolled together into a composite score known as an F1 score, and we would like this score to be as large as possible. If F1 is high, then both recall, and precision are also likely to be high. You won't find a situation where a model has good precision but bad recall, or vice versa.

So, we can compute the F1 score by using the `f1_score()` function, as follows:

```
In [12]: from sklearn.metrics import f1_score

In [13]: f1_score(y_true=actual, y_pred=predicted)

Out[13]: 0.6875

In [14]: # Again, depends on the label of interest
         f1_score(y_true=actual, y_pred=predicted, pos_label=0)

Out[14]: 0.8245614035087719
```

The first output is the F1 score for survivorship, and the second one is the F1 score for those who died.

# Classification report

Now, we've seen a few common metrics for evaluating an algorithm, and it turns out that there is a `classification_report()` function that `sklearn` provides that can quickly deliver all of these scores, all of these metrics; you can use this to evaluate your algorithm.

We can import this function using the following code:

```
In [15]: from sklearn.metrics import classification_report
```

Then, we will view the classification report, as follows:

```
In [16]:  print(classification_report(y_true=actual, y_pred=predicted))

                   precision    recall  f1-score   support

                0       0.78      0.87      0.82        54
                1       0.76      0.63      0.69        35

       micro avg       0.78      0.78      0.78        89
       macro avg       0.77      0.75      0.76        89
    weighted avg       0.77      0.78      0.77        89
```

# Bayes factor

The **Bayes factor** is a metric used to decide between two competing models that describe a process: in our case, a predictive algorithm. I demonstrate how a Bayes factor can be used to decide whether a sophisticated algorithm outperforms a Naive algorithm that simply predicts the most common label.

Let $M_1$ and $M_2$ be two competing models. $M_1$ is likely to be the model we are considering replacing $M_2$, and a larger K indicates more evidence that $M_1$ is the better model. If $M_1$ denotes our predictive algorithm, a large K indicates that our algorithm does a good job of predicting the target variable.

Now recall that, in Bayesian statistics, we have a prior distribution, we collect data, and we compute a posterior distribution for an event. Here, the event of interest will be whether a certain model is appropriate. $M_1$ is the event that our table-lookup algorithm does a better job than the naive algorithm, while $M_2$ is the event that the naive algorithm is better than our table-lookup algorithm. Let $p_1$ denote the accuracy of the table-lookup algorithm, and $p_2$ the accuracy of the naive algorithm. $M_1$ corresponds to the event that $p_1$ is greater than $p_2$, while $M_2$ corresponds to the event that $p_1$ is less than $p_2$. So, we're going to use conjugate priors, like we did in Chapter 1, *Classical Statistical Analysis*.

We're going to assume that these two parameters, which are like random variables, are independent under this prior distribution. We're also going to use the B(3,3) distribution for our prior for both of these. Now, I'm not going to explain why, but it's not that hard to show that these assumptions lead to the prior probabilities for both $M_1$ and $M_2$ being 1/2, and this is not necessarily true in general. So, what does that mean? It means that this factor is going to be canceled out and just turn into 1.

So, let's go ahead and compute a Bayes factor:

1. You may remember that we need the number of successes and the total sample size in order to compute the posterior distribution's parameters. Here, I compute those parameters:

```
In [17]:  N = len(actual)
          M = (actual == predicted).sum()
          (M, N)

Out[17]:  (69, 89)
```

2. Now, we will see the posterior distribution of the parameters for the lookup algorithm's accuracy:

```
In [18]:  post_params_lookup = (3 + M, 3 + N - M)
          post_params_lookup

Out[18]:  (72, 23)
```

3. Now, let's do the same thing for the naive algorithm. We will generate the values as follows:

```
In [19]:  ds = pd.Series(actual).value_counts()
          ds

Out[19]:  0    54
          1    35
          Name: Survived, dtype: int64
```

Here are the number of individuals who died and the number of individuals who survived the disaster. The naive algorithm predicts that everybody died. 62 is the number of correct predictions, and 27 is the number of incorrect predictions.

4. We will compute the parameters for the posterior distribution as follows:

```
In [20]:  post_params_naive = (3 + ds[0], 3 + ds[1])
          post_params_naive

Out[20]:  (57, 38)
```

We end up with these parameters for the posterior distribution of the accuracy of the naive algorithm.

5. Once again, it's pretty difficult to explicitly compute this probability. So, we are going to use the simulation trick that we looked at in Chapter 1, *Classical Statistical Analysis*, to estimate the probability that p1 is less than p2, as follows:

```
In [21]:  from scipy.stats import beta

In [22]:  N = 10000     # Number of simulations
          p_1 = beta.rvs(67, 28, size=N)
          p_2 = beta.rvs(64, 31, size=N)
          trial = p_1 > p_2

          pm1 = trial.mean()
          pm2 = 1 - pm1
          (pm1, pm2)

Out[22]:  (0.6666, 0.33340000000000003)
```

There's a 68% chance that $M_1$ is appropriate—the model that says that our new algorithm does a better job than the naive algorithm—and a 32% chance that that is not true.

6. So now, we can use this to compute the Bayes factor:

```
In [23]:  K = pm1 / pm2
          K

Out[23]:  1.9994001199760045
```

So, what do we make of this number? Well, we have what's called the **Jeffreys' scale** to give an interpretation to the Bayes factor that we computed, which is as follows:

| K | Strength of evidence |
|---|---|
| >1 | Evidence for $M_2$ |
| 1 to $10^{1/2}$ ($\approx$3.2) | Negligible |
| $10^{1/2}$ to 10 | Substantial |
| 10 to $10^{3/2}$ ($\approx$31.6) | Strong |
| $10^{3/2}$ to 100 | Very strong |
| >100 | Decisive |

Our K falls into the **negligible** range. Our algorithm seems to do barely better than the naive algorithm at predicting who survived the *Titanic*, and is not worth the computational effort.

# Summary

This brings us to the end of the chapter. In this chapter, we looked at the principles of machine learning, the various types of machine learning, and we also learned about supervised learning. We then trained a supervised learning model and then, finally, learned how to evaluate it using various performance metrics.

In the next chapter, we will start to look at actual machine learning models.

# 3
# Binary Prediction Models

In this chapter, we will look at various methods for classifying data, and focus on binary data. We will start with a simple algorithm—the k-nearest neighbors algorithm. Next, we will move on to decision trees. We will then look at an ensemble method and combine multiple decision trees into a random forest classifier. After that, we will move on to linear classifiers, the first being the Naive Bayes algorithm. Then, we will see how to train support vector machines. Following this, we will look at another well-known and extensively used classifier—logistic regression. Finally, we will see how we can extend algorithms for binary classification to algorithms that are capable of multiclass classification.

The following topics will be covered in this chapter:

- K-nearest neighbors classifier
- Decision trees
- Random forests
- Naive Bayes
- Support vector machines
- Logistic regression
- Extending beyond binary classifiers

# K-nearest neighbors classifier

Our first learning system will be the **k-nearest neighbors** (**kNN**) classifier. I will describe how the classifier makes predictions, the important hyperparameters it uses, and the problems that are faced by the classifier. Throughout, I will be using the classifier to predict species of iris flowers. So, let's go ahead and start a Jupyter Notebook for this classifier:

1. The first thing we're going to do is load in the dataset and other required functions, as follows:

```
In [ ]:  from sklearn.datasets import load_iris
         from sklearn.model_selection import train_test_split, cross_validate
         from sklearn.metrics import classification_report
```

The iris dataset is provided with sklearn. It is one of their example datasets, and is well known.

2. Then, we will load in an object that contains the iris data and save that into Python objects:

```
In [ ]:  iris_obj = load_iris()

         flower, species = iris_obj.data, iris_obj.target
```

3. Then, we will divide the dataset into training and test data by using the following lines of code:

```
In [ ]:  flower_train, flower_test, species_train, species_test = train_test_split(flower, species, test_size = 0.1)
         flower_train[:5]
```

Here are the first five rows of the training data:

```
Out[3]:  array([[5. , 3.5, 1.3, 0.3],
                [6.1, 2.8, 4. , 1.3],
                [5.8, 2.7, 5.1, 1.9],
                [6. , 3. , 4.8, 1.8],
                [4.8, 3.4, 1.9, 0.2]])
```

Here are the first five labels of the training data:

```
In [4]:  species_train[:5]

Out[4]:  array([1, 1, 2, 0, 1])
```

Throughout this chapter, we will be doing an inappropriate practice. You aren't supposed to be repeatedly looking at the test set; however, we are going to do so throughout this entire section so that you can get an idea of how well these algorithms do on test sets. We are only doing this to demonstrate these algorithms, as well as some things that you might be thinking about when you're training algorithms, just so that we have some way to evaluate an algorithm without actually looking at how it's performing on just the training set.

In a real project, looking at the test set would be the very last thing that you would do, and would be when you were presenting the results of your work to your boss. You would have already picked a classifier; you can only choose one. Getting statistics from the test set is only for academic purposes so that you have some idea of how your classifier is going to behave on your dataset. You might have a test set that isn't actually the test set that you are free to look at as often as you like, but remember that every time you're looking at the test set, it is no longer acting as data that the algorithm has not seen before. Every time you look at it, it is now acting like seen data that is affecting the algorithm that you're training.

All in all, we're going to be doing some sloppy things in this chapter, but that's just because I'm trying to teach you these methods, give you some sense of what's going on, and give you something to think about when you're trying to decide what algorithm you should be using and what you're looking for.

# Training a kNN classifier

Training a kNN classifier is easy. First, you need to load in the training data, which will be used for every classification. After we do this, we receive a new data point that we want to classify, as shown in the following diagram:

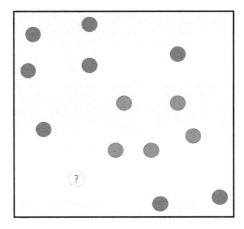

We compute the distance of the data point from each point in the training set, as shown in the following diagram:

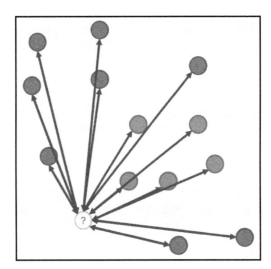

Then, we determine the *k* nearest points, as shown in the following diagram:

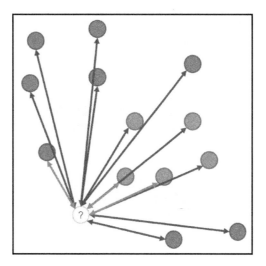

In this diagram, we can see that *k* is 3.

The most common class among those nearest points is the predicted label for the point. Let's see how this looks in Python:

1. We're going to use the kNN classifier provided by `scikit-learn`. This is implemented in the `KNeighborsClassifier` class. First, we will import this class:

```
In [5]:  from sklearn.neighbors import KNeighborsClassifier
         import numpy as np
```

2. Then, we will create an object that will implement the kNN algorithm:

```
In [6]:  knn1 = KNeighborsClassifier(n_neighbors=1)
         knn1.fit(flower_train, species_train)
         knn1.predict(np.array([[7, 3, 5, 2]]))
```

In this case, we have a `n_neighbors` parameter, which we have set to 1. In this case, *k*, the number of neighbors that you check, is equal to 1. Then, we fit this algorithm, which in effect is just loading in the training data, before we demonstrate prediction with it. Here, we will provide a point with a sepal length of 7, a sepal width of 3, a petal length of 5, and a petal width of 2 (in centimeters). This results in the following output:

```
Out[6]:  array([2])
```

It predicted the label 2, which in this case corresponds to the virginica species.

3. Let's go ahead and see what the prediction looks like on the entire flower training set, as follows:

```
In [7]:  pred1 = knn1.predict(flower_train)
         pred1

Out[7]:  array([1, 1, 2, 0, 1, 1, 1, 0, 0, 1, 0, 2, 1, 2, 1, 2, 1, 0, 0, 1, 1, 1, 1,
                1, 2, 0, 1, 2, 0, 2, 0, 2, 0, 0, 0, 1, 2, 2, 2, 0, 1, 0, 0, 1, 2, 0,
                1, 2, 2, 2, 0, 0, 1, 2, 1, 0, 1, 2, 1, 0, 2, 2, 0, 1, 0, 0, 0, 2, 2,
                1, 1, 1, 0, 2, 1, 1, 0, 1, 2, 1, 2, 1, 0, 2, 1, 1, 2, 0, 2, 1, 1, 0,
                2, 1, 2, 2, 1, 2, 0, 1, 2, 2, 2, 0, 1, 2, 1, 0, 2, 0, 0, 1, 0, 2, 0,
                0, 0, 2, 2, 1, 0, 0, 1, 2, 0, 1, 0, 2, 2, 2, 2, 0, 0, 1, 2])
```

Notice that we get an array with a bunch of labels—these are all predicted labels.

4. Now, we will look at a classification report so that we can see how well this algorithm is doing on the training set, as follows:

```
In [8]:  print(classification_report(species_train, pred1))

                    precision    recall  f1-score   support

              0         1.00      1.00      1.00        44
              1         1.00      1.00      1.00        46
              2         1.00      1.00      1.00        45

     avg / total        1.00      1.00      1.00       135
```

Not surprisingly, it does perfectly. Why? Because the nearest point to an observation is the observation, so it's going to predict exactly the same label as that observation has. This means that it's going to have perfect performance on the training set.

# Hyperparameters in kNN classifiers

There are two key hyperparameters for kNN classifiers. One is obvious—*k*, or how many neighbors to use when making predictions. The other is less obvious—how do we define the distance between two points?

**Euclidean distance** is not our only option, and in some situations, such as text classification, we may want to use different metrics. We can use **domain knowledge**, which is our knowledge about the underlying problem we're trying to solve, to answer this question. We can also use **cross-validation**.

With kNN, there are three problems to watch out for, as follows:

- The first is that you need to store the entire dataset in order to make predictions. The algorithm is memory expensive.
- This algorithm also uses a lot of computing power when making predictions, since a new data point needs to be compared to every data point in the training set to determine which are closest, and thus make a prediction.
- Finally, kNN struggles when we have lots of features. This is known as the **curse of dimensionality**. In high-dimensional spaces, our intuitive notion of distance no longer describes the space well. It seems as if distances are large in general, when there are lots of dimensions.

Let's use cross-validation for choosing k by using the following steps:

1. First, we will import a `pandas DataFrame`, as follows:

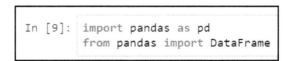

```
In [9]:  import pandas as pd
         from pandas import DataFrame
```

Then, we will define our candidate *ks*. I'm considering all possible ks between 1 and 10. We will then create a dictionary that's going to contain the results of cross-validation. This dictionary is eventually going to be turned into a `pandas DataFrame`. We're going to train this classifier for every possible choice of k.

2. Let's go ahead and implement cross-validation:

```
In [10]:  k_candidate = [1, 2, 3, 4, 5, 6, 7, 8, 9, 10]
          res = dict()

          for k in k_candidate:
              pred2 = KNeighborsClassifier(n_neighbors=k)
              res[k] = cross_validate(estimator=pred2,
                                      X=flower_train,
                                      y=species_train,
                                      cv=10,
                                      return_train_score=False,
                                      scoring='accuracy')
```

3. Now, let's see the results:

Out[11]:

| | | 0 | 1 | 2 | 3 | 4 | 5 | 6 | 7 | 8 | 9 |
|---|---|---|---|---|---|---|---|---|---|---|---|
| 1 | fit_time | 0.001004 | 0.001003 | 0.000000 | 0.001002 | 0.001002 | 0.000000 | 0.001003 | 0.000000 | 0.000000 | 0.001003 |
| | score_time | 0.001000 | 0.001008 | 0.002005 | 0.001004 | 0.000000 | 0.001003 | 0.000000 | 0.001003 | 0.001003 | 0.000000 |
| | test_score | 1.000000 | 0.933333 | 0.866667 | 1.000000 | 0.928571 | 0.846154 | 1.000000 | 1.000000 | 1.000000 | 1.000000 |
| 2 | fit_time | 0.000000 | 0.001003 | 0.000000 | 0.000517 | 0.000504 | 0.000000 | 0.001004 | 0.000502 | 0.000501 | 0.000504 |
| | score_time | 0.001001 | 0.000000 | 0.001004 | 0.000490 | 0.000500 | 0.000997 | 0.000500 | 0.000518 | 0.001002 | 0.000506 |
| | test_score | 1.000000 | 0.933333 | 0.866667 | 0.933333 | 0.928571 | 0.846154 | 0.916667 | 1.000000 | 0.916667 | 1.000000 |
| 3 | fit_time | 0.000000 | 0.000000 | 0.000000 | 0.000000 | 0.001289 | 0.001002 | 0.000000 | 0.000000 | 0.000996 | 0.000000 |
| | score_time | 0.000501 | 0.000501 | 0.000501 | 0.000500 | 0.000000 | 0.000000 | 0.001000 | 0.001016 | 0.000000 | 0.000000 |
| | test_score | 1.000000 | 0.933333 | 0.866667 | 1.000000 | 0.928571 | 0.846154 | 1.000000 | 1.000000 | 1.000000 | 1.000000 |
| 4 | fit_time | 0.001003 | 0.001003 | 0.000000 | 0.000000 | 0.001003 | 0.001003 | 0.001003 | 0.001003 | 0.000000 | 0.000000 |
| | score_time | 0.000000 | 0.000000 | 0.000000 | 0.000000 | 0.000000 | 0.000000 | 0.000000 | 0.000000 | 0.002006 | 0.000998 |
| | test_score | 1.000000 | 0.933333 | 0.866667 | 0.933333 | 0.928571 | 0.846154 | 1.000000 | 1.000000 | 0.833333 | 1.000000 |

This is going to be a measure of how well our algorithm performed. The `DataFrame` displays all the ks that we tried along the rows. It shows us how long it took to fit the data, the `score_time`, which tells us how long it took to get a score, and the actual score for the classifier in cross-validation. In this case, the score is just going to be accuracy.

4. We don't want all of this information; all we want is the test score, which can be seen as follows:

```
In [12]: resdf.loc[(slice(None), 'test_score'), :]
Out[12]:
```

|   |            | 0   | 1        | 2        | 3        | 4        | 5        | 6        | 7   | 8        | 9   |
|---|------------|-----|----------|----------|----------|----------|----------|----------|-----|----------|-----|
| 1 | test_score | 1.0 | 0.933333 | 0.866667 | 1.000000 | 0.928571 | 0.846154 | 1.000000 | 1.0 | 1.000000 | 1.0 |
| 2 | test_score | 1.0 | 0.933333 | 0.866667 | 0.933333 | 0.928571 | 0.846154 | 0.916667 | 1.0 | 0.916667 | 1.0 |
| 3 | test_score | 1.0 | 0.933333 | 0.866667 | 1.000000 | 0.928571 | 0.846154 | 1.000000 | 1.0 | 1.000000 | 1.0 |
| 4 | test_score | 1.0 | 0.933333 | 0.866667 | 0.933333 | 0.928571 | 0.846154 | 1.000000 | 1.0 | 0.833333 | 1.0 |
| 5 | test_score | 1.0 | 0.933333 | 0.866667 | 1.000000 | 0.928571 | 0.846154 | 1.000000 | 1.0 | 1.000000 | 1.0 |
| 6 | test_score | 1.0 | 1.000000 | 0.866667 | 0.933333 | 0.928571 | 0.846154 | 1.000000 | 1.0 | 0.916667 | 1.0 |
| 7 | test_score | 1.0 | 1.000000 | 0.933333 | 0.933333 | 0.928571 | 0.846154 | 1.000000 | 1.0 | 0.916667 | 1.0 |
| 8 | test_score | 1.0 | 1.000000 | 0.933333 | 0.933333 | 0.928571 | 0.923077 | 1.000000 | 1.0 | 0.916667 | 1.0 |
| 9 | test_score | 1.0 | 1.000000 | 0.933333 | 0.933333 | 0.928571 | 0.923077 | 0.916667 | 1.0 | 0.916667 | 1.0 |
| 10 | test_score | 1.0 | 1.000000 | 0.933333 | 0.933333 | 0.928571 | 0.923077 | 1.000000 | 1.0 | 0.916667 | 1.0 |

The preceding screenshot shows the test scores for each run of cross-validation. These are all the different runs. Remember, we were doing cross-validation 10 times, so we have 10 folds, and each fold is held out in each run of the cross-validation. We have treated this as a test set, while the remaining folds are treated as training data.

5. By doing this, we can see the average performance of this classifier, as follows:

```
In [13]: resdf.loc[(slice(None), 'test_score'), :].mean(axis=1)
Out[13]: 1    test_score    0.957473
         2    test_score    0.934139
         3    test_score    0.957473
         4    test_score    0.934139
         5    test_score    0.957473
         6    test_score    0.949139
         7    test_score    0.955806
         8    test_score    0.963498
         9    test_score    0.955165
         10   test_score    0.963498
         dtype: float64
```

It seems like we get good performance when we choose *k=8*.

6. Now, let's see how our classifier performs when we actually assign *k* as 8:

```
In [14]:  pred3 = KNeighborsClassifier(n_neighbors=8)
          pred3.fit(flower_train, species_train)
          species_test_predict = pred3.predict(flower_test)
          print(classification_report(species_test, species_test_predict))
```

This results in the following output:

```
In [14]:  pred3 = KNeighborsClassifier(n_neighbors=8)
          pred3.fit(flower_train, species_train)
          species_test_predict = pred3.predict(flower_test)
          print(classification_report(species_test, species_test_predict))
```

|  | precision | recall | f1-score | support |
|---|---|---|---|---|
| 0 | 1.00 | 1.00 | 1.00 | 6 |
| 1 | 1.00 | 1.00 | 1.00 | 4 |
| 2 | 1.00 | 1.00 | 1.00 | 5 |
| avg / total | 1.00 | 1.00 | 1.00 | 15 |

Now that we're looking at test data, it looks like our classifier does pretty well. It doesn't make any mistakes on the test dataset.

Now, let's go ahead and actually visualize what kNN is doing:

1. We will import `matplotlib`, as follows:

```
In [15]:  import matplotlib.pyplot as plt
          %matplotlib inline
```

2. Then, we will plot the predictions by using the following lines of code:

```
In [16]: marker_map = {0: 'o', 1: 's', 2: '^'}
         var1, var2 = 0, 1    # Sepal length and sepal width variables
         for length, width, species in zip(flower_train[:, var1], flower_train[:, var2], species_train[:]):
             plt.scatter(x=length, y=width, marker=marker_map[species], c="black")
         # Plot correct prediction
         correct = (species_test == species_test_predict)
         for length, width, species in zip(flower_test[correct, var1], flower_test[correct, var2], species_test[correct]):
             plt.scatter(x=length, y=width, marker=marker_map[species], c="blue")
         for length, width, species in zip(flower_test[np.logical_not(correct), var1],
                                           flower_test[np.logical_not(correct), var2],
                                           species_test[np.logical_not(correct)]):
             plt.scatter(x=length, y=width, marker=marker_map[species], c="red")
         plt.xlabel(iris_obj.feature_names[var1])
         plt.ylabel(iris_obj.feature_names[var2])
         plt.show()
```

Here, we can see the observations for sepal length and sepal width:

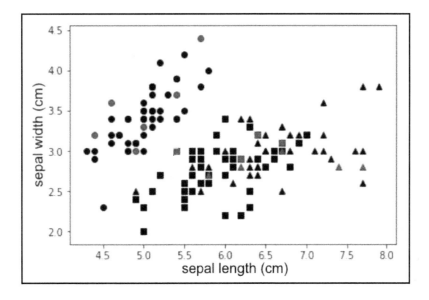

We have the species being marked with the shape—black is the training set and blue is correctly labeled training data. We can also see that every species that was predicted by the algorithm was the correct species.

3. We can also see it for petal length and petal width, as follows:

```
In [17]:  marker_map = {0: 'o', 1: 's', 2: '^'}
          var1, var2 = 2, 3    # Petal length and petal width variables
          for length, width, species in zip(flower_train[:, var1], flower_train[:, var2], species_train[:]):
              plt.scatter(x=length, y=width, marker=marker_map[species], c="black")
          # Plot correct prediction
          correct = (species_test == species_test_predict)
          for length, width, species in zip(flower_test[correct, var1], flower_test[correct, var2], species_test[correct]):
              plt.scatter(x=length, y=width, marker=marker_map[species], c="blue")
          for length, width, species in zip(flower_test[np.logical_not(correct), var1],
                                            flower_test[np.logical_not(correct), var2],
                                            species_test[np.logical_not(correct)]):
              plt.scatter(x=length, y=width, marker=marker_map[species], c="red")
          plt.xlabel(iris_obj.feature_names[var1])
          plt.ylabel(iris_obj.feature_names[var2])
          plt.show()
```

This results in the following output:

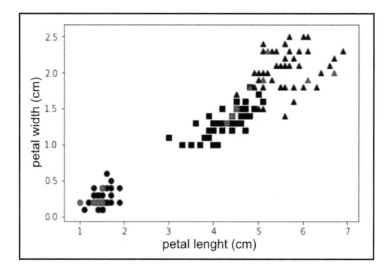

That's it for the kNN classifier. Next up are decision trees—another simple classifier.

# Decision trees

Let's take a look at decision trees, another intuitive classifier. In this section, we will see how decision trees make predictions. We will discuss important decision tree hyperparameters, and when decision trees may go awry. While we do this, I will demonstrate decision trees by using them to predict who did or did not survive the sinking of the Titanic.

A decision tree is a classification algorithm that asks a series of true or false questions. It uses those questions to decide how to classify a data point. Decision trees are implemented using the `scikit-learn` object `DecisionTreeClassifier`. Let's go over this now:

1. The first thing we will do is load in the Titanic dataset, along with some useful functions:

```
In [1]:  import pandas as pd
         from pandas import DataFrame
         from sklearn.model_selection import train_test_split, cross_validate
         from sklearn.metrics import classification_report
```

2. Then, we will load in the first few rows of the Titanic dataset with `pandas`, as follows:

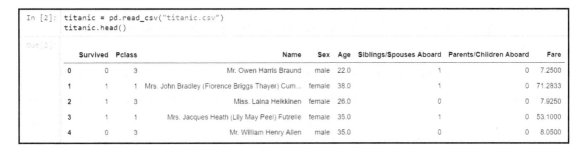

```
In [2]:  titanic = pd.read_csv("titanic.csv")
         titanic.head()
```

| | Survived | Pclass | Name | Sex | Age | Siblings/Spouses Aboard | Parents/Children Aboard | Fare |
|---|---|---|---|---|---|---|---|---|
| 0 | 0 | 3 | Mr. Owen Harris Braund | male | 22.0 | 1 | 0 | 7.2500 |
| 1 | 1 | 1 | Mrs. John Bradley (Florence Briggs Thayer) Cum... | female | 38.0 | 1 | 0 | 71.2833 |
| 2 | 1 | 3 | Miss. Laina Heikkinen | female | 26.0 | 0 | 0 | 7.9250 |
| 3 | 1 | 1 | Mrs. Jacques Heath (Lily May Peel) Futrelle | female | 35.0 | 1 | 0 | 53.1000 |
| 4 | 0 | 3 | Mr. William Henry Allen | male | 35.0 | 0 | 0 | 8.0500 |

3. We're also going to see the first few rows of the training data:

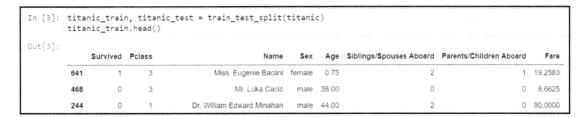

```
In [3]:  titanic_train, titanic_test = train_test_split(titanic)
         titanic_train.head()
```

| | Survived | Pclass | Name | Sex | Age | Siblings/Spouses Aboard | Parents/Children Aboard | Fare |
|---|---|---|---|---|---|---|---|---|
| 641 | 1 | 3 | Miss. Eugenie Baclini | female | 0.75 | 2 | 1 | 19.2583 |
| 468 | 0 | 3 | Mr. Luka Cacic | male | 38.00 | 0 | 0 | 8.6625 |
| 244 | 0 | 1 | Dr. William Edward Minahan | male | 44.00 | 2 | 0 | 90.0000 |

# Fitting the decision tree

A decision tree is a hierarchy for making predictions. A new data point for which we want to make a prediction starts at the top of the decision tree. We then test a condition. If the condition is true, we move down the left-hand side of the tree. Otherwise, we move down the right-hand side of the tree. We repeat this for each node. When we reach the bottom of the tree, we predict a label, as shown in the following diagram:

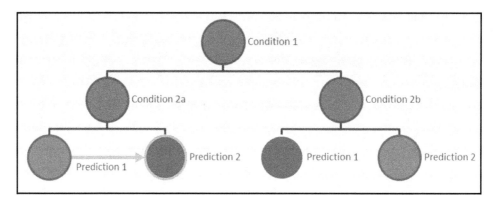

Let's see how we fit a decision tree:

1. We are going to load in some useful packages, mostly for visualizing:

```
In [4]:  from sklearn.tree import DecisionTreeClassifier
         from sklearn.externals.six import StringIO
         from IPython.display import Image
         from sklearn.tree import export_graphviz
         import pydotplus
```

2. Now, we are going to create an object for a decision tree classifier. We are going to fit the Titanic dataset. We will replace males with 0 and females with 1 so that it's easier for the decision tree to train. We'll have the variable that we are trying to predict as whether someone survived or not. We are also going to exclude the Name variable, because I don't think a person's name has anything to do with whether they survived. This can be summarized in the following code:

```
In [ ]:  tree1 = DecisionTreeClassifier()

         tree1 = tree1.fit(X=titanic_train.replace({'Sex': {'male': 0, 'female': 1}}
                                    ).drop(["Survived", "Name"], axis=1),
                    y=titanic_train.Survived)

         # Example prediction
         tree1.predict([[2, 0, 26, 0, 0, 30]])
```

3. By doing this, we can see what the tree would predict given a male in second class, age 26, with no spouse or children on board, who paid $30 in fare:

```
# Example prediction
tree1.predict([[2, 0, 26, 0, 0, 30]])
```

This results in the following output:

```
Out[5]:  array([0], dtype=int64)
```

According to the decision tree, this individual would have died.

4. Now, let's see the accuracy of the decision tree on the training set by using the following code:

```
In [ ]:  pred1 = tree1.predict(titanic_train.replace({'Sex': {'male': 0, 'female': 1}}
                                    ).drop(["Survived", "Name"], axis=1))
         print(classification_report(titanic_train.Survived, pred1))
```

This results in the following output:

|             | precision | recall | f1-score | support |
|-------------|-----------|--------|----------|---------|
| 0           | 0.98      | 1.00   | 0.99     | 403     |
| 1           | 1.00      | 0.96   | 0.98     | 262     |
| avg / total | 0.99      | 0.98   | 0.98     | 665     |

As we can see here, it is very accurate on the training set.

# Visualizing the tree

There's a good chance that this model overfitted the data. We can drive this point home by visualizing the decision tree. You will see that this tree is so complicated that it is almost certainly overfitting. For this, you're going to need to install an application called **Graphviz**, which can be found at https://www.graphviz.org/, and set up some Python packages so that Graphviz works. You can install them via conda.

On Linux, this is very easy to do. You can just install the package using apt-get graphviz, and everything will work fine.

On Windows, this is a bit of a pain. You have to install the program, install the Python package, and then you have to add the path where the application is stored so that you can interact with it in Python.

Once everything has been set, we're going to use the following lines of code to see the tree:

```
In [ ]:  # From here: https://medium.com/@rnbrown/creating-and-visualizing-decision-trees-with-python-f8e8fa394176
         dot_data = StringIO()

         export_graphviz(tree1,      # Function for exporting a visualization of the tree
                         out_file=dot_data,
                         # Data controlling the display of the graph
                         filled=True, rounded=True,
                         special_characters=True,
                         feature_names=["Pclass", "Sex", "Age", "Siblings/Spouses Aboard", "Parents/Children Aboard",
                                        "Fare"],     # Use the name of the features
                         proportion=True)    # Show proportions for labels

         # Display graph in Jupyter notebook
         graph1 = pydotplus.graph_from_dot_data(dot_data.getvalue())
         Image(graph1.create_png())
```

This results in the following tree:

Out[7]:

This is an extremely complicated rule for predicting whether someone survived the sinking of the Titanic or not. Looking at a tree such as this, you can almost certainly guess that this algorithm is overfitting.

In fact, let's go ahead and take a peek and see how well this algorithm does on the test dataset, as follows:

```
In [8]:  pred2 = tree1.predict(titanic_test.replace({'Sex': {'male': 0, 'female': 1}}
                                    ).drop(["Survived", "Name"], axis=1))
         print(classification_report(titanic_test.Survived, pred2))

                      precision    recall  f1-score   support

                  0       0.85      0.75      0.80       142
                  1       0.64      0.76      0.69        80

         avg / total      0.77      0.76      0.76       222
```

We can see that it is nowhere near as accurate as it was on the training data, so it is absolutely overfitting. It's overfitting as much as it possibly can.

# Restricting tree depth

A key hyperparameter for decision trees is the maximum tree depth. We may decide that we want to make a maximum number of decisions before we predict. By default, the tree will be as deep as it can be. If we restrict the depth, we are trying to fight overfitting in our decision tree. The main pitfall to decision trees is that, in general, they have a propensity to overfit. The best way to combat this overfitting is to restrict the maximum depth of the tree. Smaller, simpler trees do less overfitting than deep, complex trees.

Let's see how we can restrict tree depth and decide what tree depth is appropriate. Although I have stated that we might want to restrict the depth, I haven't said what depth is best. For that, we might want to actually use cross-validation.

But first, let's go ahead and see what a smaller tree looks like:

```
In [ ]:  tree2 = DecisionTreeClassifier(max_depth=3)

         tree2 = tree2.fit(X=titanic_train.replace({'Sex': {'male': 0, 'female': 1}}    # Replace strings with numbers
                                        ).drop(["Survived", "Name"], axis=1),
                           y=titanic_train.Survived)

         dot_data = StringIO()

         export_graphviz(tree2,    # Function for exporting a visualization of the tree
                         out_file=dot_data,
                         # Data controlling the display of the graph
                         filled=True, rounded=True,
                         special_characters=True,
                         feature_names=["Pclass", "Sex", "Age", "Siblings/Spouses Aboard", "Parents/Children Aboard",
                                        "Fare"],
                         proportion=True)

         # Display graph in Jupyter notebook
         graph2 = pydotplus.graph_from_dot_data(dot_data.getvalue())
         Image(graph2.create_png())
```

The following screenshot shows the result:

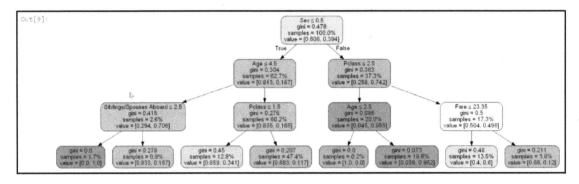

One thing that's kind of nice about decision trees is that they're very easily interpreted. You can print this out, and given an observation, such as an individual's age, their sex, which passenger class they were on, and so on, you could make the prediction about whether they survived the Titanic or not. In this case, when you reach the bottom row and you see `value = [0.833, 0.167]`, this means that 83% of people who landed down on the second node did not survive the Titanic—only 16% did. In this case, if you were to reach this node, you would predict that the person did not survive. You can print the tree and everyone in the office will know what this model is doing, and they could also do the predictions themselves. It gives you a nice heuristic for prediction.

We can also use cross-validation to decide on a good maximum depth on to try and balance our desire to have high accuracy, while not overfitting. Let's go through the cross-validation procedure here.

Here is a `pandas` DataFrame with the results for different tree depths:

```
In [ ]:  m_candidate = [2, 3, 4, 5, 6, 7, 8, 9, 10]    # Candidate depths
         res = dict()

         for m in m_candidate:
             pred3 = DecisionTreeClassifier(max_depth=m)
             res[m] = cross_validate(pred3,
                                     X=titanic_train.replace({'Sex': {'male': 0, 'female': 1}}
                                                     ).drop(["Survived", "Name"], axis=1),
                                     y=titanic_train.Survived,
                                     cv=10,
                                     return_train_score=False,
                                     scoring='accuracy')

         resdf = DataFrame({(i, j): res[i][j]
                                    for i in res.keys()
                                    for j in res[i].keys()}).T

         resdf.loc[(slice(None), 'test_score'), :]
```

This results in the following DataFrame:

|    |            | 0 | 1 | 2 | 3 | 4 | 5 | 6 | 7 | 8 | 9 |
|----|------------|---|---|---|---|---|---|---|---|---|---|
| 2  | test_score | 0.779412 | 0.647059 | 0.776119 | 0.787879 | 0.727273 | 0.833333 | 0.818182 | 0.863636 | 0.727273 | 0.787879 |
| 3  | test_score | 0.823529 | 0.720588 | 0.805970 | 0.833333 | 0.818182 | 0.863636 | 0.848485 | 0.893939 | 0.818182 | 0.833333 |
| 4  | test_score | 0.838235 | 0.720588 | 0.805970 | 0.833333 | 0.818182 | 0.863636 | 0.878788 | 0.878788 | 0.818182 | 0.833333 |
| 5  | test_score | 0.838235 | 0.735294 | 0.791045 | 0.833333 | 0.818182 | 0.863636 | 0.878788 | 0.833333 | 0.772727 | 0.833333 |
| 6  | test_score | 0.838235 | 0.676471 | 0.776119 | 0.833333 | 0.787879 | 0.848485 | 0.878788 | 0.848485 | 0.787879 | 0.833333 |
| 7  | test_score | 0.852941 | 0.705882 | 0.776119 | 0.833333 | 0.803030 | 0.833333 | 0.833333 | 0.863636 | 0.803030 | 0.833333 |
| 8  | test_score | 0.808824 | 0.705882 | 0.731343 | 0.833333 | 0.787879 | 0.833333 | 0.863636 | 0.878788 | 0.772727 | 0.833333 |
| 9  | test_score | 0.823529 | 0.705882 | 0.746269 | 0.818182 | 0.772727 | 0.833333 | 0.818182 | 0.878788 | 0.787879 | 0.818182 |
| 10 | test_score | 0.823529 | 0.676471 | 0.776119 | 0.803030 | 0.818182 | 0.848485 | 0.818182 | 0.833333 | 0.787879 | 0.833333 |

We will then display the mean accuracy, as follows:

```
In [11]:  resdf.loc[(slice(None), 'test_score'), :].mean(axis=1)

Out[11]:  2   test_score    0.774804
          3   test_score    0.825918
          4   test_score    0.828904
          5   test_score    0.819791
          6   test_score    0.810901
          7   test_score    0.813797
          8   test_score    0.804908
          9   test_score    0.800295
          10  test_score    0.801854
          dtype: float64
```

In this run, we actually have good accuracy—around depth 4.

We will then display the tree with a maximum depth of 4 by using the following code:

```
In [ ]:  tree4 = DecisionTreeClassifier(max_depth=4)

         tree4 = tree4.fit(X=titanic_train.replace({'Sex': {'male': 0, 'female': 1}}    # Replace strings with numbers
                            ).drop(["Survived", "Name"], axis=1),
                        y=titanic_train.Survived)

         dot_data = StringIO()

         export_graphviz(tree4,       # Function for exporting a visualization of the tree
                        out_file=dot_data,
                        # Data controlling the display of the graph
                        filled=True, rounded=True,
                        special_characters=True,
                        feature_names=["Pclass", "Sex", "Age", "Siblings/Spouses Aboard", "Parents/Children Aboard",
                                "Fare"],
                        proportion=True)

         # Display graph in Jupyter notebook
         graph3 = pydotplus.graph_from_dot_data(dot_data.getvalue())
         Image(graph3.create_png())
```

This results in the following output:

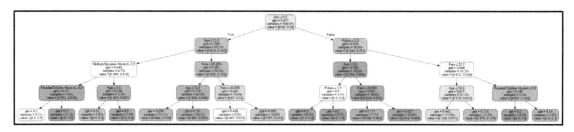

It seems to have a good balance between being able to predict well without overfitting. This is better viewed in the actual Notebook.

Now, let's see how well this tree does on the test set by using the following lines of code:

```
In [ ]:   survived_test_predict = tree4.predict(X=titanic_test.replace(
              {'Sex': {'male': 0, 'female': 1}}
          ).drop(["Survived", "Name"], axis=1))

In [ ]:   print(classification_report(titanic_test.Survived, survived_test_predict))
```

This results in the following output:

|  | precision | recall | f1-score | support |
|---|---|---|---|---|
| 0 | 0.82 | 0.90 | 0.86 | 142 |
| 1 | 0.79 | 0.65 | 0.71 | 80 |
| avg / total | 0.81 | 0.81 | 0.81 | 222 |

It doesn't do badly—it actually does a lot better than the tree that was allowed to grow without bounds and ended up overfitting the training set ridiculously. Now, it actually has a reasonable prediction rate of 81%. Now that we have finished discussing decision trees, we will look at a useful extension of them—random forests.

# Random forests

In this section, we will extend decision trees to random forests, which are an example of an approach to machine learning called **ensemble learning**. We also see how we can train these models when applying them to the Titanic dataset.

In ensemble learning, we train multiple classifiers for our dataset. For random forests, we train decision trees on random subsets of the dataset. The classifier is fed a data point that we want to predict the class for. The data point is fed to each classifier that's trained on the dataset. Each classifier then makes a prediction. The predictions are then aggregated in some way to form a final prediction. This diagram shows the steps to do this:

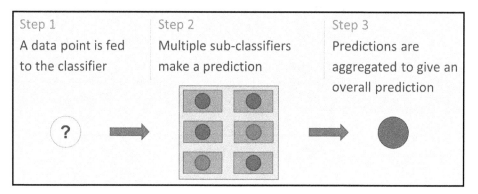

For random forests, the class that was predicted the most often is the final prediction. Let's get right into the action by following these steps:

1. First, let's load in the Titanic dataset and some required functions by using the following lines of code:

```
In [1]:  import pandas as pd
         from pandas import DataFrame
         from sklearn.model_selection import train_test_split, cross_validate
         from sklearn.metrics import classification_report
         from random import seed     # Set random seed for reproducible results
```

2. We will then set the seed for the Notebook so that we have more reproducible results, read in the dataset, and create train and test sets:

```
In [2]:  seed(110717)     # Set the seed
         titanic = pd.read_csv("titanic.csv")
         titanic_train, titanic_test = train_test_split(titanic)
```

3. Now, let's import the `RandomForestClassifier` object, which is used in `scikit-learn` for training random forest classifiers:

```
In [3]:  from sklearn.ensemble import RandomForestClassifier
```

4. We're going to train a random forest. We have 10 trees, and these trees are restricted to a maximum depth of 5. Other than this, it looks a lot similar to training a decision tree classifier:

```
In [4]:  forest1 = RandomForestClassifier(n_estimators=10,     # Number of trees
                                          max_depth=5)         # Maximum depth of
         forest1.fit(X=titanic_train.replace({'Sex': {'male': 0, 'female': 1}}
                                             ).drop(["Survived", "Name"], axis=1),
                     y=titanic_train.Survived)

         # Example prediction
         forest1.predict([[2, 0, 26, 0, 0, 30]])
```

This results in the following output:

```
Out[4]:  array([0], dtype=int64)
```

In fact, our random forest predicted the same value for our hypothetical individual—that this individual did not survive the disaster.

5. Now, we will look at our classification report for the random forest:

```
In [5]:  pred1 = forest1.predict(titanic_train.replace({'Sex': {'male': 0, 'female': 1}}
                                                       ).drop(["Survived", "Name"], axis=1))
         print(classification_report(titanic_train.Survived, pred1))
```

This results in the following output:

| | precision | recall | f1-score | support |
|---|---|---|---|---|
| 0 | 0.85 | 0.93 | 0.89 | 400 |
| 1 | 0.87 | 0.75 | 0.81 | 265 |
| avg / total | 0.86 | 0.86 | 0.86 | 665 |

It's not as high as it was for the decision tree, but our decision tree was overfitting, so that's not a bad thing. It appears that the ability of this classifier to predict whether a person survived or not is fairly decent.

# Optimizing hyperparameters

For random forests, I will highlight two hyperparameters. One is the maximum tree depth of a single tree. This would be a situation where you want even more shallow trees, as opposed to when you had one decision tree making all the decisions, where you might want a bunch of very shallow trees when training a random forest. The other hyperparameter novel to the random forest is the number of trees to grow.

Here, we are going to be optimizing multiple hyperparameters. When we do this, we have some additional considerations regarding how exactly we're going to optimize them. We have a few ways we could possibly proceed, as follows:

- We could use cross-validation to see which combinations of hyperparameters perform the best. You pick combinations at the same time—you try out every combination of possible hyperparameters and every maximum tree depth for every possible number of trees; however, there could be a lot of combinations for you to check. In this particular case, I'm going to be checking 7 different forest sizes and 10 different depths. This makes 70 combinations that I would need to check, which would take a very long time.
- Another approach we might try to use is optimize one parameter first and then the next, and so on. The result will not be path independent. Which hyperparameter you decide to optimize first will likely affect later ones. We can't guarantee that you're going to get a globally optimal result when you're doing this, but there's a good chance the result that you'll get is good enough.

- A third approach that you might consider is randomly picking combinations of hyperparameters and using the results of this random procedure to guess what a good combination of hyperparameters would be. This is very similar to the first case, where we were trying all possible combinations, but it's less work. However, you would need to think about how you're going to pick the actual hyperparameters based on random choices.

In the Notebook for this section, we will work with option 2. I'm going to optimize the number of trees to use first, and then the maximum tree depth:

1. First, we optimize the number of trees and display the results using the following lines of code:

```
In [6]:  n_candidate = [10, 20, 30, 40, 60, 80, 100]    # Candidate forest sizes
         res1 = dict()

         for n in n_candidate:
             pred3 = RandomForestClassifier(n_estimators=n, max_depth=5)
             res1[n] = cross_validate(pred3,
                                 X=titanic_train.replace({'Sex': {'male': 0, 'female': 1}}
                                             ).drop(["Survived", "Name"], axis=1),
                                 y=titanic_train.Survived,
                                 cv=10,
                                 return_train_score=False,
                                 scoring='accuracy')

         res1df = DataFrame({(i, j): res1[i][j]
                             for i in res1.keys()
                             for j in res1[i].keys()}).T

         res1df.loc[(slice(None), 'test_score'), :]
```

This results in the following DataFrame:

```
Out[6]:
```

|  |  | 0 | 1 | 2 | 3 | 4 | 5 | 6 | 7 | 8 | 9 |
|---|---|---|---|---|---|---|---|---|---|---|---|
| 10 | test_score | 0.835821 | 0.805970 | 0.820896 | 0.850746 | 0.850746 | 0.803030 | 0.878788 | 0.787879 | 0.818182 | 0.787879 |
| 20 | test_score | 0.820896 | 0.805970 | 0.835821 | 0.820896 | 0.850746 | 0.787879 | 0.848485 | 0.772727 | 0.848485 | 0.757576 |
| 30 | test_score | 0.835821 | 0.761194 | 0.850746 | 0.820896 | 0.850746 | 0.803030 | 0.863636 | 0.787879 | 0.818182 | 0.772727 |
| 40 | test_score | 0.820896 | 0.776119 | 0.865672 | 0.835821 | 0.835821 | 0.833333 | 0.863636 | 0.818182 | 0.818182 | 0.772727 |
| 60 | test_score | 0.835821 | 0.776119 | 0.820896 | 0.835821 | 0.850746 | 0.787879 | 0.863636 | 0.818182 | 0.848485 | 0.787879 |
| 80 | test_score | 0.820896 | 0.776119 | 0.835821 | 0.820896 | 0.850746 | 0.818182 | 0.848485 | 0.803030 | 0.818182 | 0.772727 |
| 100 | test_score | 0.835821 | 0.776119 | 0.820896 | 0.850746 | 0.850746 | 0.818182 | 0.863636 | 0.803030 | 0.818182 | 0.772727 |

2. We will then compute the mean scores, as follows:

```
In [7]: res1df.loc[(slice(None), 'test_score'), :].mean(axis=1)

Out[7]: 10   test_score    0.823994
        20   test_score    0.814948
        30   test_score    0.816486
        40   test_score    0.824039
        60   test_score    0.822546
        80   test_score    0.816508
        100  test_score    0.821009
        dtype: float64
```

The preceding screenshot shows the scores. It seems that choosing 100 trees seems to do well, and that choosing 60 trees also seems to do well. Choosing 40 trees seems to do the best, so that's going to be what we pick from this point on.

3. Next, we will optimize the maximum depth. After I have set the number of trees to 40, I will go through the cross-validation procedure using the following lines of code:

```
In [9]: res2 = dict()

        for m in m_candidate:
            pred3 = RandomForestClassifier(max_depth=m, n_estimators=40)
            res2[m] = cross_validate(pred3,
                            X=titanic_train.replace({'Sex': {'male': 0, 'female': 1}}
                                        ).drop(["Survived", "Name"], axis=1),
                            y=titanic_train.Survived,
                            cv=10,
                            return_train_score=False,
                            scoring='accuracy')

        res2df = DataFrame({(i, j): res2[i][j]
                                for i in res2.keys()
                                for j in res2[i].keys()}).T

        res2df.loc[(slice(None), 'test_score'), :]
```

This results in the following DataFrame:

```
Out[9]:
```

| | | 0 | 1 | 2 | 3 | 4 | 5 | 6 | 7 | 8 | 9 |
|---|---|---|---|---|---|---|---|---|---|---|---|
| 1 | test_score | 0.820896 | 0.746269 | 0.835821 | 0.791045 | 0.805970 | 0.757576 | 0.787879 | 0.818182 | 0.727273 | 0.742424 |
| 2 | test_score | 0.776119 | 0.716418 | 0.850746 | 0.746269 | 0.820896 | 0.757576 | 0.818182 | 0.848485 | 0.772727 | 0.757576 |
| 3 | test_score | 0.880597 | 0.746269 | 0.880597 | 0.791045 | 0.776119 | 0.818182 | 0.803030 | 0.818182 | 0.803030 | 0.742424 |
| 4 | test_score | 0.835821 | 0.776119 | 0.835821 | 0.880597 | 0.820896 | 0.818182 | 0.863636 | 0.757576 | 0.803030 | 0.757576 |
| 5 | test_score | 0.865672 | 0.791045 | 0.850746 | 0.835821 | 0.850746 | 0.818182 | 0.848485 | 0.818182 | 0.818182 | 0.772727 |
| 6 | test_score | 0.850746 | 0.805970 | 0.835821 | 0.865672 | 0.865672 | 0.803030 | 0.863636 | 0.772727 | 0.803030 | 0.772727 |
| 7 | test_score | 0.850746 | 0.820896 | 0.850746 | 0.850746 | 0.865672 | 0.787879 | 0.848485 | 0.772727 | 0.818182 | 0.772727 |
| 8 | test_score | 0.820896 | 0.865672 | 0.850746 | 0.865672 | 0.850746 | 0.833333 | 0.848485 | 0.818182 | 0.818182 | 0.772727 |
| 9 | test_score | 0.805970 | 0.850746 | 0.850746 | 0.865672 | 0.835821 | 0.863636 | 0.848485 | 0.772727 | 0.848485 | 0.833333 |
| 10 | test_score | 0.835821 | 0.850746 | 0.850746 | 0.850746 | 0.865672 | 0.833333 | 0.863636 | 0.757576 | 0.848485 | 0.818182 |

4. Here is the average accuracy:

```
In [10]: res2df.loc[(slice(None), 'test_score'), :].mean(axis=1)
Out[10]: 1   test_score    0.783333
         2   test_score    0.786499
         3   test_score    0.805948
         4   test_score    0.814925
         5   test_score    0.826979
         6   test_score    0.823903
         7   test_score    0.823881
         8   test_score    0.834464
         9   test_score    0.837562
         10  test_score    0.837494
         dtype: float64
```

5. It seems as if choosing a maximum tree depth of 9 does well, so that will be what we pick. Now, we will train our random forest classifier and see how well it does on the test set, as follows:

```
In [11]: forest2 = RandomForestClassifier(max_depth=9, n_estimators=40)
         forest2.fit(X=titanic_train.replace({'Sex': {'male': 0, 'female': 1}}
                                  ).drop(["Survived", "Name"], axis=1),
                 y=titanic_train.Survived)

         survived_test_predict = forest2.predict(X=titanic_test.replace(
             {'Sex': {'male': 0, 'female': 1}}
         ).drop(["Survived", "Name"], axis=1))
```

We can see that it does reasonably well, as shown in the following output:

```
In [12]:  print(classification_report(titanic_test.Survived, survived_test_predict))

                  precision    recall  f1-score   support

             0        0.84      0.90      0.87       145
             1        0.78      0.68      0.72        77

    avg / total       0.82      0.82      0.82       222
```

This concludes our path regarding random forests. Next up, we will see our first linear classifier—the Naive Bayes classifier.

# Naive Bayes classifier

Now, we will look at the Naive Bayes classifier. We will begin by looking at how the classifier works. Then, we will look at the linear separability assumptions that are used not only by the Naive Bayes algorithm, but also other important classifiers. Finally, we will train the classifier on the Titanic dataset.

The Naive Bayes classifier's big idea is to assume that the features used for prediction are independent of one other, but not of the class that we are trying to predict. To make a prediction, we estimate the likelihood that a data point would have the observed values for its features, given each possible class it belongs to. We predict the class that maximizes this likelihood.

Training consists of estimating the quantities that are used in forming these likelihoods. The independence assumption makes this task relatively painless. The Naive Bayes classifier makes two assumptions:

- The first is that all features are independent of each other, though not independent of the target variable. This is a very strong assumption and likely to be wrong, though the classifier may yield good results anyway.
- The other assumption is that the data is in some way linearly separable. This is an assumption that's frequently seen in machine learning, and the Naive Bayes classifier is not the only one to make it.

We can say that a dataset is linearly separable if instances of two classes can be separated by a hyperplane, which is a generalized notion of a straight line. Let's take a look at the following diagram to understand this better:

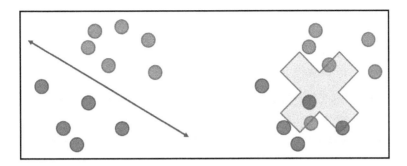

The dataset on the left is linearly separable. Here, there's a line dividing the blue dots from the red dots. The dataset on the right, though, is not.

Classifiers that require linear separability are referred to as **linear classifiers**. It turns out that the Naive Bayes classifier is a linear classifier. It's possible to train classifiers even if this assumption does not hold, but their predictive performance may degrade. If you want to know a little bit more about the Naive Bayes classifier, I have some notes in the Notebook for this section. As you can imagine, it's based on Bayes' theorem. The predictor that I actually showed is not a proper probability because it's not being divided by a number that would normalize this number to 1, but it's good enough because, in the end, we end up maximizing this, and that's how we make our predictions.

We choose $y$ so that the following formula, which is related to the likelihood of a particular class, is maximized:

$$\hat{y} = \arg\max_{y} P(Y = y) \prod_{k=1}^{K} P(X_k = x_k | Y = y)$$

Here, I have it written out in such a way that it works for binary variables, variables of a finite number of classes, or discrete variables, but this does not work for continuous variables.

For continuous variables, we replace this quantity with a density function. A common choice for the density function is the Gaussian density. I have the Gaussian density written here:

$$f_k(x_k | y) = \frac{1}{\sqrt{2\pi\sigma_{k,y}^2}} \exp\left(-\frac{(x_k - \mu_{k,y})^2}{2\sigma_{k,y}^2}\right)$$

It depends on a parameter, μ, and another parameter, σ, which correspond to a mean and a standard deviation, respectively. Here, we need to estimate these quantities from the dataset for each parameter for each possible class. Once we've done this, we'll be able to come up with our likelihood functions.

The following formula is a general description of this likelihood that a Naive Bayes classifier will use to make predictions:

$$\hat{y} = \arg\max_{y} P(Y = y) \prod_{i=1}^{I} P(U_i = u_i | Y = y) \prod_{j=1}^{J} f_j(v_j | y)$$

Regardless of what $y$ leads to, the largest value of this quantity will be the predictive class.

# Preprocessing the data

We don't have a `scikit-learn` function that mixes continuous and discrete values, like I have done here. Instead, you have the `BernoulliNB` object, which is good for binary data. We also have `MultinomialNB` and `GaussianNB`. Here, we're going to use `BernoulliNB` for a particular class of Naive Bayes classification:

1. First, we will import all the required functions, as follows:

```
In [ ]:  import pandas as pd
         from pandas import DataFrame
         from sklearn.model_selection import train_test_split, cross_validate
         from sklearn.metrics import classification_report
```

2. Let's process our Titanic dataset:

```
In [2]:  titanic = pd.read_csv("titanic.csv")
         titanic.head()
```

Out[2]:

| | Survived | Pclass | Name | Sex | Age | Siblings/Spouses Aboard | Parents/Children Aboard | Fare |
|---|---|---|---|---|---|---|---|---|
| 0 | 0 | 3 | Mr. Owen Harris Braund | male | 22.0 | 1 | 0 | 7.2500 |
| 1 | 1 | 1 | Mrs. John Bradley (Florence Briggs Thayer) Cum... | female | 38.0 | 1 | 0 | 71.2833 |
| 2 | 1 | 3 | Miss. Laina Heikkinen | female | 26.0 | 0 | 0 | 7.9250 |
| 3 | 1 | 1 | Mrs. Jacques Heath (Lily May Peel) Futrelle | female | 35.0 | 1 | 0 | 53.1000 |
| 4 | 0 | 3 | Mr. William Henry Allen | male | 35.0 | 0 | 0 | 8.0500 |

3. We're also going to discretize the `Age` and `Fare` variables. Then, we're going to turn these into binary variables, as shown here:

```
In [3]:  pd.cut(titanic.Age, bins=[-1, 2, titanic.Age.max() + 1]).head()

Out[3]:  0     (2.0, 81.0]
         1     (2.0, 81.0]
         2     (2.0, 81.0]
         3     (2.0, 81.0]
         4     (2.0, 81.0]
         Name: Age, dtype: category
         Categories (2, interval[float64]): [(-1.0, 2.0] < (2.0, 81.0]]

In [4]:  pd.cut(titanic.Fare, bins=[0, 23.35, titanic.Fare.max() + 1]).head()

Out[4]:  0        (0.0, 23.35]
         1     (23.35, 513.329]
         2        (0.0, 23.35]
         3     (23.35, 513.329]
         4        (0.0, 23.35]
         Name: Fare, dtype: category
         Categories (2, interval[float64]): [(0.0, 23.35] < (23.35, 513.329]]
```

The following screenshot shows the output for `Fare`:

```
In [5]:  titanic = titanic.assign(Age_cat=(titanic.Age <= 2), Fare_cat=(titanic.Fare <= 23.35))
         titanic.replace({'Sex': {'male': 0, 'female': 1}}, inplace=True)
         titanic.drop(['Age', 'Fare', 'Name'], axis=1, inplace=True)
         titanic.head()

Out[5]:
```

| | Survived | Pclass | Sex | Siblings/Spouses Aboard | Parents/Children Aboard | Age_cat | Fare_cat |
|---|---|---|---|---|---|---|---|
| 0 | 0 | 3 | 0 | 1 | 0 | False | True |
| 1 | 1 | 1 | 1 | 1 | 0 | False | False |
| 2 | 1 | 3 | 1 | 0 | 0 | False | True |
| 3 | 1 | 1 | 1 | 1 | 0 | False | False |
| 4 | 0 | 3 | 0 | 0 | 0 | False | True |

4. Then, we will transform the DataFrame by using the following code:

```
In [6]:  titanic_train, titanic_test = train_test_split(titanic)
         titanic_train.head()
```

This results in the following output:

```
Out[6]:
```

| | Survived | Pclass | Sex | Siblings/Spouses Aboard | Parents/Children Aboard | Age_cat | Fare_cat |
|---|---|---|---|---|---|---|---|
| 776 | 1 | 3 | 1 | 0 | 0 | False | True |
| 490 | 0 | 1 | 0 | 0 | 0 | False | False |
| 235 | 0 | 2 | 0 | 1 | 0 | False | False |
| 546 | 1 | 2 | 0 | 1 | 1 | False | False |
| 195 | 0 | 3 | 0 | 0 | 0 | False | True |

I have categorical variables for `Age` and `Fare`, where the categorical variable for `Fare` is `True` if you paid less than $23.35, and the `Age` variable is `True` if your age is less than or equal to 2 years. Why did I choose these? I could have used cross-validation to choose these cutoffs. In this case, I was basing my decision off of what I was seeing with the decision trees. It looks like they were choosing some good age and fare cutoffs. In any case, we split up our dataset into a training and test set.

# Training the classifier

Now, let's train a Naive Bayes classifier:

1. First, we import the object, as follows:

```
In [7]:  from sklearn.naive_bayes import BernoulliNB
```

2. Here, we train the classifier and see how it's performing on the training set:

```
In [8]:  bnb = BernoulliNB(alpha=0,      # Additive smoothing parameter; setting to 0 for no smoothing
                           fit_prior=False,    # Don't learn a prior distribution for the label
                           class_prior=None)   # Don't have prior distributions for features
         bnb = bnb.fit(titanic_train.drop("Survived", axis=1), titanic_train.Survived)
         print(classification_report(titanic_train.Survived, bnb.predict(titanic_train.drop("Survived", axis=1))))
```

This results in the following output:

|            | precision | recall | f1-score | support |
|------------|-----------|--------|----------|---------|
| 0          | 0.82      | 0.78   | 0.80     | 418     |
| 1          | 0.66      | 0.71   | 0.68     | 247     |
| avg / total | 0.76     | 0.75   | 0.76     | 665     |

It doesn't seem to be doing particularly well on the training set, which means that I'm not too optimistic that it's going to do well on the test set either.

3. We will still run it on the test set, as follows:

```
In [9]:  survived_test_predict = bnb.predict(titanic_test.drop("Survived", axis=1))
         print(classification_report(titanic_test.Survived, survived_test_predict))
```

This results in the following output:

|            | precision | recall | f1-score | support |
|------------|-----------|--------|----------|---------|
| 0          | 0.81      | 0.77   | 0.79     | 127     |
| 1          | 0.71      | 0.76   | 0.73     | 95      |
| avg / total | 0.77     | 0.77   | 0.77     | 222     |

We can see that it's not doing much better. This might lead us to think that a Naive Bayes algorithm is probably not the best choice; however, we could have done more to make this classifier work; for example, we could have fiddled around with some hyperparameters, such as priors. The next linear classifier we will look at is the famous **support vector machine** (**SVM**).

# Support vector machines

In this section, we will look at SVMs, what they are, and how they classify data. We will discuss important hyperparameters, including how kernel methods are used. Finally, we will see their use by training them on the Titanic dataset.

With SVMs, we seek to find a hyperplane that best separates instances of two classes. These classes are assumed to be linearly separable. All data on one side of the hyperplane is predicted to belong to one class. All others belong to the other class. By best line, we mean that the plane separates classes while at the same time maximizing the distance between the line and the nearest data point, as shown in the following diagram:

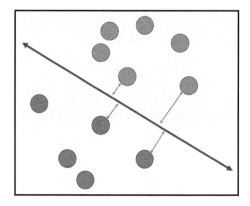

The hope is that by doing this, the SVM will generalize well to data that hasn't been seen. There are two hyperparameters that are of interest to SVMs:

- One is a tolerance parameter of C that controls the SVM's tolerance for overfitting. A smaller C hopefully leads to less overfitting.
- The other hyperparameter is the kernel function that's used. Kernel functions allow linear classifiers to possibly fit nonlinear patterns in data. On the left is a linear kernel, and on the right is a polynomial kernel, as shown in the following diagram:

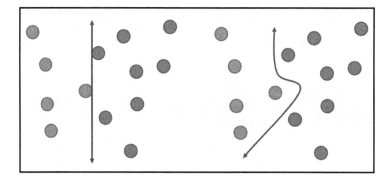

Notice that the boundary separating individuals on the right is no longer linear.

Other kernel functions are also supported by `scikit-learn`. Let's see the SVM in action:

1.  Let's import all the required functions using the following lines of code:

```
In [*]:   import pandas as pd
          from pandas import DataFrame
          from sklearn.model_selection import train_test_split, cross_validate
          from sklearn.metrics import classification_report
          from random import seed
```

2.  Let's load in our Titanic dataset by using the following lines of code:

```
In [ ]:   seed(110717)

          titanic = pd.read_csv("titanic.csv")
          titanic.replace({'Sex': {'male': 0, 'female': 1}}, inplace=True)
          titanic.drop("Name", axis=1, inplace=True)
          titanic.head()
```

This results in the following output:

```
Out[2]:
```

|   | Survived | Pclass | Sex | Age | Siblings/Spouses Aboard | Parents/Children Aboard | Fare |
|---|----------|--------|-----|------|--------------------------|---------------------------|---------|
| 0 | 0 | 3 | 0 | 22.0 | 1 | 0 | 7.2500 |
| 1 | 1 | 1 | 1 | 38.0 | 1 | 0 | 71.2833 |
| 2 | 1 | 3 | 1 | 26.0 | 0 | 0 | 7.9250 |
| 3 | 1 | 1 | 1 | 35.0 | 1 | 0 | 53.1000 |
| 4 | 0 | 3 | 0 | 35.0 | 0 | 0 | 8.0500 |

Here, I am bothered by the fact that the passenger class has values of 1, 2, and 3. This is not actually a good thing. You see, we don't want our classifier to think that there is something significant about the number 1, the number 2, and the number 3. We could call the classes A, B, and C, and it will be equally meaningful. The actual number 3 doesn't mean anything. The same thing goes for the number 1—the magnitude of that number means nothing.

3. So, what we actually want are dummy variables for each possible passenger class, which can be done using the following lines of code:

```
In [3]: pd.get_dummies(titanic.Pclass).head()
```

This results in the following output:

```
Out[3]:
          1  2  3
       0  0  0  1
       1  1  0  0
       2  0  0  1
       3  1  0  0
       4  0  0  1
```

These are variables that take the values 0 or 1, depending on whether the individual actually belongs to that class. For the first few rows, the dummy variable 3 is 1 because this individual belongs to passenger class 3, and all others are 0.

4. We're going to take this set of dummies and add them to our dataset by using the following lines of code:

```
In [4]: titanic = titanic.join(pd.get_dummies(titanic.Pclass, prefix='Pclass')).drop("Pclass", axis=1)
        titanic.head()
```

This results in the following output:

```
Out[4]:
```

| | Survived | Sex | Age | Siblings/Spouses Aboard | Parents/Children Aboard | Fare | Pclass_1 | Pclass_2 | Pclass_3 |
|---|---|---|---|---|---|---|---|---|---|
| 0 | 0 | 0 | 22.0 | 1 | 0 | 7.2500 | 0 | 0 | 1 |
| 1 | 1 | 1 | 38.0 | 1 | 0 | 71.2833 | 1 | 0 | 0 |
| 2 | 1 | 1 | 26.0 | 0 | 0 | 7.9250 | 0 | 0 | 1 |
| 3 | 1 | 1 | 35.0 | 1 | 0 | 53.1000 | 1 | 0 | 0 |
| 4 | 0 | 0 | 35.0 | 0 | 0 | 8.0500 | 0 | 0 | 1 |

This is what we will use, instead, to account for a person's passenger class.

5. We will then print out the dataset that we will be using for training, as follows:

```
In [5]: titanic_train, titanic_test = train_test_split(titanic)
        titanic_train.head()

Out[5]:
```

| | Survived | Sex | Age | Siblings/Spouses Aboard | Parents/Children Aboard | Fare | Pclass_1 | Pclass_2 | Pclass_3 |
|---|---|---|---|---|---|---|---|---|---|
| 95 | 0 | 0 | 71.0 | 0 | 0 | 34.6542 | 1 | 0 | 0 |
| 581 | 0 | 0 | 16.0 | 0 | 0 | 8.7125 | 0 | 0 | 1 |
| 267 | 1 | 1 | 35.0 | 0 | 0 | 135.6333 | 1 | 0 | 0 |
| 138 | 0 | 0 | 24.0 | 0 | 0 | 79.2000 | 1 | 0 | 0 |
| 663 | 0 | 0 | 25.0 | 0 | 0 | 13.0000 | 0 | 1 | 0 |

# Training a SVM

Now, let's train our SVM by using the following steps:

1. First, we will import the `SVC` object by using the following code:

```
In [6]:   from sklearn.svm import SVC
```

This is the object in `scikit-learn` for training SVMs.

2. Then, we define the `SVC`. We will specify a parameter, C, which is our tolerance for overfitting; we will also say that we want a `linear` kernel. We will then fit and predict the model by using the following lines of code:

```
In [7]: svm1 = SVC(C=1.0,
                    kernel='linear')
        svm1.fit(X=titanic_train.drop("Survived", axis=1), y=titanic_train.Survived)

        svm1.predict([[0, 26, 0, 0, 30, 0, 1, 0]])
```

I am actually not going to use cross-validation to decide whether these are appropriate choices or not. The only reason why is time. It may take a while to fit models and also check all the possible hyperparameters. Consider this as an exercise to you to see if a different C and a different kernel leads to better results than what you can see in this section. You've already seen what cross-validation for these classifiers looks like. It's not going to be any different here—it's just going to be a different classifier and different hyperparameters.

This results in the following output:

```
Out[7]: array([0], dtype=int64)
```

Once again, it predicts that this individual did not survive the disaster.

3. Now, let's see how well this classifier does on the training set by using the following code:

```
In [8]: print(classification_report(titanic_train.Survived, svm1.predict(titanic_train.drop("Survived", axis=1))))
```

This results in the following output:

|  | precision | recall | f1-score | support |
| --- | --- | --- | --- | --- |
| 0 | 0.80 | 0.87 | 0.83 | 404 |
| 1 | 0.76 | 0.67 | 0.71 | 261 |
| avg / total | 0.79 | 0.79 | 0.79 | 665 |

4. Now, let's see how it does on the test set:

```
In [9]: survived_test_predict = svm1.predict(titanic_test.drop("Survived", axis=1))
        print(classification_report(titanic_test.Survived, survived_test_predict))
```

This results in the following output:

|            | precision | recall | f1-score | support |
|------------|-----------|--------|----------|---------|
| 0          | 0.83      | 0.81   | 0.82     | 141     |
| 1          | 0.68      | 0.72   | 0.70     | 81      |
| avg / total | 0.78     | 0.77   | 0.78     | 222     |

SVMs are not known to overfit. They are believed to generalize pretty well to future data. Maybe we were overfitting just a little bit too much with our SVM, but the result is about the same. Personally, I'm not particularly impressed by what the SVM is doing for the Titanic dataset, but we will look at another classifier and see whether it does any better. That's it for SVMs. Next up is logistic regression.

# Logistic regression

In this section, we will look at another linear classifier—logistic regression.

Logistic regression is also referred to as **logit models**. In this section, we will look at the basic idea of prediction using logistic regression and how to train and use these models. Our applications still involve the Titanic dataset. So, let's get right into it:

1. First, we will import all the required functions:

```
In [1]: import pandas as pd
        from pandas import DataFrame
        from sklearn.model_selection import train_test_split, cross_validate
        from sklearn.metrics import classification_report
```

2. Then, we're going to load in the dataset:

```
In [ ]: titanic = pd.read_csv("titanic.csv")
        titanic.replace({'Sex': {'male': 0, 'female': 1}}, inplace=True)
        titanic.drop("Name", axis=1, inplace=True)
        titanic = titanic.join(pd.get_dummies(titanic.Pclass, prefix='Pclass')).drop("Pclass", axis=1)
        titanic_train, titanic_test = train_test_split(titanic)
        titanic_train.head()
```

This results in the following output:

```
Out[2]:
```

| | Survived | Sex | Age | Siblings/Spouses Aboard | Parents/Children Aboard | Fare | Pclass_1 | Pclass_2 | Pclass_3 |
|---|---|---|---|---|---|---|---|---|---|
| 254 | 1 | 1 | 29.0 | 0 | 2 | 15.2458 | 0 | 0 | 1 |
| 200 | 0 | 0 | 17.0 | 8 | 2 | 69.5500 | 0 | 0 | 1 |
| 635 | 0 | 1 | 41.0 | 0 | 5 | 39.6875 | 0 | 0 | 1 |
| 741 | 0 | 0 | 70.0 | 1 | 1 | 71.0000 | 1 | 0 | 0 |
| 611 | 0 | 0 | 35.0 | 0 | 0 | 8.0500 | 0 | 0 | 1 |

Some further comments about logistic regression—this is something that's not just common in machine learning. It's also a generally popular statistical model for regressions so that you can predict probabilities, so it's no wonder that this type of regression has been around for a long time. It has appeared in fields such as economics and medicine, among others.

We are still using dummies for the passenger class. This is the appropriate thing to do for logit models for SVMs, and if we were using kNN on this dataset, we would do that for kNN as well. It's not really a problem for decision trees, nor a problem for Naive Bayes.

# Fitting a logit model

Logit models are functions that, given inputs about an observation's characteristics, yield the probability that the observation belongs to a particular class. Again, they are linear classifiers. Let's look at the following graph:

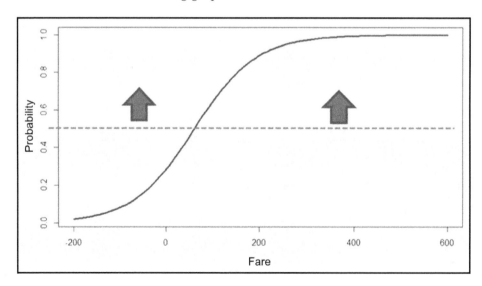

If this probability for an observation is above a certain threshold—likely, 0.5—then we predict that the observation belongs to the class the model was designed to detect. Otherwise, we predict that the observation belongs to the other class.

Logit models have other characteristics. They are linear classifiers, like Naive Bayes classifiers and SVMs. They can also be calibrated with the c tolerance parameter, just like SVMs. A smaller c implies less tolerance to overfitting. Let's see how we can fit a logit model using scikit-learn:

1. We're going to be using the LogisticRegression object that's provided by the package:

```
In [ ]:  from sklearn.linear_model import LogisticRegression
```

2. Now, we will create an instance of this object and fit a dataset to it, along with an example prediction:

```
In [4]:  logit = LogisticRegression()
         logit.fit(X=titanic_train.drop("Survived", axis=1),
                   y=titanic_train.Survived)
         logit.predict([[0, 26, 0, 0, 30, 0, 1, 0]])
```

This results in the following output:

```
Out[4]:  array([0], dtype=int64)
```

Once again, this hypothetical individual is not predicted to have survived the disaster.

3. Now, we can actually see the probability that the model is assigning to this individual by using the following code:

```
In [5]:  logit.predict_proba([[0, 26, 0, 0, 30, 0, 1, 0]])
Out[5]:  array([[ 0.70767761,  0.29232239]])
```

It is saying that there's a 70% chance that this individual did not survive the disaster. There's only a roughly 30% chance that this individual actually did survive.

4. Now, let's see how this model does on the training set:

```
In [6]: print(classification_report(titanic_train.Survived, logit.predict(titanic_train.drop("Survived", axis=1))))
```

This results in the following output:

|           | precision | recall | f1-score | support |
|-----------|-----------|--------|----------|---------|
| 0         | 0.83      | 0.88   | 0.86     | 413     |
| 1         | 0.79      | 0.70   | 0.74     | 252     |
| avg / total | 0.81    | 0.82   | 0.81     | 665     |

It gets an average result of 81% or 82%, depending on which of these metrics you're looking at, which is what the Naive Bayes classifier and the SVM got in terms of performance.

5. Let's move on to a full-on classification report:

```
In [7]: print(classification_report(titanic_test.Survived, logit.predict(titanic_test.drop("Survived", axis=1))))
```

This results in the following output:

|           | precision | recall | f1-score | support |
|-----------|-----------|--------|----------|---------|
| 0         | 0.77      | 0.87   | 0.82     | 132     |
| 1         | 0.76      | 0.61   | 0.68     | 90      |
| avg / total | 0.77    | 0.77   | 0.76     | 222     |

It looks like this model is overfitting to a great extent, so we would want to take some steps to try and combat that. We could have done some cross-validation to work with the parameter seed that is responsible for that. I'm going to leave it as an exercise for you, to implement cross-validation and possibly do better with this classifier. That's it for logit models. We're now done looking at particular classifiers. Next, we are going to see how we can take what we have seen for binary prediction and try to make multiclass predictions.

# Extending beyond binary classifiers

In this section, we will see how to go beyond binary prediction and try to predict more than one possible outcome. Here, we will shift our attention from predicting one of two classes to predicting one of multiple classes. We will see classifiers that are inherently multiclass, and those that need one-versus-one or one-versus-all approaches in order to work on multiclass data. We will be demonstrating how classifiers can predict the species of flowers in the iris dataset.

First, let's load in the iris dataset, and then let's start talking about multiclass classifiers. Some of the classifiers that we have already seen are already set up effectively for multiclass classification, because we never made an assumption that required two classes. Classifiers that are already set up for multiclass classification include kNNs, decision trees, random forests, and Naive Bayes. These are all ready for multiclass classification. In fact, we have already seen kNNs being applied to the iris dataset, so I'm not going to repeat it in this section.

# Multiple outcomes for decision trees

Let's see what the decision tree does:

1. Let's load in some packages that are useful for visualization:

```
In [4]:  from sklearn.tree import DecisionTreeClassifier
         from sklearn.externals.six import StringIO
         from IPython.display import Image
         from sklearn.tree import export_graphviz
         import pydotplus
```

2. Let's train our tree to predict which species a flower belongs to:

```
In [5]:  tree = DecisionTreeClassifier(max_depth=3)
         tree = tree.fit(flower_train, species_train)
         print(classification_report(species_test, tree.predict(flower_test)))
```

This results in the following output:

| | precision | recall | f1-score | support |
|---|---|---|---|---|
| 0 | 1.00 | 1.00 | 1.00 | 5 |
| 1 | 1.00 | 1.00 | 1.00 | 4 |
| 2 | 1.00 | 1.00 | 1.00 | 6 |
| avg / total | 1.00 | 1.00 | 1.00 | 15 |

The tree does extremely well on the test set. It hasn't made a single error.

3. We will now visualize the tree by using the following function:

```
In [ ]: dot_data = StringIO()

        export_graphviz(tree,     # Function for exporting a visualization
                        out_file=dot_data,
                        # Data controlling the display of the graph
                        filled=True, rounded=True,
                        special_characters=True,
                        feature_names=["Sepal Length", "Sepal Width",
                                       "Petal Length", "Petal Width"],
                        proportion=True)    # Show proportions for labels

        # Display graph in Jupyter notebook
        graph = pydotplus.graph_from_dot_data(dot_data.getvalue())
        Image(graph.create_png())
```

This results in the following output:

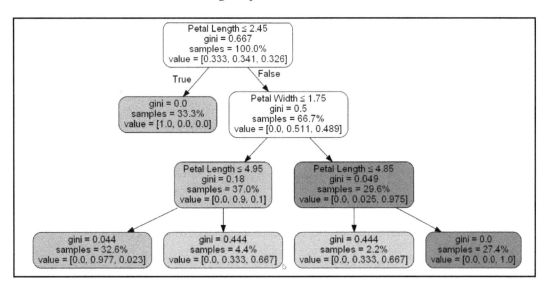

Notice that it's now working with multiple classes. It's very nice to read this image and know how we can decide what species a flower belongs to. If our petal length is less than 2.45, then we predict that the flower is setosa. Otherwise, we move on to the next test. If the petal width is less than 1.75, then we're going to check if the petal length is less than 4.95, and if that's the case, we're going to predict versicolor; otherwise, we predict virginica. Finally, if the petal length is less than 4.85, it appears that there's a prediction for virginica, regardless of other factors.

# Multiple outcomes for random forests

Now, we will implement this for a random forest. If the decision tree did well, we might suspect that the random forest will also do well because it's based on decision trees.

We will import the classifier using the following code:

```
In [7]:  from sklearn.ensemble import RandomForestClassifier
```

We will then run the classification report for the forest, as follows:

```
In [8]:  forest = RandomForestClassifier(n_estimators=20, max_depth=2)
         forest.fit(flower_train, species_train)
         print(classification_report(species_test, forest.predict(flower_test)))
```

This results in the following output:

|              | precision | recall | f1-score | support |
|--------------|-----------|--------|----------|---------|
| 0            | 1.00      | 1.00   | 1.00     | 5       |
| 1            | 1.00      | 1.00   | 1.00     | 4       |
| 2            | 1.00      | 1.00   | 1.00     | 6       |
| avg / total  | 1.00      | 1.00   | 1.00     | 15      |

And lo and behold, the random forest does a perfect job on the dataset as well.

# Multiple outcomes for Naive Bayes

Now, we will move on to the Naive Bayes classifier. Here, I'm going to use the Gaussian variant of the Naive Bayes classifier, which I talked about earlier. This is because we're working with continuous variables. In this case, we're working with the lengths and widths of flower sepals and flower petals, so that means that likelihoods are actually using the Gaussian function and the Gaussian density.

We will import the object using the following code:

```
In [ ]:  from sklearn.naive_bayes import GaussianNB
```

We train this using the following lines of code:

```
In [ ]:  nb = GaussianNB()
         nb = nb.fit(flower_train, species_train)
         print(classification_report(species_test, nb.predict(flower_test)))
```

This results in the following output:

|          | precision | recall | f1-score | support |
|----------|-----------|--------|----------|---------|
| 0        | 1.00      | 1.00   | 1.00     | 5       |
| 1        | 1.00      | 1.00   | 1.00     | 4       |
| 2        | 1.00      | 1.00   | 1.00     | 6       |
| avg / total | 1.00   | 1.00   | 1.00     | 15      |

As we can see, this classifier does pretty well on the test set.

# One-versus-all and one-versus-one classification

Now, we will move on to the classifiers that are not inherently multiclass. If we have a classifier and it is intended for binary classification, then we need to use either one-versus-one or one-versus-all schemes.

**One-versus-all** classification trains classifiers for each class that predicts that an observation does or doesn't belong to that class. There should be only one classifier that predicts that an observation belongs to its respective class in the end, and that will be our prediction for the label of the observation, as illustrated in the following graph:

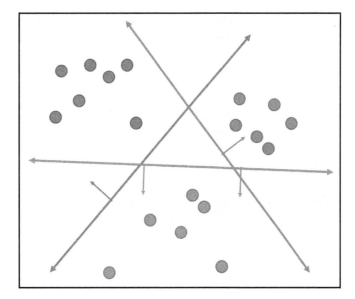

In comparison, **one-versus-one** classification trains a classifier for each pair of classes. When a prediction needs to be made, all these classifiers make a prediction. The label that's predicted the most frequently is the model's overall prediction, as shown in the following graph:

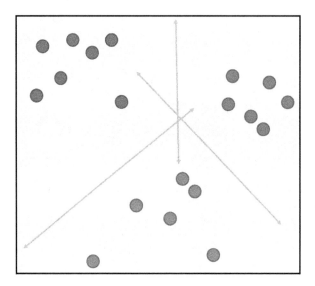

So, when we have one-versus-all, we will have as many classifiers as we have classes, which is nice because that's not very many classifiers. If we have $k$ classes, we will have $k$ classifiers, which sounds good to me. Now, we may run into problems if our classifier is very sensitive to how much data we have. If it takes a long time to train this classifier when there's lots of data, maybe the one-versus-one classifier is better because we're actually restricting our datasets. Also, when we're doing one-versus-all classification, we are assuming that the data is linearly separable for every class, and this is a strong assumption that doesn't need to hold.

With one-versus-one classification, we have a classifier for every combination of classes. This means that if we have $k$ classes, then we will have almost K-squared classifiers, something resembling K-squared, which means that the number of classifiers we need grows quadratically with the number of classes in our dataset, which isn't desirable. However, if our classifiers tend to have low performance when they need to be trained on lots of data points, then this might be preferable because we're cutting up our dataset into many smaller datasets, and that might speed up the training of these classifiers. Also, this mode of classification doesn't have as strong a linearity assumption.

`scikit-learn` has functions that are dedicated for turning binary classifiers into multiclass classifiers that are provided in the multiclass module. We have `OneVsRestClassifier` and `OneVsOneClassifier`, but the documentation makes it clear that they prefer that you use the support for multiclass classification that's already built into all of their binary classifiers. This includes SVC and logistic regression. They're already set up for multiclass classification. However, they don't do multiclass classification the same way. SVC implements the one-versus-one method, while logistic regression uses the one-versus-all method. Let's see how we can train an SVM that uses one-versus-one:

1. First, we import the `SVC` class, as follows:

```
In [11]:   from sklearn.svm import SVC
```

2. Then, we will see how well this class does by using a classification report:

```
In [12]:   svm = SVC()
           svm.fit(flower_train, species_train)
           print(classification_report(species_test, svm.predict(flower_test)))
```

This results in the following output:

```
             precision    recall  f1-score   support

          0       1.00      1.00      1.00         5
          1       1.00      1.00      1.00         4
          2       1.00      1.00      1.00         6

avg / total       1.00      1.00      1.00        15
```

Look at that—it does a perfect job on the dataset. It seems like one-versus-one classification using an SVM does a good job.

3. Now, let's take a look at logistic regression:

```
In [14]:   logit = LogisticRegression()
           logit.fit(flower_train, species_train)
           print(classification_report(species_test, logit.predict(flower_test)))
```

This results in the following output:

```
                precision    recall  f1-score   support

           0         1.00      1.00      1.00         5
           1         1.00      1.00      1.00         4
           2         1.00      1.00      1.00         6

avg / total          1.00      1.00      1.00        15
```

Logistic regression also did very well. It seems like it was pretty easy to predict the species of the flower from the test set. However, this is not always the case. I have seen times where the classifiers did not do a perfect job on the test set. Our results were not guaranteed; it looks like we got lucky. That's it for classification.

# Summary

In this chapter, we learned all about kNN classifiers and how to train them. We looked at decision trees and how to fit and visualize it. Then, we learned about random forests and how to train them. We looked at Naive Bayes classifiers, and trained one using the Titanic dataset. We then used SVMs on the Titanic dataset and learned how they work. We also looked at logistic regression. Finally, we learned how to find out multiple outcomes for all the classifiers that we worked on in this chapter.

In this next chapter, we will move on to regression, where we want to predict the value of a continuous variable, not a discrete class.

# Regression Analysis and How to Use It

4

Welcome to regression analysis! This chapter covers a different type of supervised learning, where the variable of interest is not categorical but quantitative. We will focus on different modes of linear regression. We will start by learning what linear models do and how they are estimated, using one of the oldest and simplest procedures—**ordinary least squares** (**OLS**). Next, we will evaluate how well a model fits data using `statsmodels`. Then, we will move on to the Bayesian linear regression model and ridge regression; this is a means of regularized linear regression. This is followed by **least absolute shrinkage and selection operator** (**LASSO**) regression, which is another regularized regression approach. Finally, we will discuss spline interpolation. While this is technically not considered to be a type of regression, it's still a useful topic to explore, with some similarities to regression.

This chapter covers the following topics:

- Linear models
- Evaluating linear models
- Bayesian linear models
- Ridge regression
- LASSO regression
- Spline interpolation

# Linear models

Let's start by discussing the basics of linear models. In this section, we will examine the objectives of regression, what a linear model is, and how to evaluate the quality of a fit. We will explore estimation with the help of OLS. Additionally, we will take a look at the OLS method of estimation in action by trying to predict the price of homes in Boston.

Classification and regression are both methods of prediction, but they each predict variables of different natures. For instance, classification predicts whether a data point belongs to one of a finite number of classes, such as whether a viewer clicks on an ad on a web page or not. On the other hand, regression predicts a value from a continuum, such as how much a customer will spend on a website. The following diagram demonstrates the difference between classification and regression:

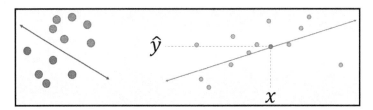

Linear models are regression models that multiply the value of each element with a weight, and then add the product to produce a prediction. Linear models almost always include an intercept term. At first, linear models may seem restrictive, but they are actually quite expressive. Polynomials and other functions are also linear models. Here are some examples of linear models:

$$\checkmark \quad \hat{y} = \beta_0 + \beta_1 x$$
$$\checkmark \quad \hat{y} = \beta_0 + \beta_1 x + \beta_2 x^2$$
$$\checkmark \quad \hat{y} = \alpha e^{\beta x} \Leftrightarrow \log \hat{y} = \log \alpha + \beta x$$
$$\times \quad \hat{y} = \beta_0 + \frac{1}{1 + \beta_1 x}$$

In comparison to linear models, nonlinear models are more difficult to handle. We can evaluate regression models by their errors. We define an error as the difference between the predicted and actual values for data points in the dataset. The errors of all the data points are combined to form the sum of squared errors. We can then use a linear model to minimize this quantity. The least squares procedure, in fact, does this for a dataset by finding the coefficients of the model that will minimize the sum of squared errors for the data it uses in the fit, as shown in the following diagram:

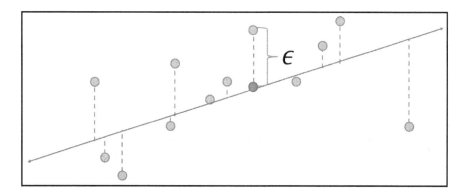

However, we can't necessarily guarantee that this future data has a smaller sum of squared errors. There are hyperparameters to consider with linear models that are fitted with OLS (or other methods). The first is what features to include in the model; for example, should we use age, race, and sex when predicting people's incomes? Another hyperparameter to consider is the possible transformation in the model; that is, should our model take a nonlinear functional form such as a quadratic function, or other interaction terms?

# Fitting a linear model with OLS

In the Jupyter Notebook for this section, we will see how we can obtain OLS fits using the `scikit-learn` library:

1. First, we will load the Boston dataset and other required functions:

```
In [5]:   from sklearn.datasets import load_boston
          from sklearn.model_selection import train_test_split
```

2. After loading in this dataset, we can take a look at the objects that it contains:

```
In [6]:   boston_obj = load_boston()
          data, price = boston_obj.data, boston_obj.target
          data[:5, :]
```

This results in the following output:

```
Out[2]:  array([[6.3200e-03, 1.8000e+01, 2.3100e+00, 0.0000e+00, 5.3800e-01,
                 6.5750e+00, 6.5200e+01, 4.0900e+00, 1.0000e+00, 2.9600e+02,
                 1.5300e+01, 3.9690e+02, 4.9800e+00],
                [2.7310e-02, 0.0000e+00, 7.0700e+00, 0.0000e+00, 4.6900e-01,
                 6.4210e+00, 7.8900e+01, 4.9671e+00, 2.0000e+00, 2.4200e+02,
                 1.7800e+01, 3.9690e+02, 9.1400e+00],
                [2.7290e-02, 0.0000e+00, 7.0700e+00, 0.0000e+00, 4.6900e-01,
                 7.1850e+00, 6.1100e+01, 4.9671e+00, 2.0000e+00, 2.4200e+02,
                 1.7800e+01, 3.9283e+02, 4.0300e+00],
                [3.2370e-02, 0.0000e+00, 2.1800e+00, 0.0000e+00, 4.5800e-01,
                 6.9980e+00, 4.5800e+01, 6.0622e+00, 3.0000e+00, 2.2200e+02,
                 1.8700e+01, 3.9463e+02, 2.9400e+00],
                [6.9050e-02, 0.0000e+00, 2.1800e+00, 0.0000e+00, 4.5800e-01,
                 7.1470e+00, 5.4200e+01, 6.0622e+00, 3.0000e+00, 2.2200e+02,
                 1.8700e+01, 3.9690e+02, 5.3300e+00]])
```

Here, we see the first five rows of the dataset.

3. We can now see the first five prices that we would need to predict, as follows:

```
In [3]:  price[:5]
Out[3]:  array([24. , 21.6, 34.7, 33.4, 36.2])
```

4. We can split our dataset as we did previously, when we were working with data that could take one of a finite number of values, using the following code:

```
In [8]:  data_train, data_test, price_train, price_test = train_test_split(data, price)
         data_train[:5, :]
```

This results in the following array:

```
Out[4]: array([[5.60200e-02, 0.00000e+00, 2.46000e+00, 0.00000e+00, 4.88000e-01,
                7.83100e+00, 5.36000e+01, 3.19920e+00, 3.00000e+00, 1.93000e+02,
                1.78000e+01, 3.92630e+02, 4.45000e+00],
               [8.30800e-02, 0.00000e+00, 2.46000e+00, 0.00000e+00, 4.88000e-01,
                5.60400e+00, 8.98000e+01, 2.98790e+00, 3.00000e+00, 1.93000e+02,
                1.78000e+01, 3.91000e+02, 1.39800e+01],
               [8.71675e+00, 0.00000e+00, 1.81000e+01, 0.00000e+00, 6.93000e-01,
                6.47100e+00, 9.88000e+01, 1.72570e+00, 2.40000e+01, 6.66000e+02,
                2.02000e+01, 3.91980e+02, 1.71200e+01],
               [8.79212e+00, 0.00000e+00, 1.81000e+01, 0.00000e+00, 5.84000e-01,
                5.56500e+00, 7.06000e+01, 2.06350e+00, 2.40000e+01, 6.66000e+02,
                2.02000e+01, 3.65000e+00, 1.71600e+01],
               [7.84200e-01, 0.00000e+00, 8.14000e+00, 0.00000e+00, 5.38000e-01,
                5.99000e+00, 8.17000e+01, 4.25790e+00, 4.00000e+00, 3.07000e+02,
                2.10000e+01, 3.86750e+02, 1.46700e+01]])
```

5. We will then print the first five rows of the training dataset for prices, as follows:

```
In [5]: price_train[:5]

Out[5]: array([50. , 26.4, 13.1, 11.7, 17.5])
```

We'll go ahead and use all the features available to us for prediction in our linear model. In general, this doesn't necessarily produce better models. There are some features that may introduce only noise and make prediction more difficult, not less; however, we're going to go ahead and ignore that wrinkle for now.

6. We're going to import the LinearRegression object from sklearn, along with the mean_squared_error metric, using the following lines of code:

```
In [10]: from sklearn.linear_model import LinearRegression
         from sklearn.metrics import mean_squared_error
         import numpy as np
```

This is the go-to metric to evaluate how well a model is predicting the target variable.

7. Now we can fit the model and see an individual prediction:

```
In [11]:  ols1 = LinearRegression()
          ols1.fit(data_train, price_train)    # Fitting a linear model
          ols1.predict([[    # An example prediction
              1,       # Per capita crime rate
              25,      # Proportion of land zoned for large homes
              5,       # Proportion of land zoned for non-retail business
              1,       # Tract bounds the Charles River
              0.3,     # NOX concentration
              10,      # Average number of rooms per dwelling
              2,       # Proportion of owner-occupied units built prior to 1940
              10,      # Weighted distance to employment centers
              3,       # Index for highway accessibility
              400,     # Tax rate
              15,      # Pupil/teacher ratio
              200,     # Index
              5        # % lower status of population
          ]])
```

Here, we have the per capita crime rate, the proportion of land that has been zoned, and a number of other variables. We're simply making up a possible value for this, and seeing what the predicted price of the home will be. This results in the following output:

```
Out[7]:  array([40.59396201])
```

In this case, the predicted price is 40.5939.

8. Once we have this prediction, we can make predictions for every row in our training data, as follows:

```
In [12]:  predprice = ols1.predict(data_train)
          predprice[:5]
```

The array of predicted values is as follows:

```
Out[8]:  array([36.60268045, 22.74630558, 20.19610388, 14.04474667, 17.14567269])
```

9. Once we have this one-dimensional array, we can then compute the
   mean_squared_error metric, which results in the following output:

```
In [9]:  mean_squared_error(price_train, predprice)

Out[9]:  19.24697544587027
```

10. If we were to take the square root of the mean_squared_error metric, we could
    interpret the resulting number as the average amount of error, that is, the
    average difference between the home's actual price and the price that was
    predicted by our model. This is shown in the following screenshot:

```
In [10]:  np.sqrt(mean_squared_error(price_train, predprice))

Out[10]:  4.387137500223838
```

# Performing cross-validation

Now we can perform cross-validation to see how well things are going.

We will use the cross_val_score() function instead of what we've been using so far.
This wraps up a lot of the cross-validation procedure into one nice function. We will import
this function as follows:

```
In [15]:  from sklearn.model_selection import cross_val_score
```

The following function will give us all of the **mean squared error** (**MSE**) values for the folds
that it creates; in our case, we want 10 folds:

```
In [16]:  ols2 = LinearRegression()
          ols_cv_mse = cross_val_score(ols2, data_train, price_train, scoring='neg_mean_squared_error', cv=10)
          ols_cv_mse.mean()
```

This results in the following output:

```
Out[12]:  -21.336072658144275
```

The reason why we see a negative of the MSE is that, ideally, we want the MSE to be as small as possible. So, if we make the negative MSE as large as possible, then we will achieve our goal. This is like saying we would like our classification accuracy to be as high as possible—we would like our negative MSE to be as high as possible as well.

So, we just saw how well the model was doing on the training data. Here is how well the model does on the test data:

```
In [13]: testpredprice = ols1.predict(data_test)
         mean_squared_error(price_test, testpredprice)

Out[13]: 30.480706235794237
```

We can see the square root of this MSE, as follows:

```
In [14]: np.sqrt(mean_squared_error(price_test, testpredprice))

Out[14]: 5.520933456925037
```

So, it doesn't seem like the test data is making that much more of an error, although it appears that it may have overfitted slightly on our training data. In the next section, we will look at a number of techniques for determining how well a linear model performs, and for deciding between models.

# Evaluating linear models

In this section, we will examine a number of metrics that we can use to evaluate the performance of a linear model other than using the MSE and cross-validation. We will look at some of the statistical tests and metrics that are used to evaluate how well a linear model performs, and to help decide between different linear model forms.

There are two statistical tests to be aware of for linear models, as follows:

- First, is the test for whether one particular coefficient in the model is 0 or not. Failing to reject the null hypothesis indicates that the feature does not seem to contribute much to predictions. The following formulas show these hypotheses:

$$H_0 : \beta = 0$$
$$H_A : \beta \neq 0$$

- Second, is an overall test, that is, the F-test. This tests whether any features have coefficients that are nonzero. Rejecting the null hypothesis suggests that your model has some predictive ability. The following formulas show these hypotheses:

$$H_0 : \beta_0 = \beta_1 = \ldots = \beta_K = 0$$
$$H_A : H_0 \text{ is false}$$

Let's evaluate the model using the following steps:

1. We'll import the Boston dataset and the splitting function, as follows:

```
In [1]:   from sklearn.datasets import load_boston
          from sklearn.model_selection import train_test_split
```

2. We're going to split the dataset into training and testing data, using the following code:

```
In [2]:  boston_obj = load_boston()
         data_train, data_test, price_train, price_test = train_test_split(boston_obj.data, boston_obj.target)
```

From this point on, we will use `statsmodels` instead of `scikit-learn`. The reason for this is because `statsmodels` makes it easier to evaluate the quality of a fit, using metrics that we will introduce shortly.

3. Let's import the libraries, as follows:

```
In [3]:  import statsmodels.api as sm
         import numpy as np
```

Now, before we continue, `statsmodels` does do OLS, but it does it a little bit differently. We will need to manually add a constant to our dataset. This is something that is done automatically by `sklearn` behind the scenes; however, here, we have to add a constant column to our dataset in order for this constant to be fitted.

4. We will now display the first five rows of the training set, as follows:

```
Out[4]: array([[1.00000e+00, 7.67202e+00, 0.00000e+00, 1.81000e+01, 0.00000e+00,
                6.93000e-01, 5.74700e+00, 9.89000e+01, 1.63340e+00, 2.40000e+01,
                6.66000e+02, 2.02000e+01, 3.93100e+02, 1.99200e+01],
               [1.00000e+00, 6.91100e-02, 4.50000e+01, 3.44000e+00, 0.00000e+00,
                4.37000e-01, 6.73900e+00, 3.08000e+01, 6.47980e+00, 5.00000e+00,
                3.98000e+02, 1.52000e+01, 3.89710e+02, 4.69000e+00],
               [1.00000e+00, 3.68940e-01, 2.20000e+01, 5.86000e+00, 0.00000e+00,
                4.31000e-01, 8.25900e+00, 8.40000e+00, 8.90670e+00, 7.00000e+00,
                3.30000e+02, 1.91000e+01, 3.96900e+02, 3.54000e+00],
               [1.00000e+00, 7.61620e-01, 2.00000e+01, 3.97000e+00, 0.00000e+00,
                6.47000e-01, 5.56000e+00, 6.28000e+01, 1.98650e+00, 5.00000e+00,
                2.64000e+02, 1.30000e+01, 3.92400e+02, 1.04500e+01],
               [1.00000e+00, 1.51902e+00, 0.00000e+00, 1.95800e+01, 1.00000e+00,
                6.05000e-01, 8.37500e+00, 9.39000e+01, 2.16200e+00, 5.00000e+00,
                4.03000e+02, 1.47000e+01, 3.88450e+02, 3.32000e+00]])
```

Here, you can see that the first entry of every row is 1. This means that every row now has a constant term, which doesn't change. So, that serves as the intercept in our regression model.

5. If we print out the first column of the first five rows, here is the result:

```
In [5]:  data_train[:5, 0]

Out[5]:  array([1., 1., 1., 1., 1.])
```

6. We can now fit the linear model using OLS, using the following code:

```
In [6]:  ols1 = sm.OLS(price_train, data_train)
         model1 = ols1.fit()
         model1.params
```

This results in the following output:

```
Out[6]: array([ 3.72034520e+01, -1.08373524e-01,  5.32398554e-02,  7.13335371e-02,
                3.19363160e+00, -2.13738034e+01,  3.76094998e+00,  3.56314642e-03,
               -1.42530066e+00,  2.84001139e-01, -1.12664749e-02, -9.15548827e-01,
                7.55580272e-03, -5.13539339e-01])
```

7. Let's make a single prediction, using the following code:

```
In [7]: model1.predict([[    # An example prediction
            1,        # Intercept term; always 1
            10,       # Per capita crime rate
            25,       # Proportion of land zoned for large homes
            5,        # Proportion of land zoned for non-retail business
            1,        # Tract bounds the Charles River
            0.3,      # NOX concentration
            10,       # Average number of rooms per dwelling
            2,        # Proportion of owner-occupied units built prior to 1940
            10,       # Weighted distance to employment centers
            3,        # Index for highway accessibility
            400,      # Tax rate
            15,       # Pupil/teacher ratio
            200,      # Index
            5         # % lower status of population
        ]])
```

This results in the following output:

```
Out[7]:  array([39.50813578])
```

8. We can look at a summary of the model, as follows:

```
In [8]:  print(model1.summary())
```

```
                            OLS Regression Results
==============================================================================
Dep. Variable:                      y   R-squared:                       0.725
Model:                            OLS   Adj. R-squared:                  0.715
Method:                 Least Squares   F-statistic:                     74.03
Date:                Mon, 06 May 2019   Prob (F-statistic):           8.44e-94
Time:                        09:12:09   Log-Likelihood:                -1132.3
No. Observations:                 379   AIC:                             2293.
Df Residuals:                     365   BIC:                             2348.
Df Model:                          13
Covariance Type:            nonrobust
==============================================================================
                 coef    std err          t      P>|t|      [0.025      0.975]
------------------------------------------------------------------------------
const         37.2035      6.003      6.197      0.000      25.399      49.008
x1            -0.1084      0.036     -2.998      0.003      -0.179      -0.037
x2             0.0532      0.016      3.279      0.001       0.021       0.085
x3             0.0713      0.072      0.995      0.320      -0.070       0.212
x4             3.1936      0.993      3.217      0.001       1.241       5.146
x5           -21.3738      4.716     -4.532      0.000     -30.647     -12.100
x6             3.7609      0.493      7.633      0.000       2.792       4.730
x7             0.0036      0.016      0.225      0.822      -0.028       0.035
```

Here, `statsmodels` gives us a nice statistical summary of our fit. Looking at the summary, we can see that we have quite a few metrics to consider:

- **R-squared ($R^2$)**: This is the ability of the model to explain variation in the target variable. Ideally, we would like $R^2$ to be high to indicate that our model does a good job of predicting the target variable. It is always possible to increase $R^2$ by adding more variables, even if they're just adding noise to your data. Many people prefer not to use $R^2$, because it doesn't take into account how complex your model is and how many parameters it includes. They often prefer **adjusted R-squared ($\bar{R}^2$)**, which includes a penalty term for more parameters. Here, the more parameters you add (all else being equal), the smaller the adjusted R-squared value will be.
- **F-statistic**: This is a statistic test to determine whether any coefficients in the model are not zero. We also have the **p-value**, which is associated with the F-statistic. This p value is small and indicates that at least one of these coefficients is nonzero.
- **The Akaike information criterion (AIC) and Bayesian information criterion (BIC)**: These are two information criteria, which can help you to decide between models; we'll discuss them in more detail later.

We can do t-tests for every single coefficient to decide whether a coefficient is statistically different from 0 or not. By doing so, we will see that many of the coefficients are, in fact, statistically different from 0. However, there are a few coefficients that are not, such as $x3$ and $x7$. So, whatever variables correspond to $x3$ and $x7$, we should consider removing these from our model, as this may give us a better fit. However, even a statistical test such as this doesn't mean that the best procedure for deciding what parameters to keep is by sequentially doing tests and then removing the coefficients that are not statistically different from 0. That doesn't necessarily produce good results, because it's possible that, in the process, this very path-dependent process, you might discover that other coefficients are not statistically different from 0, and are, in fact, different models.

# Using AIC to pick models

The best way to decide between models is to use AIC and BIC. Let's focus mainly on AIC because BIC is very similar. If we have a collection of candidate models, the best model should minimize AIC. We want models to predict data well but adding too many features leads to overfitting. AIC rewards accuracy but punishes complexity, so it helps to choose models that balance these competing desires. So, let's start working with AIC and BIC, and explore how they can help us to predict models.

I'm going to fit another model, which doesn't include the features that are not statistically different from 0. We can do this using the following code:

```
In [9]: ols2 = sm.OLS(price_train, np.delete(data_train, [3, 7], axis=1))
        model2 = ols2.fit()
        print(model2.summary())
```

This results in the following output:

```
                          OLS Regression Results
==============================================================================
Dep. Variable:                      y   R-squared:                       0.724
Model:                            OLS   Adj. R-squared:                  0.716
Method:                 Least Squares   F-statistic:                     87.63
Date:                Mon, 06 May 2019   Prob (F-statistic):           1.59e-95
Time:                        09:12:09   Log-Likelihood:                -1132.8
No. Observations:                 379   AIC:                             2290.
Df Residuals:                     367   BIC:                             2337.
Df Model:                          11
Covariance Type:            nonrobust
==============================================================================
                 coef    std err          t      P>|t|      [0.025      0.975]
------------------------------------------------------------------------------
const         36.6868      5.958      6.157      0.000      24.970      48.403
x1            -0.1101      0.036     -3.056      0.002      -0.181      -0.039
x2             0.0508      0.016      3.198      0.002       0.020       0.082
x3             3.3004      0.986      3.348      0.001       1.362       5.239
x4           -19.9543      4.401     -4.534      0.000     -28.609     -11.300
x5             3.7602      0.477      7.888      0.000       2.823       4.698
x6            -1.4893      0.223     -6.686      0.000      -1.927      -1.051
x7             0.2612      0.075      3.491      0.001       0.114       0.408
x8            -0.0093      0.004     -2.322      0.021      -0.017      -0.001
x9            -0.8979      0.152     -5.903      0.000      -1.197      -0.599
x10            0.0076      0.003      2.466      0.014       0.002       0.014
```

So, here is the new model, where we have a different AIC and BIC. Ideally, we want a smaller AIC. This means that the second model, where we removed the coefficients, might be a better one. Now, there's actually a nice interpretation for a different AIC. You cannot universally compare AIC between completely different problems. However, if you are staying within a localized problem (such as the Boston dataset using linear regression estimated through OLS), you can use these different criteria and make statements, such as which model is more likely to be true; which model is more likely to minimize information loss; and which model is a concept from information theory that's relatively common in statistics and data science, and accounts for not only how well a model is able to predict your target variable, but also how complex your model is.

We want models that are very likely to minimize information loss. We can use the following formula to find out which model is more likely to do so, given two of them:

$$\exp((\text{AIC}_2 - \text{AIC}_1)/2)$$

We can find the performance of model 2 against model 1 as follows:

```
In [10]: np.exp((model2.aic - model1.aic)/2)

Out[10]: 0.23044709840835434
```

Then, we can find the performance for model 1 against model 2:

```
In [11]: np.exp((model1.aic - model2.aic)/2)

Out[11]: 4.3393907187670075
```

Here, we can see that model 1 is only 0.23 times (so, a number less than 1) more likely to minimize information loss than model 2; whereas, if we take the inverse of this, then model 2 is four times more likely to minimize information loss than model 1. So, by this metric, model 2 is four times better than model 1, which suggests that we should be using model 2 instead of model 1.

So, let's import the `mean_squared_error` metric and look at the predictions of model 2 on the training data:

```
In [12]: from sklearn.metrics import mean_squared_error

In [13]: price_train_pred = model2.predict(np.delete(data_train, [3, 7], axis=1))
         mean_squared_error(price_train, price_train_pred)
```

This results in the following output:

```
Out[13]: 23.10725806084707
```

This is the MSE for the training data.

Additionally, here is the MSE for the test data:

```
In [14]:  price_test_pred = model2.predict(np.delete(data_test, [3, 7], axis=1))
          mean_squared_error(price_test, price_test_pred)
```

This results in the following output:

```
Out[14]:  18.820105467553404
```

Here, we can see that the MSE is slightly larger, but not by much.

Now we can compare this to model 1, as follows:

```
In [15]:  price_test_pred_mod1 = model1.predict(data_test)
          mean_squared_error(price_test, price_test_pred_mod1)

Out[15]:  19.147546993735563
```

Here, we see that there is not that much of a difference. Technically, model 1 did have a larger MSE than model 2 on the test dataset, so model 2 did perform better. So, this is another way for you to decide between models. It can also help you to decide which features to include in a model and which features to exclude. Additionally, if you wanted to explore different functional forms such as a quadratic term, adding a quadratic term or a cubic term, or interaction terms, then you could use AIC or BIC to decide between the different models. In the next section, we will move away from OLS and discuss its alternatives. We will explore our first alternative to OLS—the Bayesian approach to linear models.

# Bayesian linear models

Occam's razor is an idea that appears not just in data science, but in science in general. It's a problem-solving principle, which suggests that we should prefer simple models that explain phenomena to complex models that also explain the same phenomena. The idea is that a simple model, without much complexity and without extraneous features, is more likely to be correct than an overly complicated model. The hope with some of these regularization methods, such as Bayesian ridge regression, is to obtain simple models. These models are as simple as they need to be, and they do a decent job of explaining data without overfitting.

In comparison, out of the box, OLS is prone to overfitting. Let's take a look at the following base function, which is generating a dataset:

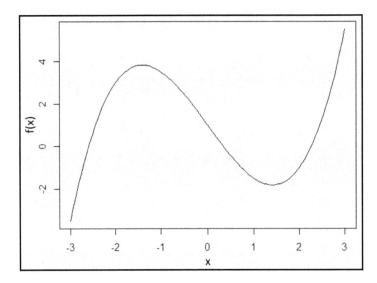

Here, we can see randomly selected points from this function, with noise added to them:

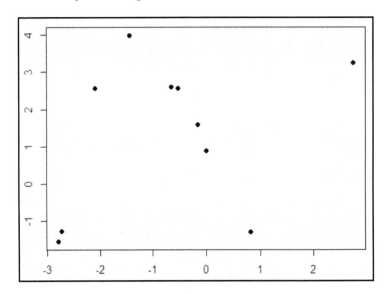

So, can we recover the original function? If we choose the wrong functional form, it is possible that we could end up underfitting:

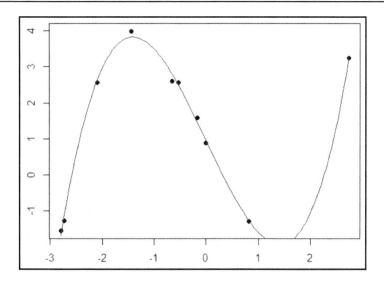

The preceding diagram shows an example of underfitting. The function that we tried to fit was misspecified. If we correctly specify the function and then perform OLS, we get a pretty good approximation as to what the actual function was. However, it's optimistic for us to think that we can obtain the exact functional form. In this instance, I generated this dataset, so I knew the correct functional form; however, in the real world, we need to decide which polynomial we should use. If we end up choosing a polynomial that is too large, then we may end up in a situation where OLS overfits the data:

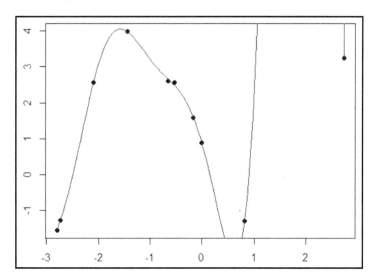

Here, we can see that the model fits individual data points very well, but it is objectively bad. It is very distant from the actual function that generated this data. In fact, notice that this function shoots off the screen; the function shoots up to over 100 before returning to the next data point. This is a very overfitted function, so any quality fit is highly overstated, and we would like to see this problem rectified in some way.

# Choosing a polynomial

In Bayesian regression, we place a prior on the coefficients of the linear regression model that biases the model parameters to 0. The hyperparameters of the model control this prior and to what extent it biases the coefficients of the model to 0. In Bayesian ridge regression, the estimated parameters are the **maximum a posteriori probability (MAP)** estimates. While I haven't discussed it, there is, in fact, a prior distribution that we are imposing upon the coefficients of the model, and Bayesian ridge regression will estimate a posterior distribution. The coefficients that maximize this posterior distribution are referred to as the MAP estimates of the coefficients. We will choose a polunomial using the following steps:

1. Let's load in a mystery function and plot it, as follows:

```
In [2]: dat = np.load("mystery_function.npy")
        x, y = dat[:, 0], dat[:, 1]
        plt.scatter(x, y)
        plt.show()
```

This results in the following output:

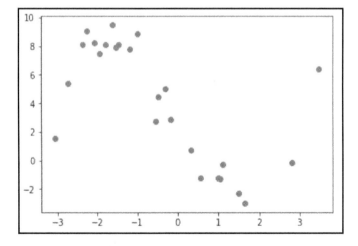

The hope is that we can use regression to recover the function that generated this data.

2. So, we're going to import `LinearRegression`, which represents OLS. Then, we'll write a function that generates a NumPy array that allows for fitting different polynomials, as follows:

```
In [4]: olsfit1, olsfit2, olsfit3, olsfit4, olsfit5, olsfit6 = (LinearRegression(),)*6

        def gen_order_mat(x, order=1):
            """Generates a matrix of x useful for fitting a polynomial of some order"""
            # Similar functionality is supplied by the vander() function in NumPy

            if order == 1:
                return x.reshape(-1, 1)
            else:
                return np.array([x**i for i in range(1, order + 1)]).T

        # The number designates the order of the fit of the polynomial
        olsfit1 = LinearRegression().fit(gen_order_mat(x, order=1), y)
        olsfit2 = LinearRegression().fit(gen_order_mat(x, order=2), y)
        olsfit3 = LinearRegression().fit(gen_order_mat(x, order=3), y)
        olsfit4 = LinearRegression().fit(gen_order_mat(x, order=4), y)
        olsfit5 = LinearRegression().fit(gen_order_mat(x, order=5), y)
        olsfit10 = LinearRegression().fit(gen_order_mat(x, order=10), y)
        olsfit12 = LinearRegression().fit(gen_order_mat(x, order=12), y)

        def plotfit(fit, order=1):
            """Plots the function estimated by OLS."""

            fx = np.linspace(x.min(), x.max(), num = 100)
            fx_mat = gen_order_mat(fx, order=order)
            yhat = fit.predict(fx_mat)
            plt.scatter(x, y)
            plt.plot(fx, yhat)
            plt.ylim(y.min() - 0.5, y.max() + 0.5)
            plt.show()

        plotfit(olsfit1, order=1)
```

This function is similar to the `vander` function provided by NumPy. Essentially, this function adds columns of data raised to various powers. The preceding function displays the following graph:

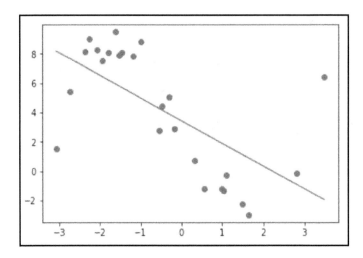

3. Let's go to `order=2`, which is a quadratic function:

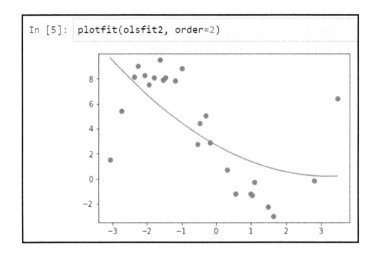

Here, we can see that the fit is slightly better, but not by much.

4. If we go to `order= 3`, then we actually have a reasonably good fit, as follows:

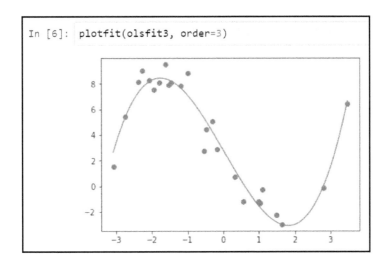

5. When we go to `order= 4`, we get a really good fit, as follows:

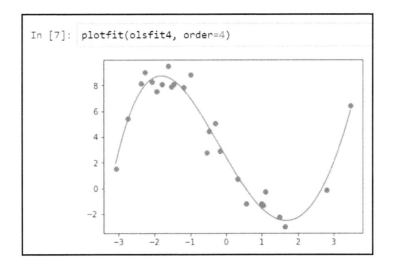

It may be that `order=4` is the correct fit.

6. Let's now take a look at `order=10`:

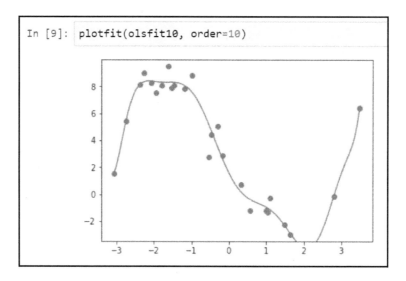

Here, the preceding graph is starting to look like a bad fit. We're starting to see wiggles that might be indicative of overfitting. This is not actually representing the function that generated this dataset.

7. If we go to `order=12`, then the overfitting problem is quite obvious:

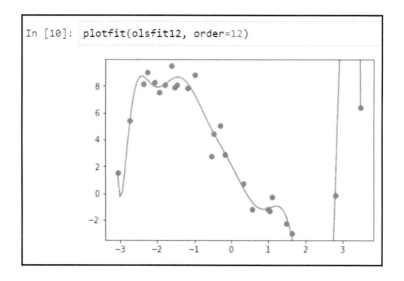

Here, it appears that the function is shooting down to a very negative number and then a very positive number in order to hit these two data points. So, increasing the order of the polynomial that we fit to this data leads to a better fit up until a certain point, that is, when new features simply lead to overfitting. Now, I know for a fact that I generated this dataset with a cubic function, so the cubic function was the most appropriate; however, in the real world, we wouldn't know that a cubic function is appropriate. It may be that the quartic function was more appropriate.

# Performing Bayesian regression

Bayesian ridge regression will help combat this overfitting by biasing all the parameters to 0. This means that when we fit a model, the parameters get non-negligible contributions to the final fit only when they help in prediction.

Bayesian ridge regression is supported by `sklearn` using the `BayesianRidge()` function, and can be imported as follows:

```
In [11]:  from sklearn.linear_model import BayesianRidge
          BayesianRidge()
```

The `BayesianRidge()` function has quite a few parameters, including `alpha_1`, `alpha_2`, `lambda_1`, and `lambda_2`. These are going to control the parameters that are associated with the prior distribution. We will fit the model through Bayesian ridge regression, as shown in the following code:

```
In [12]:  bayesfit = BayesianRidge(alpha_1 = 1, alpha_2 = 1,
                          lambda_1 = 30, lambda_2 = 50).fit(gen_order_mat(x, order=10), y)

          plotfit(bayesfit, order=10)
```

This results in the following output:

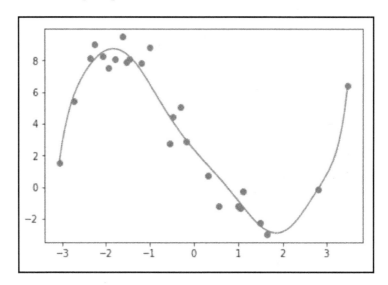

This is not bad; it looks similar to the cubic function, and it's not as bad as the original polynomial of `order=10`. So, it looks like the Bayesian ridge regression has helped to combat some of the overfitting. You will want to play around with these parameters to try to see how they might improve the fit of your model. For instance, this could be something that you could tweak through cross-validation. Next up in the linear model zoo is ridge regression.

# Ridge regression

In this section, we will discuss ridge regression, which is another alternative regression technique to OLS. We will look at the basic idea of ridge regression, the hyperparameters it introduces, and how to use it in practice.

Ridge regression adds more constraints to a linear model when attempting to fit it. It's another technique that attempts to control overfitting in linear models, more so than OLS. The strength of regularization is controlled by a parameter, α. A larger α implies less tolerance to overfitting, while an α of 0 is OLS. In some ways, ridge regression and Bayesian ridge regression are equivalent; they mainly differ in their presentation. We will now perform ridge regression using the following steps:

1. We will import the required functions, as follows:

```
In [1]:  from sklearn.datasets import load_boston
         from sklearn.model_selection import train_test_split
         import numpy as np
```

2. Now, we will load in our Boston dataset; I'm going to drop the two variables that we decided were not a valuable contribution to our predictions, using the following lines of code:

```
In [2]:  boston_obj = load_boston()
         data_train, data_test, price_train, price_test = train_test_split(boston_obj.data, boston_obj.target)
         data_train = np.delete(data_train, [2, 6], axis=1)
         data_test = np.delete(data_test, [2, 6], axis=1)

         data_train[:5, :]
```

Here is the resulting dataset:

```
Out[2]:  array([[1.27346e+00, 0.00000e+00, 1.00000e+00, 6.05000e-01, 6.25000e+00,
                 1.79840e+00, 5.00000e+00, 4.03000e+02, 1.47000e+01, 3.38920e+02,
                 5.50000e+00],
                [3.23700e-02, 0.00000e+00, 0.00000e+00, 4.58000e-01, 6.99800e+00,
                 6.06220e+00, 3.00000e+00, 2.22000e+02, 1.87000e+01, 3.94630e+02,
                 2.94000e+00],
                [8.24400e-02, 3.00000e+01, 0.00000e+00, 4.28000e-01, 6.48100e+00,
                 6.18990e+00, 6.00000e+00, 3.00000e+02, 1.66000e+01, 3.79410e+02,
                 6.36000e+00],
                [7.15100e-02, 0.00000e+00, 0.00000e+00, 4.49000e-01, 6.12100e+00,
                 3.74760e+00, 3.00000e+00, 2.47000e+02, 1.85000e+01, 3.95150e+02,
                 8.44000e+00],
                [1.10690e-01, 0.00000e+00, 1.00000e+00, 5.50000e-01, 5.95100e+00,
                 2.88930e+00, 5.00000e+00, 2.76000e+02, 1.64000e+01, 3.96900e+02,
                 1.79200e+01]])
```

3. We will now import the `Ridge` object from `sklearn` and other required functions:

```
In [3]:  from sklearn.linear_model import Ridge
         from sklearn.metrics import mean_squared_error
         from sklearn.model_selection import cross_val_score
```

4. Let's fit the model; we will use the `Ridge` object that is provided by `scikit-learn`, along with the usual collection of functions for evaluating the quality of our fits. I'm going to choose an `alpha=1` function for our ridge regression model:

```
In [4]:  ridge1 = Ridge(alpha=1)      # alpha is a hyperparameter controlling regularization
         ridge1.fit(data_train, price_train)
         ridge1.predict([[      # An example prediction
             1,         # Per capita crime rate
             25,        # Proportion of land zoned for large homes
             1,         # Tract bounds the Charles River
             0.3,       # NOX concentration
             10,        # Average number of rooms per dwelling
             10,        # Weighted distance to employment centers
             3,         # Index for highway accessibility
             400,       # Tax rate
             15,        # Pupil/teacher ratio
             200,       # Index
             5          # % lower status of population
         ]])
```

The following screenshot shows the resulting fit, along with a predicted value:

```
Out[4]:  array([40.3079661])
```

5. We can make a prediction for the entire training set, and get the MSE, using the following lines of code:

```
In [5]:  predprice = ridge1.predict(data_train)
         mean_squared_error(price_train, predprice)
```

This results in the following output:

```
Out[5]:  21.351348759006743
```

# Finding the right alpha value

Well, that was one way to pick `alpha`. I just picked a number off the top of my head, but we can go ahead and use cross-validation to decide which alpha value provides the best results.

So, first, we are going to import a `pandas` DataFrame and perform cross-validation for all of the different alphas we might want. Then, we will present the results in a DataFrame, using the following code:

```
In [7]: alpha = [.125, .25, .5, 1, 2, 4, 8, 16, 32, 64, 128]
        res = dict()

        for a in alpha:
            ridge2 = Ridge(alpha=a)
            res[a] = cross_val_score(ridge2, data_train, price_train, scoring='neg_mean_squared_error', cv = 10)

        res_df = DataFrame(res)

        res_df
```

This results in the following DataFrame:

| | 0.125 | 0.25 | 0.5 | 1.0 | 2.0 | 4.0 | 8.0 | 16.0 | 32.0 | 64.0 | 128.0 |
|---|---|---|---|---|---|---|---|---|---|---|---|
| 0 | -21.136397 | -21.174217 | -21.239738 | -21.335265 | -21.439335 | -21.512837 | -21.543107 | -21.581599 | -21.734692 | -22.127897 | -22.870870 |
| 1 | -35.295151 | -35.369547 | -35.482326 | -35.613420 | -35.691366 | -35.608797 | -35.290118 | -34.770318 | -34.242058 | -33.991896 | -34.178383 |
| 2 | -47.688921 | -47.722503 | -47.790422 | -47.916107 | -48.120480 | -48.419823 | -48.838968 | -49.409453 | -50.166443 | -51.200846 | -52.684054 |
| 3 | -14.234170 | -14.217945 | -14.196529 | -14.173981 | -14.152665 | -14.130729 | -14.124144 | -14.205387 | -14.511105 | -15.171413 | -16.178626 |
| 4 | -36.501400 | -36.581716 | -36.702679 | -36.844673 | -36.940679 | -36.893613 | -36.636722 | -36.197699 | -35.740667 | -35.559596 | -35.988827 |
| 5 | -21.158588 | -21.178485 | -21.219770 | -21.292714 | -21.395285 | -21.523307 | -21.728595 | -22.172775 | -23.078143 | -24.541200 | -26.347936 |
| 6 | -20.030027 | -19.956883 | -19.857809 | -19.750478 | -19.651889 | -19.548398 | -19.404620 | -19.218301 | -19.107265 | -19.356012 | -20.194475 |
| 7 | -10.969761 | -11.003824 | -11.079949 | -11.223218 | -11.436194 | -11.694832 | -11.988998 | -12.348718 | -12.836282 | -13.522750 | -14.393156 |
| 8 | -12.562399 | -12.441207 | -12.280951 | -12.123326 | -12.029545 | -12.037861 | -12.165042 | -12.444006 | -12.934736 | -13.673027 | -14.549999 |
| 9 | -13.282412 | -13.188090 | -13.066362 | -12.946314 | -12.854185 | -12.780166 | -12.707226 | -12.678688 | -12.840152 | -13.426312 | -14.650781 |

We are now going to take the mean of the columns, as follows:

```
In [8]:  res_df.mean()

Out[8]:  0.125      -23.285923
         0.250      -23.283442
         0.500      -23.291653
         1.000      -23.321950
         2.000      -23.371162
         4.000      -23.415037
         8.000      -23.442754
         16.000     -23.502694
         32.000     -23.719154
         64.000     -24.257095
         128.000    -25.203711
         dtype: float64
```

Here, it seems that the negative MSE is maximized for the smallest possible `alpha`, which is interesting. An `alpha` of 0 corresponds to the OLS solution, which suggests that ridge regression might not help us get better predictions.

Well, let's go ahead and pick `alpha=0.125`, as the cross-validation suggested that we should, and see how the model fitted using ridge regression performs on our test dataset:

```
In [9]:  ridge3 = Ridge(alpha=0.125)
         ridge3.fit(data_train, price_train)

         testpredprice = ridge3.predict(data_test)
         mean_squared_error(price_test, testpredprice)
```

Here is the result:

```
Out[9]:  25.896595152731784
```

If I remember correctly, this might be higher than what we got with OLS, which suggests that ridge regression isn't a superior choice and that we might actually want to consider sticking with a little less.

That's all for ridge regression in this chapter. Next, we will next discuss LASSO regression, which is another variant of regularized regression.

# LASSO regression

In this section, we will look at the basic concept of LASSO regression, including the hyperparameters that it introduces and how to use it in practice.

Put simply, LASSO regression is another method for regularizing a linear model while fitting—more so than OLS. LASSO is extremely similar to ridge regression in form, but the penalty terms are different. In many ways, the two procedures are interchangeable, but they don't necessarily get the same solutions, so you might want to consider looking at both. LASSO regression has the same alpha parameter as ridge regression, and it is used the same way. A larger alpha value penalizes overfitting. So, let's take a look at LASSO in action:

1. We will import the `Lasso` object along with the other required libraries, as follows:

```
In [3]:  from sklearn.linear_model import Lasso
         from sklearn.metrics import mean_squared_error
         from sklearn.model_selection import cross_val_score
```

2. We will then fit a LASSO regression model, choosing `alpha=1` again, using the following code:

```
In [4]:  lasso1 = Lasso(alpha=1)    # alpha is a hyperparameter controlling regularization
         lasso1.fit(data_train, price_train)
         lasso1.predict([[    # An example prediction
             1,        # Per capita crime rate
             25,       # Proportion of land zoned for large homes
             1,        # Tract bounds the Charles River
             0.3,      # NOX concentration
             10,       # Average number of rooms per dwelling
             10,       # Weighted distance to employment centers
             3,        # Index for highway accessibility
             400,      # Tax rate
             15,       # Pupil/teacher ratio
             200,      # Index
             5         # % lower status of population
         ]])
```

This results in an array with a value of `29.08`.

3. We will also make a prediction for the entire training set and compute the MSE, as follows:

```
In [5]:   predprice = lasso1.predict(data_train)
          mean_squared_error(price_train, predprice)

Out[5]:   26.186116476897762
```

This is a larger number than what we were seeing before, so it doesn't look like LASSO's doing a very good job compared to some of the other methods that we've seen.

4. Now, let's import `pandas` and the DataFrame so that we can do cross-validation once again with all of these different alpha values, and then store them in a dictionary to turn into a DataFrame. We can perform cross-validation, as follows:

```
In [7]:   alpha = [.125, .25, .5, 1, 2, 4, 8, 16, 32, 64, 128]
          res = dict()

          for a in alpha:
              lasso2 = Lasso(alpha=a)
              res[a] = cross_val_score(lasso2, data_train, price_train, scoring='neg_mean_squared_error', cv = 10)

          res_df = DataFrame(res)

          res_df
```

This results in the following output:

| | 0.125 | 0.25 | 0.5 | 1.0 | 2.0 | 4.0 | 8.0 | 16.0 | 32.0 | 64.0 | 128.0 |
|---|---|---|---|---|---|---|---|---|---|---|---|
| 0 | -15.410308 | -15.576114 | -16.239303 | -18.890937 | -24.434237 | -27.678038 | -28.240305 | -31.633401 | -46.917994 | -50.034332 | -51.303476 |
| 1 | -17.546908 | -18.013341 | -19.369314 | -23.773658 | -31.926944 | -40.712020 | -42.224214 | -48.384351 | -66.782254 | -70.657480 | -73.174571 |
| 2 | -35.770240 | -35.329683 | -35.042684 | -36.845868 | -44.128087 | -53.322653 | -55.709802 | -63.464168 | -82.109049 | -83.930715 | -84.749809 |
| 3 | -16.988829 | -16.574853 | -16.078654 | -16.413008 | -16.552518 | -16.147738 | -18.409100 | -25.043977 | -41.677179 | -44.311565 | -46.153342 |
| 4 | -12.855487 | -12.711071 | -12.693937 | -13.746736 | -17.672406 | -22.934872 | -24.453265 | -28.336625 | -40.412506 | -43.055529 | -45.002219 |
| 5 | -16.945048 | -17.132288 | -17.661655 | -19.339483 | -21.774543 | -24.691131 | -25.728358 | -29.988728 | -45.548242 | -48.157426 | -50.052946 |
| 6 | -21.524633 | -22.329022 | -24.128090 | -28.487369 | -34.135331 | -37.184960 | -39.366339 | -44.690851 | -58.573889 | -59.235519 | -58.463009 |
| 7 | -39.426794 | -40.295094 | -42.418176 | -48.210253 | -56.998427 | -65.941036 | -65.682958 | -69.865867 | -88.069363 | -90.480773 | -91.151060 |
| 8 | -56.903062 | -55.973955 | -54.262835 | -51.428866 | -49.251228 | -52.096057 | -54.887623 | -62.859961 | -80.202024 | -81.718826 | -82.134217 |
| 9 | -17.994109 | -18.620720 | -20.161896 | -24.396093 | -32.912563 | -42.747876 | -43.852608 | -48.636116 | -63.616723 | -66.633446 | -68.649208 |

5. Now we take the mean of the columns, as follows:

```
In [8]:  res_df.mean()

Out[8]:  0.125      -25.136542
         0.250      -25.255614
         0.500      -25.805654
         1.000      -28.153227
         2.000      -32.978628
         4.000      -38.345638
         8.000      -39.855457
         16.000     -45.290404
         32.000     -61.390922
         64.000     -63.821561
         128.000    -65.083386
         dtype: float64
```

Once again, the MSE gets better for smaller alpha values, which suggests that this regularization procedure isn't helping us predict the target variable any better. In fact, if I remember correctly, LASSO's doing a worse job than ridge regression was for this particular dataset. So, I'm not very confident about LASSO's abilities in this context.

6. So, let's look at what the best `alpha` choice for LASSO does and fit it to the dataset:

```
In [9]:  lasso3 = Lasso(alpha=0.125)
         lasso3.fit(data_train, price_train)

         testpredprice = lasso3.predict(data_test)
         mean_squared_error(price_test, testpredprice)
```

This results in the following output:

```
Out[9]:  24.552504055553456
```

Here, we actually did get a pretty decent MSE. This is the smallest one that we've seen so far, so we might have just gotten lucky in this particular case. In other examples, we saw an MSE that was higher than what we were getting for OLS. Well, that's enough for regression. We will now conclude this chapter with a slightly different topic, that is, spline interpolation.

# Spline interpolation

We will now wrap up this chapter with spline interpolation. In this section, we will look at interpolation using a single variable and interpolation using multiple variables. We will look at a toy example using the univariate case but also demonstrate the actual use of interpolation in image resizing.

I should probably start by saying that, even though I've included this section in this chapter about regression, interpolation and regression are not the same. With regression, we infer a function's values in the presence of noise, as shown in the following diagram:

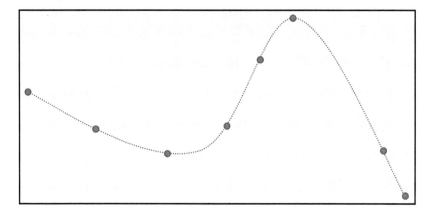

With interpolation, we have the exact values of a function at some data points, and we seek to estimate the values of the function at other locations, as shown in the following diagram:

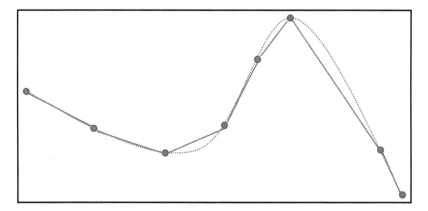

Therefore, there can be no noise with interpolation. Regression falls into the realm of statistics, whereas interpolation falls more into the realm of numerical analysis. However, both of these can appear in data science. We start with the values of a function at a collection of points. For some reason, the function's values at other points are inaccessible; perhaps they're computationally expensive to obtain, or they simply don't exist. Our interpolating function will connect these points using simpler functions. This means that when we want to estimate the function of the data points other than the ones provided, we can use the interpolating function to get these estimates. Notice that the interpolating function doesn't change the values of the data points. We have exactly the same values at the data points that we are using for the interpolation. This is not a characteristic of regression. Additionally, our interpolating functions can take different forms. The functions in the preceding screenshots were linear, but we can also use constants, quadratic, or, very commonly, cubic functions for interpolation. We might get better approximations for different functions. These illustrations are for one-dimensional examples so far, but we can interpolate functions in higher dimensions, with the logic being essentially the same.

# Using SciPy for interpolation

So, let's take a look at how we can perform spline interpolation using SciPy. Again, we have a function, *f* that is unknown, and we want to infer its values. We have its exact values for a collection of data points, and our objective is to estimate the values of *f* at values other than these points—although, whatever function we end up using, its values should exactly equal the values of the function that we observed. We can use `interp1d()` for univariate interpolation, as seen in the following steps:

1. So, we are going to import this function, along with all the other required functions:

```
In [1]:   from scipy.interpolate import interp1d
          import numpy as np
          import matplotlib
          import matplotlib.pyplot as plt
          %matplotlib inline
```

2. We will then load in a dataset containing a mystery function and plot it, using the following code:

```
In [2]:  dat = np.load("mystery_function_2.npy")
         x, y = dat[:, 0], dat[:, 1]
         # Visualize the mystery function
         plt.scatter(x, y)
         plt.show()
```

This results in the following output:

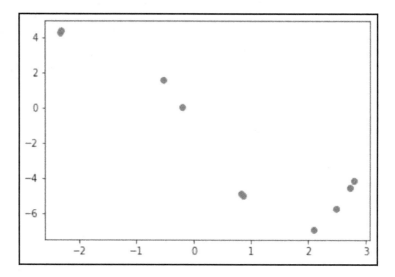

3. Now, we will interpolate this function by using the nearest kind of interpolation; this is essentially a step function:

```
In [3]:  xi = np.linspace(x.min(), x.max(), num=1000)
         fit1 = interp1d(x, y, kind='nearest')

         plt.plot(xi, fit1(xi), '-')
         plt.scatter(x, y)
         plt.show()
```

This results in the following output:

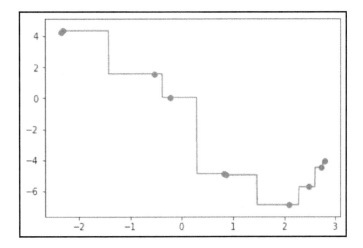

4. Now, let's take a look at a `linear` interpolator, using the following code:

```
In [4]:  fit2 = interp1d(x, y, kind='linear')

         plt.plot(xi, fit2(xi), '-')
         plt.scatter(x, y)
         plt.show()
```

This results in the following output:

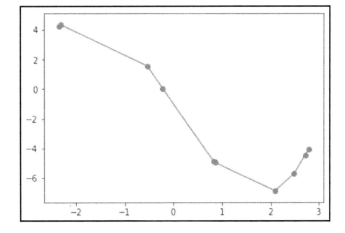

Here, we draw a straight line connecting each point.

5. Let's check whether the `quadratic` function, where we use quadratic functions to connect these points, will get a better result:

```
In [5]: fit3 = interp1d(x, y, kind='quadratic')

        plt.plot(xi, fit3(xi), '-')
        plt.scatter(x, y)
        plt.show()
```

The following graph is plotted:

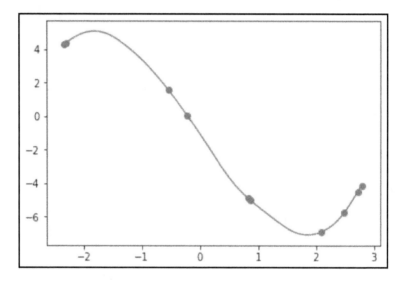

This graph looks more like what we would expect our function to be.

6. If we use the `cubic` function, it almost seems like we get an even better fit:

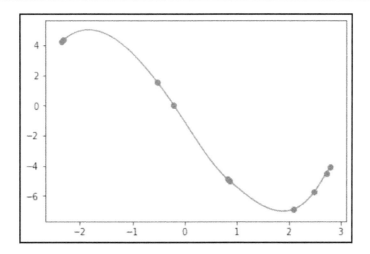

So, this will be the cubic interpolator, where everything is being connected by cubic functions.

# 2D interpolation

The preceding function is for the univariate case. There's only one variable, *x*, and one output variable, *y*, but we can do 2D interpolation. In fact, we can do interpolation for any number of dimensions. Here, we will look at only 2D interpolation and I'm going to demonstrate interpolation for image resizing. So, we have an image; we will consider this image as being in a matrix, and we'll be working with a grayscale image. A pixel's intensity will be a function's *y* value, and its location on a grid will be its *x* value, where *x* is actually a vector with two coordinates. It's easier, in my opinion, to normalize everything so that the upper-left corner is (0, 0) and the bottom-right corner is (1, 1). This means that everything is working on a square from 0 to 1. When we rescale an image, we will have the image values at particular points, but we will need the intensity of the pixels at the points that we haven't actually observed. Therefore, we will need to interpolate. We can do this type of interpolation using the `griddata` function from SciPy. We'll also use `PIL` to work with an image. Let's get started using the following steps:

1. Let's import all the required functions, using the following code:

```
In [7]:  from scipy.interpolate import griddata
         from PIL import Image
         matplotlib.rcParams['figure.figsize'] = (20, 12)
```

2. We have an image of the US Capitol, which we will load in as a grayscale image, using the following code:

```
In [8]:  capitol_png = Image.open("USCapitol.png").convert('L')
         capitol = np.array(capitol_png)

         capitol.shape
```

The preceding code also prints the shape or dimensions of the image, which is (574, 800).

3. We will now print the pixel intensities for the upper left-hand corner, consisting of a 5×5 square of pixels, as follows:

```
In [9]:  capitol[:5, :5]
```

This results in the following array:

```
Out[10]:  array([[213, 213, 214, 214, 215],
                 [215, 215, 215, 215, 215],
                 [217, 216, 216, 215, 215],
                 [217, 216, 216, 215, 216],
                 [218, 217, 217, 217, 217]], dtype=uint8)
```

We will consider this our function value.

4. We will now print out the image, using the `plt` function:

Notice that we have a number of artifacts; this is due to anti-aliasing, the fact that we're working with different pixels, and because we'd like to actually do a better job than what you see here.

Instead of pixels resizing to big squares, we may want to have a smoother transition between pixel values; this is where interpolation appears. I should mention first though, that this is a grayscale image. We don't have to display it in grayscale, though; replacing black and white with different colors can help visually pick out more information in the image.

5. Now, we will create a function, which converts a grayscale image stored in `ndarray` into a format that is acceptable for `griddata`. What will be returned is a dictionary that I can then pass on directly to `griddata`. We also have `interp_points`; this will correspond to the resized image:

```
In [13]:  def griddata_point_format(arr, normalize=True):
              """Converts grayscale image stored in ndarray arr into a format acceptable for griddata, returning a dict
              If normalize is True, coordinates are on a 0-1 scale"""

              shape = arr.shape
              x = np.arange(shape[0])
              y = np.arange(shape[1])
              coord_mat = np.transpose([np.tile(x, shape[1]), np.repeat(y, shape[0])])    # Construct a matrix of coordinates
              values = arr[coord_mat[:, 0], coord_mat[:, 1]]     # Construct a 1D array containing the intensity values of the image
                                                                 # at the given coordinates
              if normalize:
                  # All coordinates will be between 0 and 1
                  coord_mat = np.array(coord_mat, dtype=np.float64)
                  coord_mat[:, 0] = coord_mat[:, 0] / shape[0]    # Note that 1 is not actually attained; that's fine
                  coord_mat[:, 1] = coord_mat[:, 1] / shape[1]

              return {"points": coord_mat, "values": values}

          def interp_points(length, width, normalize=True):
              """Gets two NumPy arrays corresponding to the points where interpolation should occur"""

              grid_x, grid_y = np.mgrid[0:length, 0:width]
              if normalize:
                  # This option should be used if normalize is True in griddata_point_format
                  # All points will be between 0 and 1
                  grid_x = np.array(grid_x, dtype=np.float64)
                  grid_y = np.array(grid_y, dtype=np.float64)
                  grid_x = grid_x / length
                  grid_y = grid_y / width

              return (grid_x, grid_y)

          test = griddata_point_format(capitol)
          test["values"][:5]     # intensities of the first five pixels (bright)
```

This results in the following output:

```
Out[14]:  array([213, 215, 217, 217, 218], dtype=uint8)
```

6. Here are the last five values:

```
In [15]:  test["values"][-5:]

Out[15]:  array([1, 1, 2, 3, 4], dtype=uint8)
```

7. Now, we are going to create a new image of 400×400, using the following code:

```
In [17]:   im0 = griddata(xi = interp_points(400, 400), **griddata_point_format(capitol))

           plt.imshow(im0)
```

This results in the following output:

As you can see, the image has been resized; it is now a square image and you can see that it has been stretched.

8. Now let's consider just a corresponding image, where you scale both dimensions by 4. So, instead of being at 200×279, the new dimensions of the image will be 804×279. Additionally, we are using the nearest method, which produces an image that looks very similar to what we had before (with anti-aliasing):

```
In [18]: im1 = griddata(xi = interp_points(800, 4 * 279), method="nearest", **griddata_point_format(capitol))
         plt.imshow(im1, cmap="hot")
```

This results in the following output:

You will not be very satisfied with this; this is the default method that image applications use because it's relatively easy.

9. However, we can do better than that. Let's look at linear interpolation, using the following code:

```
In [19]:  im1 = griddata(xi = interp_points(800, 4 * 279), method="linear", **griddata_point_format(capitol))
          plt.imshow(im1, cmap="hot")
```

This results in the following output:

Here, we can see that around the statue at the top of the dome there has been some smoothing. The resulting image looks a little bit nicer.

10. If we now look at cubic interpolation, then the image, in my opinion, is even better:

This image is even smoother than when we were using the linear interpolator, especially around the statue.

# Summary

This brings us to the end of the chapter. In this chapter, we learned about regression and regression analysis. We learned about various techniques for performing regression analysis and how to implement them in machine learning applications. We learned about linear models, ridge regression, Bayesian ridge regression, LASSO regression, and also spline interpolation.

In the next chapter, we start discussing deep learning models, beginning with the perceptron.

# 5
# Neural Networks

In this chapter, we will talk about classification and regression using neural networks. We will start this chapter by discussing the perceptron, which is an online classifier that also serves as a building block for neural networks. We will also discuss the idea behind neural networks, including the different types of perceptrons, and what a **multilayer perceptron (MLP)** is. We will also learn how to train a neural network for various purposes.

The following topics will be covered in this chapter:

- An introduction to perceptrons
- Neural networks
- Using MLPs for classification
- Neural networks for regression

## An introduction to perceptrons

Let's start talking about perceptrons. In this section, we will discuss the perceptron algorithm, particularly as an instance of online learning. We will also look at a demonstration of training the perceptron, and show you what online training looks like.

On the surface, the perceptron classifier resembles a **support vector machine (SVM)**. It is a linear classifier and predicts that all observations lying on a particular side of a hyperplane belong to a particular class. However, perceptrons are not SVMs—that is, they do not try to maximize the gap between classes and they are not designed to train data in a batch, where all data is perceived at once and no future data is used. Batch learning uses all available data for training at once. In comparison, the classifier fits data in the best way that it can.

All algorithms that we usually see use batch learning. Online algorithms do support it as well, and they often start out being trained by batch learning. However, online algorithms can also update themselves as new data comes in. If an incorrect prediction is made, then the algorithm uses the error to change the classifier.

There are some advantages to online learning. One advantage is that, with online learning, the learning process doesn't end. This means that the classifier adapts itself based on the feedback it receives. Another advantage of online learning is that it allows for training classifiers on big datasets that don't fit in memory. Data can be loaded in when needed, and fit to the trainer without loading in all the data at once.

In `scikit-learn`, the `Perceptron` object supports training perceptrons, including allowing for online learning. We will apply perceptrons (which are binary classifiers) to predicting the species of iris flowers (perceptrons support multiclass learning using the one-versus-all approach). Let's perform the following steps to train a perceptron using `scikit-learn`:

1. Our first step is to load in the dataset and the necessary function, as follows:

```
In [ ]:  from sklearn.linear_model import Perceptron
         from sklearn.model_selection import train_test_split
         from sklearn.metrics import accuracy_score
         from sklearn.datasets import load_iris
```

2. We will then split our dataset into training and test sets, as follows:

```
In [2]:  iris_obj = load_iris()
         data_train, data_test, species_train, species_test = train_test_split(iris_obj.data, iris_obj.target)
         data_in, data_out, species_in, species_out = train_test_split(data_train, species_train, test_size=.1)
         data_in[:5,]

Out[2]:  array([[6.7, 3.1, 4.4, 1.4],
                [6.1, 2.8, 4.7, 1.2],
                [5. , 3.2, 1.2, 0.2],
                [6.3, 2.5, 4.9, 1.5],
                [5.3, 3.7, 1.5, 0.2]])
```

Here, you'll notice that I've actually split the training data twice. We have `data_in`, `data_out`, `species_in`, and `species_out`. The reason for this is because I want to demonstrate what online learning looks like—that is, the ability of an algorithm to update with new data.

3. Let's take a look at the first five elements in the `species_in` set, as follows:

```
In [3]:  species_in[:5]

Out[3]:  array([1, 1, 0, 1, 0])
```

4. Let's create a perceptron and then fit it to the first training dataset, which is `species_in`, and examine how well it does on that training set, as follows:

```
In [4]: perc = Perceptron()
        perc = perc.fit(data_in, species_in)      # Tr

        species_pred_in = perc.predict(data_in)
        accuracy_score(species_pred_in, species_in)

Out[4]: 0.87
```

Here, you can see that it's able to predict 87% correctly, which is pretty good!

5. Now, let's examine what online learning looks like. We will use the remaining data in the training data to update the perceptron that we trained. Here is how our algorithm does on out-of-sample data using the second training dataset:

```
In [5]: species_pred_out = perc.predict(data_out)
        accuracy_score(species_pred_out, species_out)

Out[5]: 0.9166666666666666
```

This dataset turns out to be 91% accurate—much to my surprise!

6. Now we can go ahead and fit our algorithm to include the information in the other dataset using `partial_fit`, which is similar to fit, but updates an algorithm rather than replacing the fit; we will do this using the following code:

```
In [6]: perc = perc.partial_fit(data_out, species_out)
```

7. Now, let's examine how well it does on the `species_out` training data, as follows:

```
In [7]: species_pred_out = perc.predict(data_out)
        accuracy_score(species_pred_out, species_out)

Out[7]: 0.5
```

We can see that it achieves low accuracy, that is, approximately 50%.

8. Now that we are done with minor tests, let's examine how the algorithm does on the entire sample:

```
In [8]:  species_pred_train = perc.predict(data_train)    #
         accuracy_score(species_pred_train, species_train)

Out[8]:  0.7053571428571429
```

Here, we can see that it has an accuracy of approximately 70%.

 Note that the accuracy values will vary every time you run the code, so please try this out for yourself, and consider these steps as just a foundation.

When we go to the test data, it should also have a similar accuracy.

Thus, we have learned about online learning, and we now understand how to use feedback in order to improve our algorithm. For example, consider that we have a website, and we're trying to predict whether a customer will add something to their shopping cart or not. In this instance, we can actually update our algorithm as a person goes to their shopping cart (or not), while it's making its predictions. Another thing that it will be able to do is scale to very large datasets, because you can load in, in principle, some of the data, update the algorithm, load in some more of the data, and update again. Now that we have learned about perceptrons, let's take a look at neural networks.

# Neural networks

This section focuses on the class of classifiers and regression algorithms known as **neural networks**. In this section, we will cover the theory behind neural networks. We will also look at one specific type of neural network—that is, the MLP.

Neural networks are inspired by a model of how the brain works. In this model, a neuron is connected with other neurons in the brain; if the signals surpass a threshold, then the neuron is induced to activate. This is better illustrated in the following diagram:

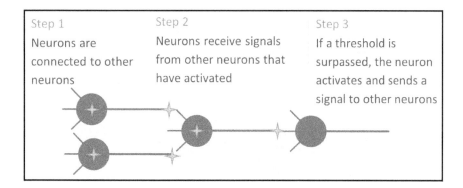

The neuron that is activated is then passed to other neurons, spreading messages. Neural networks in machine learning emulate this process; neural networks are characterized by how information is transmitted through the network.

# The structure of a neural network

A neural network may include a layer representing data as features. An output layer represents the target variables that we want to predict. In the middle, there may be hidden layers that are used for making predictions, allowing the nonlinear patterns in data to be found. The nodes in the center are the actual neurons themselves. A node may use its inputs, which could be features (or other nodes), from a lower layer or even the same layer to decide whether or not to activate. It may have an activation function, and the value of that activation function is fed forward into the next nodes in the network. The following diagram better illustrates neural networks:

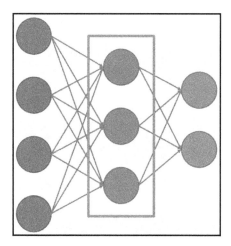

# Types of neural networks

Neural networks come in a variety of flavors, as follows:

- **MLPs**: Feed-forward networks, such as MLPs, take inputs from features, pass information through the hidden layers, and then use the result of the hidden layers as outputs:

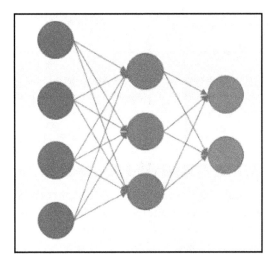

- **Recurrent neural networks**: Nodes in recurrent neural networks use their own feedback, as well as the feedback simultaneously given and received from other nodes in the network, in order to decide whether or not to activate:

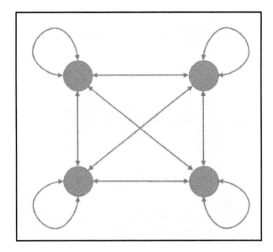

- **MLPs with lateral connections**: Sometimes, the nodes in the hidden layers are used to inform each other of whether to activate or not. These are neural networks with lateral connections:

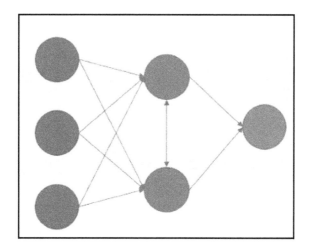

# The MLP model

Our focus, in this section, will be on the simpler neural network—the MLP. MLPs connect multiple perceptrons in multiple layers before determining the final activation. Each perceptron has an activation function whose input depends on the nodes that are fed into the network. Naturally, the number of hidden layers, the number of nodes or neurons per layer, and the choice of activation function, can be viewed as hyperparameters when training a neural network. MLPs are based on perceptrons, so they support online learning. However, unlike perceptrons, MLPs are not considered linear regressors or linear classifiers. Instead, they allow for finding nonlinear patterns in data.

Here is an example of the activation functions that are used for neurons in a network:

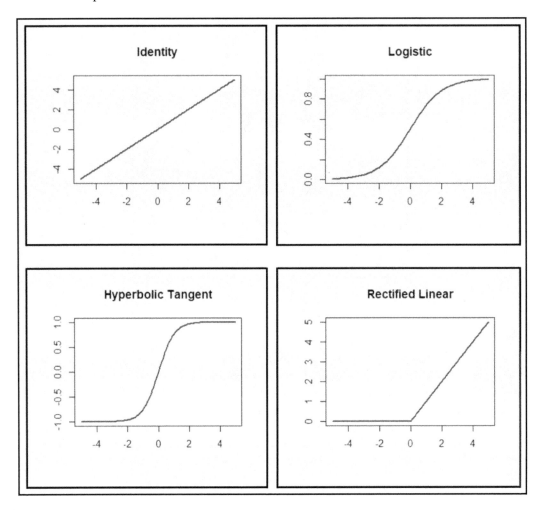

The weighted sum of a neuron's inputs is passed to the activation function to determine that function's value, which is then passed on to later nodes in the network. Notice that the logistic and hyperbolic tangent functions are restricted to values between 0 and 1, while the identity and rectified linear functions don't have this restriction. Now that we know more about what neural networks are, let's explore how to train an MLP classifier.

# MLPs for classification

In this section, we will train an MLP for classification by discussing the required hyperparameters. Additionally, we will explore the various issues in optimization.

All MLPs are required to have their shape specified. This includes the number of hidden layers and how many neurons each layer has. Each neuron, which is a perceptron, has an activation function whose value will need to be passed to later neurons in the network. Here, the activation function needs to be selected.

Finally, to control overfitting, a regularization parameter can be specified to help weed out unhelpful neurons in the network, giving them little to no weight.

# Optimization techniques

We will briefly discuss optimization procedures when fitting neural networks. Many of the algorithms that we have seen in this book rely on these procedures. I've let this occur in the background, but for neural networks, practitioners should be more aware of the process since optimization is more complicated.

All optimization procedures have the same goal. Given an objective function, such as the sum of squared errors or the likelihood, you can find the global maximum or minimum value and the parameters used to attain that value. Neural networks use a gradient descent technique called **backpropagation for fitting**. Randomization may be involved when this technique is used, which means that no two runs may necessarily produce the same neural network.

With neural networks, the problem of finding a local minimum instead of a global one is especially acute. In some sense, the optimizer can find the wrong solution. While this is true for any optimization procedure, it's a particular concern for neural networks, given their complexity. Optimization procedures are iterative; this means they take steps to reach an optimal value, until some criterion that is intended to detect convergence is attained. It's possible that the algorithm takes a long time to see this criterion (if it happens at all). These are some of the issues that developers who are training neural networks should be aware of. Packages for fitting neural networks also include parameters to control the optimization process. But enough of that, let's now actually start training an MLP.

# Training the network

In this section, we're actually going to work with two datasets. We're going to work with the iris dataset, and we're also going to load the digits dataset. Additionally, I'm going to import some functions for plotting so that we can see the digits dataset. So, let's get started, using the following steps:

1. First, let's load in the datasets and the various functions we will use, using the following code:

```
In [1]:  from sklearn.datasets import load_iris, load_digits
         from sklearn.model_selection import train_test_split
         import numpy as np
         import matplotlib.pyplot as plt
         %matplotlib inline
```

2. Now, let's actually call in both datasets, using the following code:

```
In [2]:  # First, the iris dataset
         iris_obj = load_iris()
         iris_data_train, iris_data_test, species_train, species_test = train_test_split(iris_obj.data, iris_obj.target)

         # Next, the digits dataset
         digits_obj = load_digits()
         print(digits_obj.DESCR)
```

Here, we are printing out the digits dataset in order to get familiar with it; this results in the following output:

```
Optical Recognition of Handwritten Digits Data Set
===================================================

Notes
-----
Data Set Characteristics:
    :Number of Instances: 5620
    :Number of Attributes: 64
    :Attribute Information: 8x8 image of integer pixels in the range 0..16.
    :Missing Attribute Values: None
    :Creator: E. Alpaydin (alpaydin '@' boun.edu.tr)
    :Date: July; 1998
```

As you can see, the digits dataset consists of handwritten digits with 5,620 examples. Additionally, there are 64 attributes, which correspond to a pixel in an 8 x 8 grid.

3. We will then print out the dataset shape, as follows:

```
In [3]:  digits_obj.data.shape
Out[3]:  (1797, 64)
```

4. We will then see the first few rows, containing the numbers that people have actually written down, as follows:

```
In [4]:  digits_data_train, digits_data_test, number_train, number_test = train_test_split(digits_obj.data, digits_obj.target)
         number_train[:5]
Out[4]:  array([6, 3, 4, 5, 6])
```

Here, people have written down digits, such as 6, 3, 4, 5, and 6.

5. We will then display the first row of the dataset in an array, as follows:

```
In [5]:  digits_data_train[0, :]
Out[5]:  array([ 0.,   0.,   0.,   8.,  15.,   2.,   0.,   0.,   0.,   0.,   6.,  16.,   5.,
                 0.,   0.,   0.,   0.,   0.,  12.,   8.,   0.,   0.,   0.,   0.,   0.,   0.,
                13.,   6.,   0.,   0.,   0.,   0.,   0.,   0.,  12.,  12.,  16.,  14.,   0.,
                 0.,   0.,   0.,  14.,  15.,   6.,   8.,  11.,   0.,   0.,   3.,  12.,  14.,
                 5.,  10.,  13.,   0.,   0.,   0.,   0.,   9.,  16.,  13.,   5.,   0.])
```

6. Then, we can see the pixel if we actually put it into a shape:

```
In [6]:  digits_data_train[0, :].reshape((8, 8))
Out[6]:  array([[ 0.,   0.,   0.,   8.,  15.,   2.,   0.,   0.],
                [ 0.,   0.,   6.,  16.,   5.,   0.,   0.,   0.],
                [ 0.,   0.,  12.,   8.,   0.,   0.,   0.,   0.],
                [ 0.,   0.,  13.,   6.,   0.,   0.,   0.,   0.],
                [ 0.,   0.,  12.,  12.,  16.,  14.,   0.,   0.],
                [ 0.,   0.,  14.,  15.,   6.,   8.,  11.,   0.],
                [ 0.,   3.,  12.,  14.,   5.,  10.,  13.,   0.],
                [ 0.,   0.,   0.,   9.,  16.,  13.,   5.,   0.]])
```

7. Now, we can actually plot the image that this array represents, using the following code:

```
In [7]: plt.imshow(digits_data_train[0, :].reshape((8, 8)))
```

Here, we can see that this is a handwritten digit of 6:

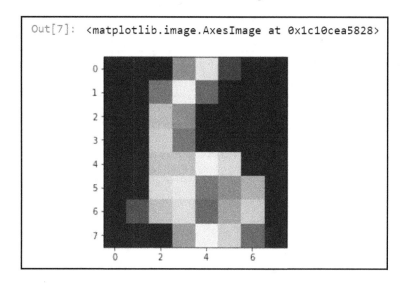

```
Out[7]: <matplotlib.image.AxesImage at 0x1c10cea5828>
```

Now, our goal is to train an MLP to detect a 6 when it sees a 6, or a 5, or a 7, or a 4, or a 2, and so on. This is a common example for MLPs, since these are nonlinear classifiers. This means that they don't require linearity, and it seems that being able to predict digits is a nonlinear problem.

# Fitting an MLP to the iris dataset

So, let's work with the iris dataset because this is a familiar dataset that we've been working with so far:

1. Let's import the MLP classifier; I'm also going to use accuracy_score, as follows:

```
In [8]: from sklearn.neural_network import MLPClassifier
        from sklearn.metrics import accuracy_score
```

2. For this network, we only have one hidden layer, which has 20 neurons; it uses the logistic activation function. We will use an alpha parameter of 1, and specify the maximum number of iterations of the optimization procedure to be 1,000, to make sure that the procedure does, in fact, terminates and attains it when it terminates the solution, which is very similar to the optimal solution. This can be summarized using the following code:

```
In [9]:  mlp_iris = MLPClassifier(hidden_layer_sizes=(20,),
                                  activation='logistic',
                                  alpha=1,
                                  max_iter=1000)
         mlp_iris = mlp_iris.fit(iris_data_train, species_train)
         mlp_iris.predict(iris_data_train[:1,:])
```

3. Now, let's go ahead and fit this classifier on the training set:

```
In [10]:  species_pred_train = mlp_iris.predict(iris_data_train)
          accuracy_score(species_pred_train, species_train)

Out[10]:  0.9910714285714286
```

Here's the prediction of the first few rows; you can see that this classifier is 99% accurate on the training dataset. So, how does it do on the testing dataset?

4. We will use a similar function to fit the classifier on the test set, as follows:

```
In [11]:  species_pred_test = mlp_iris.predict(iris_data_test)
          accuracy_score(species_pred_test, species_test)

Out[11]:  0.9473684210526315
```

As you can see here, we have really high accuracy scores.

This classifier has essentially learned how to predict the species of flower for an iris flower, given these four inputs. Therefore, the MLP classifier does extremely well for this dataset.

# Fitting an MLP to the digits dataset

Now, let's take a look at how it works on the `digits` dataset:

1.  Here, we have 50 neurons in a single hidden layer. However, we're still using the logistic activation function and we're still using a regularization parameter of 1, as shown in the following code:

```
In [12]:  mlp_digits = MLPClassifier(hidden_layer_sizes=(50,),
                                      activation='logistic',
                                      alpha=1)
          mlp_digits = mlp_digits.fit(digits_data_train, number_train)
```

2.  So, let's go ahead and fit the classifier. Let's predict the first row, which we know to be 6, as follows:

```
In [13]:  mlp_digits.predict(digits_data_train[[0], :])
Out[13]:  array([6])
```

Here, you can see that it does, in fact, predict 6, which is correct.

3.  Now, we will examine the accuracy score on the training dataset:

```
In [14]:  number_pred_train = mlp_digits.predict(digits_data_train)
          accuracy_score(number_pred_train, number_train)
Out[14]:  0.9977728285077951
```

We see that it's almost 100% accurate on the training dataset. Now it is still possible for these things to overfit, so how does it do on the test data?

4.  We will run the accuracy score for the test set as follows:

```
In [15]:  number_pred_test = mlp_digits.predict(digits_data_test)
          accuracy_score(number_pred_test, number_test)
Out[15]:  0.9777777777777777
```

The result is remarkable: 97%. This means that there has been just a teensy, tiny bit of overfitting, but it is not enough to really worry about.

Therefore, this classifier has essentially learned what handwritten digits actually are. If you think about it, it's pretty impressive for this classifier to predict handwritten digits with 97% accuracy, because it can be hard for humans to be able to do the same thing—and you've seen other people's handwriting! Having seen neural networks for classification, let's explore how we can use them for regression.

# MLP for regression

In this final section, we will examine how to train an MLP for regression. When it comes to regression, there is a little more to say about the MLP. As it turns out, the only thing that changes is the activation function for the final nodes in the network that produces predictions. They allow for a wide range of outputs, not just the output from a set of classes. All the issues and hyperparameters are the same, as in the case of classification. Of course, in the regression context, you may end up making different choices than for classification.

So, let's now demonstrate regression using neural networks:

1. We're going to be working with the Boston dataset. We're going to import `MLPRegressor` in order to be able to do the regression, and we're still going to be using the `mean_squared_error` metric to assess the quality of our fit, using the following code:

```
In [1]:  from sklearn.datasets import load_boston
         from sklearn.neural_network import MLPRegressor
         from sklearn.model_selection import train_test_split
         from sklearn.metrics import mean_squared_error
```

2. Let's go ahead and import the Boston dataset and split it as required:

```
In [2]:  boston_obj = load_boston()
         data_train, data_test, price_train, price_test = train_test_split(boston_obj.data, boston_obj.target)
```

3. Now, our network is going to have three layers, each with 100 neurons. So, when we say `hidden_layer_sizes`, we specify it in a tuple. The first layer has 100 neurons, the second has 100, and the third has 100. We specify the activation function using the hyperbolic tangent. Additionally, for my regularization parameter, we are going to use alpha = 10; we can fit this as follows:

```
In [3]:  mlp = MLPRegressor(hidden_layer_sizes=(100,100,100), activation='tanh', alpha=10, max_iter=1000)
         mlp = mlp.fit(data_train, price_train)
```

4. After fitting the regressor, we will make a prediction for the first row, as follows:

```
In [4]:  mlp.predict(data_train[[0], :])

Out[4]:  array([30.78134366])
```

5. Now, let's take a look at how well this did on the training data:

```
In [5]:  price_pred_train = mlp.predict(data_train)
         mean_squared_error(price_pred_train, price_train)

Out[5]:  19.064498781061268
```

Here, we can see that this is actually a reasonable mean squared error on the training data.

6. Now, let's examine what it does on the test data:

```
In [6]:  price_pred_test = mlp.predict(data_test)
         mean_squared_error(price_pred_test, price_test)

Out[6]:  20.85705171707011
```

Here, we can see that the error has certainly increased.

Therefore, it seems like this neural network is overfitting and not by an insignificant amount—this is somewhat alarming. Additionally, when looking at the mean squared error for the test dataset, I'm not particularly convinced that this neural network is doing a better job than some of the linear models that we examined previously. In addition to this, to make a point about the fact that neural networks have issues when fitting, we could run these code blocks again and we'd find that we won't get different results.

If you run the above routines multiple times you may get different predictive models and different mean-square errors. This is because of the randomization involved in initializing the model. In practice, you may want to train the network multiple times to make sure you find the best fit.

# Summary

This wraps up our discussion on neural networks. In this chapter, we learned about neural networks and their various types. We learned how they function, and we also learned all about perceptrons, more specifically, MLPs. Finally, we learned how to train an MLP for various tasks, such as classification and regression.

In the next chapter, we will look at various types of clustering techniques.

# 6
# Clustering Techniques

So far, we've been performing supervised learning. There have been labels we wished to predict correctly, and values we wished to approximate closely with a function, and were unable to. Now, we'll look at an entirely different topic, which will be the focus of both this chapter and the next: unsupervised learning, starting with clustering. This chapter starts with a brief discussion on the difference between supervised and unsupervised learning, and specifically, what clustering is. After that, we'll look at our first clustering algorithm: the k-means algorithm, a popular and simple algorithm. Before exploring some other algorithms, we'll discuss approaches to evaluating a clustering scheme. Then, we'll move on to the next two approaches for clustering; the first being hierarchical clustering. The final clustering approach we'll discuss is spectral clustering.

The following topics will be covered in this chapter:

- Introduction to clustering
- Exploring the k-means algorithm
- Evaluating clusters
- Hierarchical clustering
- Spectral clustering

# Introduction to clustering

Let's get started. In this section, we will contrast unsupervised learning with supervised learning—the latter is what we have been doing up to this point. We will then learn what clustering is.

Supervised and unsupervised learning are two different learning paradigms. So far in this book, we have been performing different kinds of supervised learning. There was a variable, which we called the target variable, that we wanted to predict. This was the case both for classification and regression. Learning consisted of finding a classifier that could accurately predict the target variable. The following diagram represents supervised learning:

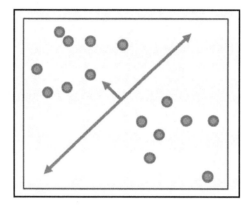

With unsupervised learning, there is no target variable. We believe there are hidden features that differentiate the data, but we don't observe them. The objective of unsupervised learning is to find these hidden features, which we never observe directly, and to assign values for these hidden features of our data and, hopefully, future data as well. The following diagram shows the premise of unsupervised learning:

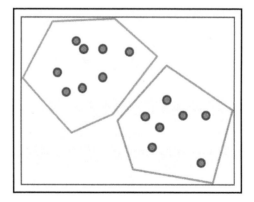

Clustering is the unsupervised learning analog to classification. We start with unlabeled data. We want to group the data into different clusters. We claim that data in a given cluster shares a common feature, even though we may not be able to describe what that feature is. The following diagram shows an example of clustering:

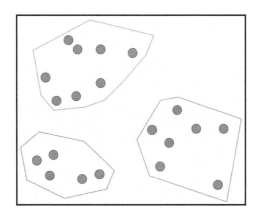

There could be many different clustering schemes. While we think similar data points should be in the same cluster, there are many ways to define similarity. Of course, another issue is how many clusters we want. Trivial clusters include one giant cluster or each data point having its own unique cluster, neither of which is useful. So, how many clusters should there be? There is no easy answer, though there are techniques for judging the quality of a cluster.

What does it mean for two points to be similar? First, consider a similar question—*what does it mean for two points to be different?* This could be the same thing, because the two points are far away or distant. There are a lot of distance notions that we can use for clustering. The following table highlights some of the key metrics:

| Name | Description |
|------|-------------|
| Euclidean | The notion of distance taught in primary and secondary school |
| Manhattan | Or taxi cab distance; the distance when you can only travel up or down and left or right |
| Hamming | The number of symbols to change to make two strings the same (For example: The Hamming distance between 100101 and 110100 is 2) |
| Angular | The size of the angle between vectors pointing to the two data points |
| Jaccard | The number of elements two sets don't have in common divided by both sets combined (excluding duplicates) |

# Computing distances

Choosing a notion of distance is important for clustering. Also, once we accept that there are different ideas of what it means to be distant, we can answer different problems more effectively. To drive home the idea of different distance metrics, I want to demonstrate how to compute different distances. The first thing I will show is how to compute Euclidean distance, which corresponds to how we normally think about distance.

We will use a function that computes the Euclidean distance for two NumPy vectors, presumably of the same length, using the following lines of code:

```
In [2]: def euclidean_distance(v1, v2):
            return np.sqrt(np.sum((v1 - v2) ** 2))
```

Now, let's create two vectors: vec1 and vec2; imagine these as being in a three-dimensional space. How far away are these points from one another? We can see that using the following lines of code:

```
In [3]: vec1 = np.array([1, 2, 3])
        vec2 = np.array([1, -1, 0])

        euclidean_distance(vec1, vec2)
```

This results in the following output:

```
Out[3]: 4.242640687119285
```

They're about 4.2426 units away.

The Manhattan distance, however, views distance differently. This is the distance between two points when you can only travel horizontally or vertically; you're not allowed to travel diagonally. We will use the following function to find out the Manhattan distance:

```
In [4]: def manhattan_distance(v1, v2):
            return np.sum(np.abs(v1 - v2))
```

We then compute the Manhattan distance between vec1 and vec2, as follows:

```
In [5]: manhattan_distance(vec1, vec2)
Out[5]: 6
```

In this case, the Manhattan distance between these two points is 6.

How about the angular distance? The angular distance is defined as follows: if you have two vectors that point to different points, what is the angle between the two points? Whatever angle that is, that would be the angular distance. We can find the angular distance between two points using the following function:

```
In [6]:   from numpy.linalg import norm

          def angular_distance(v1, v2):
              sim = v1.dot(v2)/(norm(v1) * norm(v2))
              return np.arccos(sim)/np.pi
```

Now, I would like to point out that there are certain rules that a function must satisfy in order to be considered a distance. For vec1 and vec2 we have an angular distance, which is as follows:

```
In [7]:   angular_distance(vec1, vec2)

Out[7]:   0.5605188591618384
```

And here is the angular distance between vec1 and vec1:

```
In [8]:   angular_distance(vec1, vec1)

Out[8]:   0.0
```

The angular distance for the same vector is 0, and any distance must satisfy this property. The distance between a point and itself is 0; but we also have the characteristic that the angular distance between a point and two times that vector is also 0, and that would make angular distance not a distance in the mathematical notion of what a distance must satisfy. The distance between two points is 0 if, and only if, the two points are the same. If we can find two points where they're not the same but the distance between them is 0, then that makes this not a distance, according to mathematicians. And yet, at the same time, if these points were to lie along a unit circle (so, a circle of radius 1), if those are the only points we consider, then we could consider this a distance along the unit circle; this acts a lot like a distance, even though it doesn't have the property that mathematicians would like.

Now, on to Hamming distance. If you have two strings, the Hamming distance is the number of characters you need to change to make one string the same as the other. We will use the following function for Hamming distance:

```
In [10]: def hamming_distance(s1, s2):
             if len(s1) != len(s2):
                 raise ValueError("Undefined for sequences of unequal length")
             return sum(el1 != el2 for el1, el2 in zip(s1, s2))
```

 For further information, you can refer to the Wikipedia site for Hamming distance: https://en.wikipedia.org/wiki/Hamming_distance.

We will define two strings, `11101` and `11011`, and find the distance between them:

```
In [11]: hamming_distance("11101", "11011")

Out[11]: 2
```

So, the Hamming distance between these two strings should be 2, which is in fact what this function reports.

Now, let's look at Jaccard distance. This is defined for collections, or sets. It is the number of objects the two sets do not have in common, divided by the total number of objects in the union of the sets. We will define the function using the following lines of code:

```
In [12]: def jaccard_distance(s1, s2):
             s1, s2 = set(s1), set(s2)
             diff = len(s1.union(s2)) - len(s1.intersection(s2))
             return diff / len(s1.union(s2))
```

Now, we define two collections: `["cow", "pig", "horse"]` and `["cow", "donkey", "chicken"]`. So, there are five unique objects when you combine these two sets together and both of these sets have `"cow"` in common, but otherwise there are four elements that differentiate the sets. So, the Jaccard distance between these two sets should be about four-fifths:

```
In [13]: jaccard_distance(["cow", "pig", "horse"], ["cow", "donkey", "chicken"])

Out[13]: 0.8
```

This is exactly what we find: four-fifths is `0.8`.

Now, remember that we're talking about sets. Sets have exactly one copy of each element.

As an exercise, try to compute the Jaccard distance between two binary strings containing 1s and 0s.

This concludes the introduction to clustering. Now, let's look at our first clustering algorithm: the famous k-means algorithm.

# Exploring the k-means algorithm

In this section, we will look at applying the k-means clustering algorithm. We will learn about the k-means algorithm, and demonstrate how it's used.

When clustering with k-means, we start with a dataset we want to cluster, as seen here:

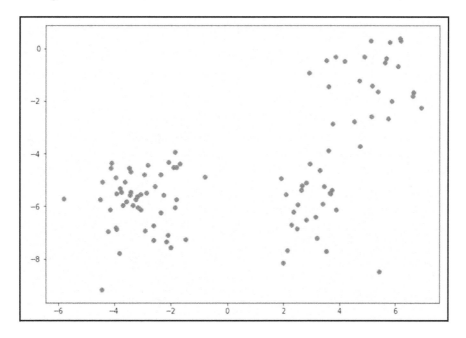

We choose the initial cluster centers. This is an important step, as badly chosen centers can lead to bad clusters, as shown in the following diagram:

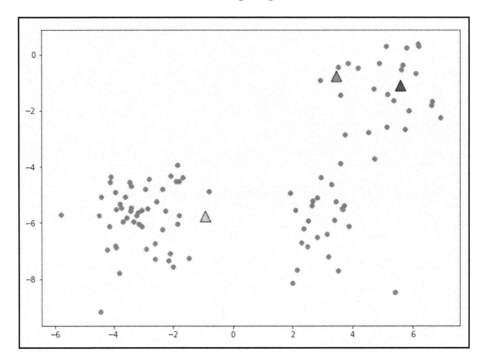

The default options for the KMeans class in scikit-learn, however, helps you to avoid the problems associated with badly chosen starting-cluster centers. I won't go into the details of how this class does this. In this section, all I'm going to do is choose a random subset of the dataset to serve as the initial cluster points. This is not necessarily the best approach, and you probably shouldn't deviate from what the class is doing by default, but it's fine for now.

Next, we use these centers to assign points to clusters based on which center the points are nearest to, as seen in the following diagram:

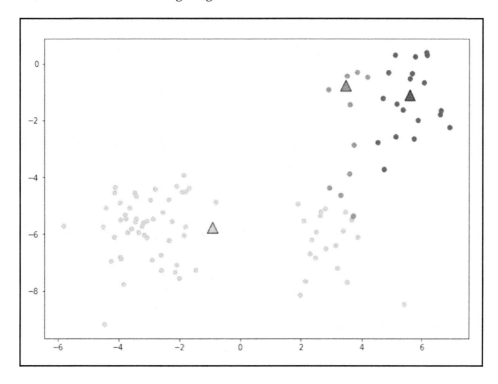

Using the clusters, we compute new cluster centers by averaging the data points in the assigned clusters, as follows:

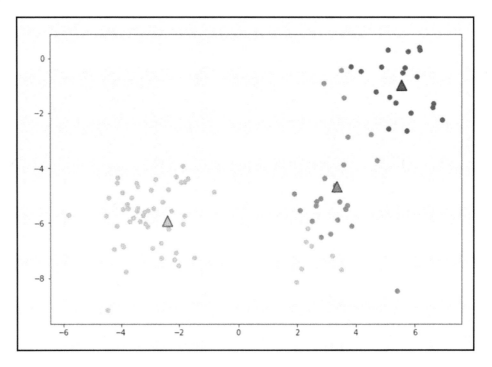

The cluster centers have moved. We then repeat this process, assigning data points to new centers and recomputing centers. This process continues until either the clusters stop changing or they stop changing enough. There is no guarantee that the process will terminate, however, and it is possible that bad clusters will be found.

# Clustering the iris dataset

Now, let's perform k-means clustering on the iris dataset:

1. Import the dataset and the required functions:

```
In [1]:  from sklearn.datasets import load_iris
         import matplotlib.pyplot as plt
         %matplotlib inline
```

2. Load in the dataset, as follows:

```
In [2]:  iris_obj = load_iris()
         iris_data = iris_obj.data
         species = iris_obj.target
         iris_data[:5,:]
```

3. Plot the dataset, including labels for the different species:

```
In [3]:  plt.scatter(iris_data[:, 0], iris_data[:, 1], c=species, cmap=plt.cm.brg)
         plt.xlabel("Sepal Length")
         plt.ylabel("Sepal Width")
         plt.show()
```

Here is the plot:

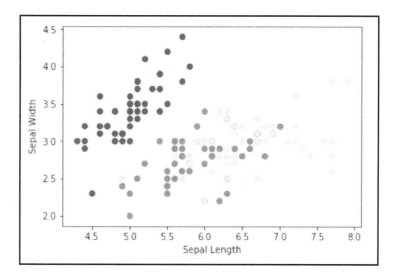

We have the different species plotted in blue, green, and red. Here, we're showing only **Sepal Width** and **Sepal Length**, and you can kind of tell that there is a difference between versicolor and virginica, and that setosa is kind of an outlier of these other two classes.

As an exercise, I invite you to look at the petal length and the petal width on your own; you can see a very stark difference between the setosa species and the versicolor and virginica species.

4. Import the `KMeans` class:

```
In [4]:  from sklearn.cluster import KMeans
```

5. Tell the class to create an object that's going to do clustering when there are three clusters; `init='random'` tells it to choose random points from the dataset. We will also the fit the dataset, as follows:

```
In [5]:  irisclust = KMeans(n_clusters=3, init='random')
         irisclust.fit(iris_data)
         irisclust.cluster_centers_
```

This results in the following output:

```
Out[5]:  array([[6.85       , 3.07368421, 5.74210526, 2.07105263],
                [5.006      , 3.418      , 1.464      , 0.244      ],
                [5.9016129  , 2.7483871  , 4.39354839, 1.43387097]])
```

When finding clusters using k-means we may restart the algorithm completely, using new initial cluster centers, and find a new clustering. We may repeat this process several times, starting the algorithm over with new initial centers and finding several clustering schemes. We do so to help ensure we find the best possible clustering scheme. It's possible for the algorithm to get stuck in a bad clustering scheme, and by restarting we can help avoid this problem. There is a quantity that the k-means algorithm attempts to minimize and after several restarts we will keep the clustering scheme that produced this minimal score. Thus by restarting more, we can help make sure we get good clusters.

6. Predict the clusters and print out the plot, as shown in the following code block:

```
In [6]: # Visualizing the clustering
        plt.scatter(iris_data[:, 0], iris_data[:, 1], c=irisclust.predict(iris_data), cmap=plt.cm.brg)
        plt.scatter(irisclust.cluster_centers_[:, 0], irisclust.cluster_centers_[:, 1],
                    c=irisclust.predict(irisclust.cluster_centers_), cmap=plt.cm.brg, marker='^', s=200,
                    edgecolors='k')
        plt.xlabel("Sepal Length")
        plt.ylabel("Sepal Width")
        plt.show()
```

This results in the following output:

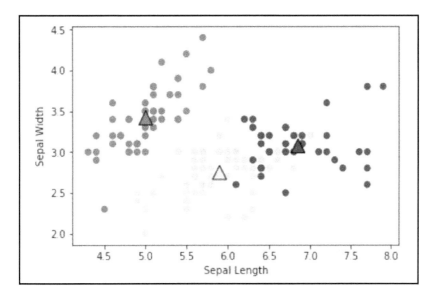

The cluster centers are triangles; let's go ahead and look at the original image. Bear in mind that the color map has been swapped. We now have red where there used to be blue, green where there used to be red, and blue where there used to be green. There are a couple of errors in these two plots, which should be expected; for example, there is no overlap, some versicolor flowers look like virginica flowers, and vice versa. It seems like a bit too much to ask our algorithm to correctly predict these flowers.

 As an exercise, look at petal length and petal width on your own, and you'll see an even more stark differentiation of clusters.

# Compressing images with k-means

Now, let's move on to image compression. Image compression is another application of k-means. The idea is that you've got a lot of different colors in your picture but, perhaps, instead of having thousands of different colors, you could reduce your image down to 10; then you'd have to store less information when you want to distribute and then render the image. So, this is a way to simplify an image while preserving some of its features, and you can judge by the results how well the k-means algorithm finds a reasonable compression for the image. Let's get started:

1. Import all the required functions, as follows:

```
In [7]:   from sklearn.datasets import load_sample_image
          from PIL import Image
          import numpy as np
```

2. We will be looking at an image of a frog, as defined here:

```
In [9]:   frog = np.array(Image.open("frog.png").convert("RGB")) / 255
```

As seen here, we're storing it as a NumPy array.

3. Print out the shape, as follows:

```
In [10]:   frog.shape
Out[10]:   (750, 1024, 3)
```

It is a 750x1024 pixel image. It communicates colors via RGB—so red, green, and blue tuples. That is how images are very commonly communicated.

4. Print the red channel for the upper-leftmost 5x5 block of pixels, as follows:

```
In [11]:   frog[:5, :5, 0]
```

This results in the following output:

```
Out[11]:  array([[0.61568627, 0.6       , 0.6       , 0.60392157, 0.6       ],
                 [0.61568627, 0.60784314, 0.6       , 0.60392157, 0.60392157],
                 [0.61176471, 0.60784314, 0.6       , 0.6       , 0.6       ],
                 [0.61176471, 0.60784314, 0.6       , 0.60392157, 0.6       ],
                 [0.61568627, 0.61176471, 0.60784314, 0.60784314, 0.60392157]])
```

Here's the green channel:

```
In [12]:   frog[:5, :5, 1]

Out[12]:  array([[0.52156863, 0.51764706, 0.51764706, 0.52156863, 0.51764706],
                 [0.5254902 , 0.51764706, 0.51764706, 0.52156863, 0.52156863],
                 [0.52156863, 0.51764706, 0.51764706, 0.51764706, 0.51764706],
                 [0.52156863, 0.51764706, 0.51764706, 0.52156863, 0.51764706],
                 [0.5254902 , 0.52156863, 0.5254902 , 0.5254902 , 0.52156863]])
```

And here's the blue channel:

```
In [13]:   frog[:5, :5, 2]

Out[13]:  array([[0.41176471, 0.40392157, 0.40392157, 0.40784314, 0.41176471],
                 [0.40392157, 0.39607843, 0.39607843, 0.40784314, 0.40784314],
                 [0.4       , 0.39607843, 0.39607843, 0.40392157, 0.40392157],
                 [0.4       , 0.39607843, 0.39607843, 0.4       , 0.40392157],
                 [0.4       , 0.4       , 0.40392157, 0.40392157, 0.4       ]])
```

And this is what the picture looks like:

```
In [14]:  plt.imshow(frog)

Out[14]:  <matplotlib.image.AxesImage at 0x208f5abd898>
```

So, we have a little poison dart frog standing on a leaf; and we want to compress this image to 10 colors. Is there a way to reasonably represent this image using only 10 colors?

5. We will use a function that takes in `img`, which is an `ndarray`, and the number of clusters, which is going to be the number of unique colors that we want. It will spit out an `ndarray` that uses only these colors, as seen here:

```
In [15]:  def kmeans_compression(img, n_clusters):
              h, w, d = img.shape
              assert d == 3
              img_data = img.reshape(h * w, d)
              img_clust = KMeans(n_clusters=n_clusters, init='random').fit(img_data)
              centroids = img_clust.cluster_centers_
              clust_pixels = img_clust.predict(img_data)
              new_img_data = centroids[clust_pixels]
              return new_img_data.reshape(h, w, d)
```

So, if you're doing actual image compression, you'll probably be storing the different colors, and also which of those colors the function is compressing, rather than storing the value of each cluster at every pixel. The only reason I'm doing it this way is because it's easier to render in the Juypter notebook.

Here is the new frog image after we compress it:

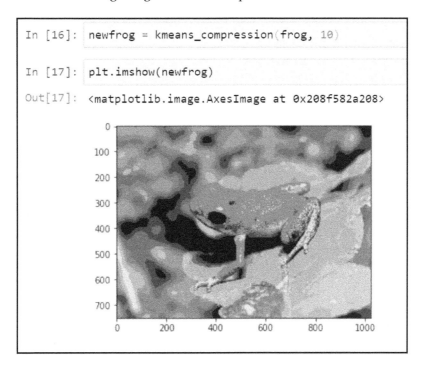

This is the compressed image; you can tell that it is not as good a picture as the original, but that should not come as a shock. What you should be see is that this is a reasonable representation of the original image, and it seems to have chosen reasonably good clusters to differentiate the different colors in the picture. Now that we know how to create clusters, how can we determine whether a clustering scheme did a good job?

# Evaluating clusters

In this section, we will look at ways to judge the quality of a clustering scheme. The two approaches we will discuss include what's known as elbow analysis and silhouette analysis.

Evaluating the quality of a clustering scheme isn't well-defined. In unsupervised learning, there is no base truth to compare against, so we cannot say that a clustering scheme does a good job when compared to that base truth. Thus, we need to define an objective that a clustering scheme tries to achieve, such as minimizing the squared distances from cluster members to centroids or maximizing a likelihood function.

In this section, when I discuss clustering evaluation, I'm concerned primarily with deciding between clustering algorithms and choosing the number of clusters. The **elbow method** is a method for choosing the number of clusters to use in a clustering scheme. Along the $x$-axis is the number of clusters, and along the $y$-axis is the within-cluster sum of squared errors, where the error is the distance of a data point to the cluster centroid. This is summarized in the following formula:

$$\sum_{k=1}^{K} \sum_{i_k=1}^{N_k} \| x_{i_k} - \mu_k \|^2$$

We look for an elbow in the plot, a point after which finding more clusters does little to reduce the within-cluster sum of squared errors, as seen here:

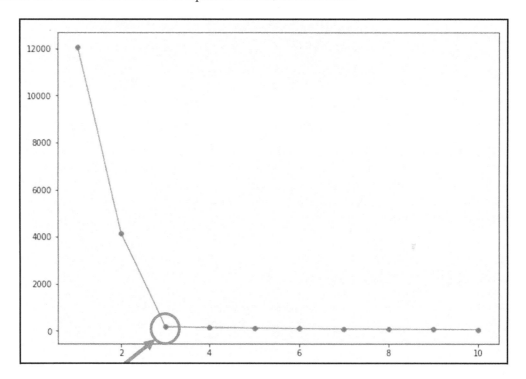

The number of clusters corresponding to the elbow is the number of clusters we should use.

# The elbow method

So, let's demonstrate the elbow method. We recap everything we did in the previous section, clustering and plotting the iris dataset. Then, we come to finding the elbow.

We will use the following code block to do so:

```
In [7]:  def wcsse_plot(data, max_clusters):
             wcsse = np.arange(max_clusters) + 1
             for k in wcsse:
                 wcsse[k - 1] = KMeans(n_clusters=k).fit(data).inertia_
             plt.plot(np.arange(max_clusters) + 1, wcsse, marker='o')
```

Keep in mind that it is always possible to make the plot function smaller by adding more clusters. That said, that doesn't necessarily mean we've found a good clustering scheme. As I said, this function will be the smallest of all if you have a single point per cluster, which is not useful clustering at all. So, we want this to be small, but not too small; thus, you have the elbow.

Now, let's go ahead and create a plot for the iris dataset, which can be seen here:

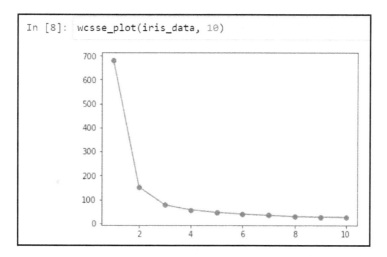

When I look at this, it looks like the elbow is around 3, and then, after that, you have a very slow tailing off of the within-cluster sum of squared errors. So, using elbow analysis, you would think that 3 is the best choice for the number of clusters.

# The silhouette method

The silhouette method requires that we first compute silhouette scores for each data point. The silhouette score for a single data point is the average dissimilarity of the data point with all other data points in the next-nearest cluster, minus the average dissimilarity of the data point to points in the same cluster, divided by the larger of these two numbers. This is represented using the following formula:

$$s(i) = \frac{b(i) - a(i)}{\max\left(a(i), b(i)\right)}$$

We plot the average silhouette score for all data points in the dataset. A large silhouette score, close to 1, means that the data point is dissimilar to data points in other clusters, and the data point seems to be where it belongs. A score of 0 means that the point is on the border between two clusters, and a negative number (the smallest number possible is -1) means the data points may be in the wrong cluster. We plot the silhouette score for each data point in each cluster in order, from smallest to largest, along with the average silhouette score. Ideally, each cluster's shape should look similar, each with a similar number of data points:

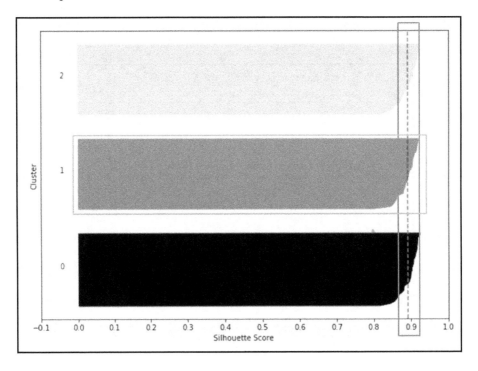

In other words, each bar should be equally wide, and there won't be any bars that are significantly smaller than the average. The preceding silhouette plot indicates that we've found a good clustering of the dataset it was generated from. Let's now look at a demonstration of silhouette analysis.

A lot of this code has been borrowed from scikit-learn's own documentation which can be found at `https://scikit-learn.org/stable/auto_examples/cluster/plot_kmeans_silhouette_analysis.html`, so have a look at that—it has a great demonstration on how to construct silhouette plots. But in many cases, you can use the following silhouette function to construct silhouette plots:

```
In [12]:  def silhouette_plot(data, labels, metric="euclidean", xticks = True):
              silhouette_avg = silhouette_score(data, labels,
                                                metric=metric)
              sample_silhouette_values = silhouette_samples(data, labels,
                                                            metric=metric)


              y_lower = 10
              for k in np.unique(labels):
                  cluster_values = sample_silhouette_values[labels == k]
                  cluster_values.sort()
                  nk = len(cluster_values)
                  y_upper = y_lower + nk
                  color = cm.Spectral(float(k) / len(np.unique(labels)))
                  plt.fill_betweenx(np.arange(y_lower, y_upper),
                                    0, cluster_values,
                                    facecolor=color, edgecolor=color)
                  plt.text(-0.05, y_lower + 0.5 * nk, str(k))
                  y_lower = y_upper + 10

              plt.axvline(x=silhouette_avg, color="red", linestyle="--")
              if xticks:
                  plt.xticks([-0.1, 0, 0.1, 0.2, 0.3, 0.4, 0.5, 0.6, 0.7, 0.8, 0.9, 1.0])
              plt.yticks([])
              plt.xlabel("Silhouette Score")
              plt.ylabel("Cluster")
              plt.show()

              print("The average silhouette score is", silhouette_avg)
```

Now, let's go ahead and look at a silhouette plot for the iris dataset we have constructed:

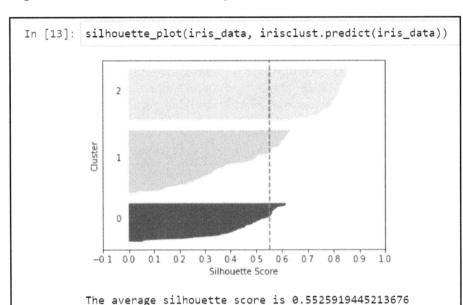

```
In [13]:  silhouette_plot(iris_data, irisclust.predict(iris_data))
```

The average silhouette score is 0.5525919445213676

Judging from this plot, it seems like the iris dataset has reasonable clustering.

Now, we will implement another function, where we provide a dataset and we tell it how many clusters we want to find, and it will construct a silhouette plot for the k-means clustering of that dataset, as follows:

```
In [14]:  def nclust_silhouette_kmeans(data, n_clusters):
              labels = KMeans(n_clusters=n_clusters, init='random').fit_predict(data)
              silhouette_plot(data=data, labels=labels)
```

We want to use the silhouette plot to try to decide between different numbers of clusters. So, let's look at a bunch of different silhouette plots.

Here is a silhouette plot when we have only two clusters for the iris dataset:

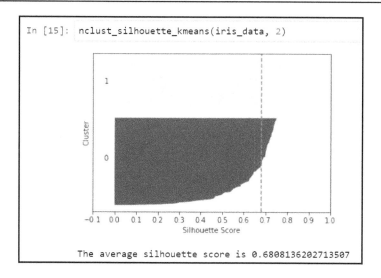

We find that most of the data is going to one cluster, and a significant portion goes to the other cluster. What do I think of this clustering? It's not bad, actually. There's nothing really abnormal about this. We know for a fact that there are three clusters in this dataset, for three different species. That said, we've looked at the dataset and we saw that the setosa species was pretty different from the versicolor and virginica species, and this is especially obvious if you look at a comparison of petal lengths and petal widths. So, two clusters aren't necessarily bad.

Now we'll look at three clusters:

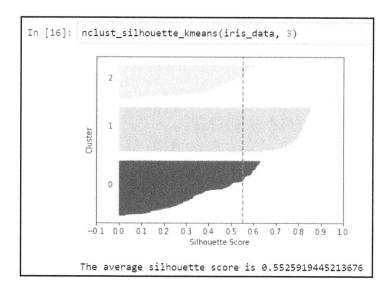

Three clusters aren't necessarily bad either.

When we go to four clusters, though, it's not ideal:

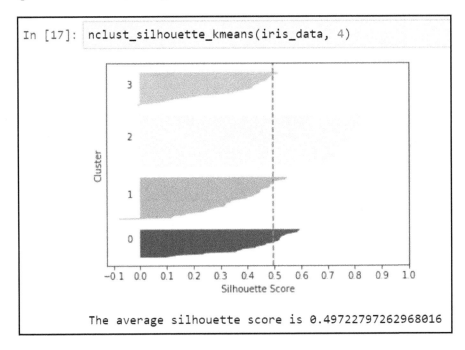

```
In [17]: nclust_silhouette_kmeans(iris_data, 4)
```

The average silhouette score is 0.49722797262968016

We have one point that, according to the silhouette analysis, might be in the wrong cluster; and a lot of points in this cluster are dragging down the overall average silhouette score, which is a little bit disturbing. This is indicative of bad clustering. So, having talked about how to judge clustering schemes, let's look at the next approach to clustering: hierarchical clustering.

# Hierarchical clustering

In this section, we will first look at similarity measures. Then, we will learn about hierarchical clustering.

We talked before about different notions of distance in the *Computing distances* section. Now, I want to talk about the idea of similarity. A **similarity score** describes how similar two objects are. There is no universal definition of the properties a similarity score has, but everyone agrees that similar objects have a high similarity score and dissimilar objects have a low similarity score. Dissimilarity is the opposite of similarity, and distance is a form of dissimilarity. Hierarchical clustering uses dissimilarity to form clusters. This means that if we can come up with similarity scores that make sense, we can cluster just about any type of data in a meaningful way.

In this section, I will be focusing on Jaccard similarity, which is related to Jaccard distance. I am going to demonstrate similarity scores by working with what I'm calling the `HNHeadlines` dataset. This is a collection of titles of posts submitted to Hacker News (http://news.ycombinator.com). We will take the following steps to find the scores:

1. Import the `pandas` library.
2. Import the `HNHeadlines.txt` file as a series, using the following lines of code:

```
In [2]:   headlines = pd.read_csv("HNHeadlines.txt", header=None, index_col=0).iloc[:, 0]
          headlines
```

This results in the following output:

```
Out[2]:  0
          0      Uber Co-Founder Travis Kalanick Said to Plan S...
          1                       Update on Meltdown and Spectre
          2      Intel Issues Updates to Protect Systems from S...
          3      Where Pot Entrepreneurs Go When the Banks Say No
          4                   Announcing the OpenWrt/LEDE merge
          5              Transpile Java Bytecode to WebAssembly
          6                             iMac Pro's T2 chip
          7      Productivity in 2017: analyzing 225 million ho...
          8      About speculative execution vulnerabilities in...
          9      "My ten hour white noise video now has five co...
          10             Site Isolation - The Chromium Projects
          11     Xerox Alto zero-day: cracking disk password pr...
          12                    The Best Things and Stuff of 2017
          13     More details about mitigations for the CPU Spe...
          14                     In pursuit of Otama's tone (2017)
          15            Show HN: PAST, a secure alternative to JWT
          16     Ink/stitch: an Inkscape extension for machine ...
```

Here, you see some of the headlines in this dataset. It's just a collection of strings—each of these strings being a headline from Hacker News—and we want to be able to cluster them. We suspect that there are some topics in this dataset, or headlines, that are very similar to one another, that could be grouped together in some way, and we will find out how to do that. But in order to do that, I'm going to have to find a way to describe what constitutes similar headlines and different headlines. To do that, we are going to use an *n*-gram. This is a concept of natural language processing. An ***n*-gram** is *n* characters that appear in sequence in a string. Let's say we have a string, `library`. The 3-grams, which are sequences of 3 characters, for library, are `lib`, `ibr`, `bra`, `rar`, and `ary`. These 3-grams can be used to describe the word `library` by forming a set that consists of all of these 3-grams.

3. We are going to use a package called **Natural Language Toolkit** (**NLTK**) to form 3-grams, as follows:

```
from nltk import ngrams
```

4. We will use the `ngrams` function from this package to form these 3-grams. `headline_sets` is a list of sets. Each of those sets consists of all 3-grams for that corresponding headline, as follows:

```
In [4]:  headline_sets = [set(''.join(u) for u in ngrams(h.lower(), 3)) for h in headlines]
         headline_sets[:3]
```

This results in the following output:

```
Out[4]: [{' 29',
          ' co',
          ' ka',
          ' of',
          ' pl',
          ' sa',
          ' st',
          ' to',
          ' tr',
          '% o',
          '-fo',
          '29%',
          '9% ',
          'aid',
          'ake',
          'ala',
          'ale',
          'an ',
          'ani',
          'avi',
          'ber',
```

Why do I want this? Well, I can use these sets to compute a similarity matrix. Now, we are going to use the Jaccard similarity. The Jaccard similarity is 1 minus the Jaccard distance. So, the easiest way to think of the Jaccard similarity is the number of elements that both sets have in common divided by the total number of elements in both sets, removing duplicates.

5. We will now create a function that prepares an affinity matrix or a similarity matrix, where each headline has its own row and its own column, and the intersection of a row and a column is the similarity between headline *i* and headline *j*. It goes through every row and every column, and it takes advantage of the fact that this matrix is symmetric. If you have the *i,j* entry, you also have the *j,i* entry, so you only have to compute the Jaccard similarity once (and that's what this line does) and assign it to both of those entries. This is summarized in the following code block:

```
In [6]:  sims = np.zeros((len(headlines), len(headlines)))
         for i in range(len(headlines)):
             for j in range(i, len(headlines)):
                 h1, h2 = headline_sets[i], headline_sets[j]
                 js = len(h1.intersection(h2))/len(h1.union(h2))
                 sims[i,j] = sims[j,i] = js

         sims[:5, :5]
```

This results in the following output:

```
Out[6]:  array([[1.        , 0.01176471, 0.02631579, 0.00980392, 0.02298851],
                [0.01176471, 1.        , 0.06097561, 0.01388889, 0.03508772],
                [0.02631579, 0.06097561, 1.        , 0.        , 0.        ],
                [0.00980392, 0.01388889, 0.        , 1.        , 0.04109589],
                [0.02298851, 0.03508772, 0.        , 0.04109589, 1.        ]])
```

This is a small subset; notice that it is symmetric, and all of these are pretty dissimilar, which is not particularly surprising. This matrix will be useful not only for hierarchical clustering but also for spectral clustering, and matrices like this—hierarchical clustering uses the distance matrix instead of the similarity matrix; spectral clustering uses the similarity matrix. But in the background, even if you don't explicitly create this matrix, this matrix is created.

# Clustering the iris dataset

With hierarchical clustering, we start with a dataset and assign each data point to its own cluster. We then take objects that are similar, and group them together into another set of clusters. This process repeats. Clusters that are considered similar to each other are grouped together, until eventually there is only one cluster remaining. The end result of hierarchical clustering looks similar to the following diagram:

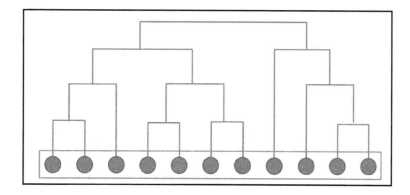

What is left is a hierarchy of clusters that can be unpacked for greater granularity, peeling them like an onion. Choosing the number of clusters amounts to deciding how far down this tree to go. What makes two clusters similar? You should not be surprised to hear that there are many ways to define this. Clearly, the dissimilarity between clusters should depend on the dissimilarity of their elements, but in what way should this be used?

One approach is to use the average dissimilarity of the elements in the clusters to decide how dissimilar the overall clusters are. Another approach is to use maximal dissimilarity, that is, the dissimilarity of the two most dissimilar elements in either cluster; there are other approaches for defining cluster dissimilarity as well.

We will first import the required functions, load the dataset, and plot it, as we have been doing so far.

Now, let's import the AgglomerativeClustering class, which is the scikit-learn implementation of hierarchical clustering (agglomerative is a different word for that) to form the cluster.

We have decided we want three clusters. We're using Euclidean distance, and we say that the average dissimilarity between two clusters is how we define cluster dissimilarity. So, we fit this to our dataset and we're also able to get the labels for our data, using the following lines of code:

```
In [11]:  irisclust1 = AgglomerativeClustering(n_clusters=3,
                                                affinity="euclidean",
                                                linkage="average")
          irisclust1 = irisclust1.fit(iris_data)

          # Visualizing the clustering
          plt.scatter(iris_data[:, 0], iris_data[:, 1], c=irisclust1.labels_, cmap=plt.cm.brg)
          plt.xlabel("Sepal Length")
          plt.ylabel("Sepal Width")
          plt.show()
```

This is the result of the clustering:

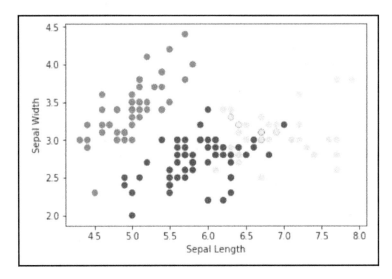

Now, if we were to choose a different affinity and linkage scheme, we may end up with different results. So, let's change the parameters, as follows, and see the result:

```
In [12]:  irisclust2 = AgglomerativeClustering(n_clusters=3,

                                      affinity="manhattan",
                                      linkage="complete")

          irisclust1 = irisclust2.fit(iris_data)

          # Visualizing the clustering
          plt.scatter(iris_data[:, 0], iris_data[:, 1], c=irisclust2.labels_, cmap=plt.cm.brg)
          plt.xlabel("Sepal Length")
          plt.ylabel("Sepal Width")
          plt.show()
```

This results in the following output:

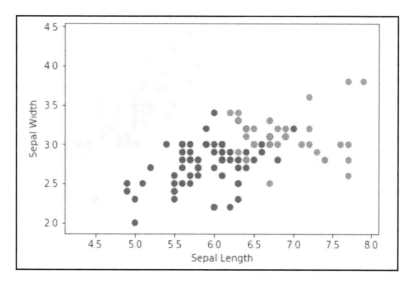

# Clustering the Headlines dataset

Now, let's look at clustering the Headlines dataset.

We're using agglomerative clustering and we want 10 clusters. The affinity is precomputed, and we're using average linkage. We want the Jaccard distance between headlines, which is 1 minus the Jaccard similarity—that's what we're going to use here. We will use the `fit_predict` method, which not only finds clusters but also returns the labels of the clusters found. The following code block summarizes this:

```
In [13]:  headlineclust = AgglomerativeClustering(n_clusters=10, affinity="precomputed", linkage="average")
          hclusters = headlineclust.fit_predict(1 - sims)

          hclusters
```

This is the result:

```
Out[13]: array([1, 0, 1, 1, 1, 1, 0, 1, 1, 1, 1, 1, 1, 1, 3, 1, 1, 1, 1, 1, 1, 4,
         1, 1, 1, 1, 1, 1, 1, 1, 1, 2, 1, 1, 1, 1, 1, 0, 5, 3, 1, 1, 1, 1,
         1, 1, 1, 1, 1, 2, 1, 3, 1, 1, 1, 1, 1, 1, 1, 1, 1, 1, 1, 1, 1, 1,
         1, 1, 1, 1, 1, 9, 0, 1, 1, 1, 1, 1, 1, 1, 1, 1, 1, 1, 1, 1, 1, 1,
         1, 1, 0, 1, 1, 1, 8, 1, 1, 1, 1, 8, 1, 1, 1, 1, 1, 1, 1, 1, 1, 0,
         1, 1, 1, 1, 1, 1, 1, 1, 1, 0, 1, 1, 1, 1, 9, 1, 1, 1, 1, 1, 1, 1,
         1, 1, 3, 1, 0, 1, 1, 0, 1, 1, 1, 1, 1, 1, 1, 1, 1, 4, 1, 2, 1, 1,
         1, 1, 1, 1, 6, 1, 4, 1, 1, 1, 1, 1, 1, 1, 2, 1, 1, 1, 1, 1, 1, 1,
         1, 1, 1, 1, 1, 1, 1, 3, 1, 1, 3, 4, 1, 1, 1, 1, 1, 1, 1, 1, 1, 1,
         1, 1, 1, 3, 1, 1, 1, 1, 1, 1, 1, 1, 0, 1, 1, 1, 1, 1, 1, 1, 1, 1,
         1, 1, 1, 1, 1, 1, 1, 1, 1, 1, 1, 4, 1, 1, 1, 1, 1, 1, 1, 1, 1, 3,
         1, 1, 3, 1, 1, 1, 1, 1, 1, 1, 1, 1, 1, 1, 1, 2, 1, 1, 1, 1, 1,
         1, 1, 0, 1, 1, 1, 1, 1, 1, 1, 1, 1, 3, 1, 1, 1, 0, 7, 1, 1, 1, 1,
         1, 1, 1, 1, 1, 1, 1, 1, 1, 4, 1, 1, 1, 1], dtype=int64)
```

Now, I want to look at some of the metrics we talked about previously. Let's look at the silhouette plot, which can be computed as follows:

```python
import matplotlib.cm as cm
import matplotlib.pyplot as plt
from sklearn.metrics import silhouette_score, silhouette_samples
%matplotlib inline

def silhouette_plot(data, labels, metric="euclidean", xticks = True):
    silhouette_avg = silhouette_score(data, labels,
                        metric=metric)
    sample_silhouette_values = silhouette_samples(data, labels,
                                    metric=metric)

    # This loop creates the silhouettes in the silhouette plot
    y_lower = 10
    for k in np.unique(labels):
        cluster_values = sample_silhouette_values[labels == k]
        cluster_values.sort()
        nk = len(cluster_values)
        y_upper = y_lower + nk
        color = cm.Spectral(float(k) / len(np.unique(labels)))
        plt.fill_betweenx(np.arange(y_lower, y_upper),
                    0, cluster_values,
                    facecolor=color, edgecolor=color)
        plt.text(-0.05, y_lower + 0.5 * nk, str(k))
        y_lower = y_upper + 10

    plt.axvline(x=silhouette_avg, color="red", linestyle="--")
    if xticks:
        plt.xticks([-0.1, 0, 0.1, 0.2, 0.3, 0.4, 0.5, 0.6, 0.7, 0.8, 0.9, 1.0])
    plt.yticks([])
    plt.xlabel("Silhouette Score")
    plt.ylabel("Cluster")
    plt.show()

    print("The average silhouette score is", silhouette_avg)
```

This results in the following plot:

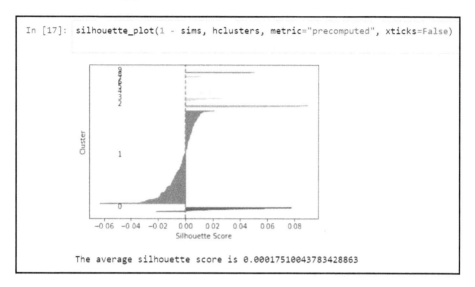

```
In [17]:  silhouette_plot(1 - sims, hclusters, metric="precomputed", xticks=False)
```

The average silhouette score is 0.00017510043783428863

Here is the silhouette plot for the dataset. For one thing, the average silhouette score is pretty darn small—it's close to 0, which isn't great. It's saying that, of the clusters that we found, it's very difficult to differentiate headlines in the two clusters. That said, it looks like we found some clusters that are OK, for example, cluster 0 and cluster 2. These might be somewhat reasonable clusters.

If we look at cluster 0, we have a lot of headlines about the `Meltdown` and `Spectre` vulnerabilities, which were major topics at the time—basically, a lot of headlines about attacks, as seen here:

```
In [19]:  headlines[hclusters == 0]

Out[19]:  0
          1                       Update on Meltdown and Spectre
          6                                    iMac Pro's T2 chip
          37            LLVM patch to fix half of Spectre attack
          72       Apple Confirms 'Meltdown' and 'Spectre' Vulner...
          90       GIMPS Project Discovers Largest Known Prime Nu...
          109            Ubuntu anouncement on Spectre/Meltdown
          119                            The Giant, Under Attack
          136                                    Mapzen Shutdown
          139                  India caste protest disrupts Mumbai
          210       Details of "Meltdown" and "Spectre" Attacks Ag...
          266                                      Spectre Attack
          280                                    iMac Pro Teardown
          Name: 1, dtype: object
```

Now let's change the `hclusters` value to 2:

```
In [20]:   headlines[hclusters == 2]

Out[20]:   0
           31                              GitHub acquires AppCanary
           49     Apple Joins AV1 Codec Effort with Mozilla, Goo...
           151                             Apple joins AV1 consortium
           168                             Apple acquires Buddybuild
           258                       Avere Systems joining Microsoft
           Name: 1, dtype: object
```

So, this cluster is talking about acquisitions.

Let's try another clustering; for example, cluster 9—I wonder what's in cluster 9:

```
In [21]:   headlines[hclusters == 9]

Out[21]:   0
           71                                            Frontmacs
           124     Don't Be Evil: Utopias, Frontiers, and Brogram...
           Name: 1, dtype: object
```

If we look at cluster 9, we don't have a lot of interesting topics here. So, the clustering isn't great; but at the same time, we did find clusters that weren't necessarily terrible. We didn't find great clusters, but we did find a few that seemed reasonable. Our final clustering topic is spectral clustering. We'll discuss that in the next section.

# Spectral clustering

The final clustering method we will look at is spectral clustering. In this section, we will learn what spectral clustering is and demonstrate how to perform it.

Of all the clustering methods mentioned in this chapter, spectral clustering may be the most opaque. Nevertheless, I will attempt to explain it. We start with a dataset, as shown in the following diagram:

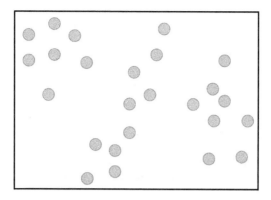

Next, we compute the similarity between the points in the dataset, as seen here:

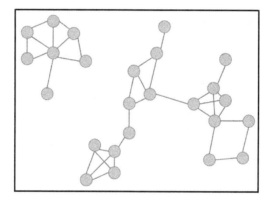

If the points are highly similar, we can infer that those points are connected:

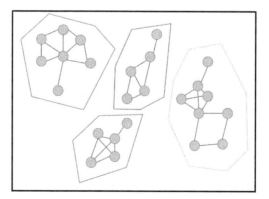

These connections form something similar to a graph. Once we have the graph, we find connections to cut. Then, nodes that are connected belong to the same cluster. So, let's go ahead and see what spectral clustering does with the iris dataset.

We will import the `SpectralClustering` class and perform spectral clustering for this dataset.

We want three clusters. Spectral clustering uses **radial basis function** (**RBF**) similarity. I'm not going to explain what that is, but it's the default option. It's basically taking the distance between two points—the Euclidean distance between two points—and making that the exponent of the exponential function. So, we fit the model and then we plot it, using the following lines of code:

```
In [5]:  irisclust = SpectralClustering(n_clusters=3,
                                          affinity="rbf")
         irisclust = irisclust.fit(iris_data)

         # Visualizing the clustering
         plt.scatter(iris_data[:, 0], iris_data[:, 1], c=irisclust.labels_, cmap=plt.cm.brg)
         plt.xlabel("Sepal Length")
         plt.ylabel("Sepal Width")
         plt.show()
```

This results in the following output:

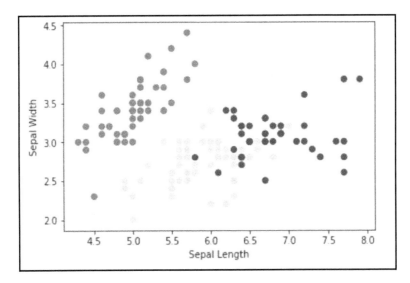

It comes up with clusters that look pretty similar to what we had earlier. Now, this is nice but, so far, our spectral clustering hasn't done anything that we haven't seen already.

# Clustering the Headlines dataset

Let's now look at clustering the Headlines dataset:

1. We will import the required functions:

```
In [6]:  import pandas as pd
         from nltk import ngrams
         import numpy as np
```

2. We also want to construct silhouette plots, so we need to compute the Jaccard similarity. For that, we will use the following lines of code:

```
In [7]:  headlines = pd.read_csv("HNHeadlines.txt", header=None, index_col=0).iloc[:, 0]
         headline_sets = [set(''.join(u) for u in ngrams(h.lower(), 3)) for h in headlines]
         sims = np.zeros((len(headlines), len(headlines)))
         for i in range(len(headlines)):
             for j in range(i, len(headlines)):
                 h1, h2 = headline_sets[i], headline_sets[j]
                 js = len(h1.intersection(h2))/len(h1.union(h2))
                 sims[i,j] = sims[j,i] = js

         headlines
```

This results in the following output:

```
Out[7]:  0
         0     Uber Co-Founder Travis Kalanick Said to Plan S...
         1                   Update on Meltdown and Spectre
         2     Intel Issues Updates to Protect Systems from S...
         3     Where Pot Entrepreneurs Go When the Banks Say No
         4                   Announcing the OpenWrt/LEDE merge
         5            Transpile Java Bytecode to WebAssembly
         6                            iMac Pro's T2 chip
         7     Productivity in 2017: analyzing 225 million ho...
         8     About speculative execution vulnerabilities in...
         9     "My ten hour white noise video now has five co...
         10             Site Isolation - The Chromium Projects
         11    Xerox Alto zero-day: cracking disk password pr...
         12              The Best Things and Stuff of 2017
         13    More details about mitigations for the CPU Spe...
         14                In pursuit of Otama's tone (2017)
         15        Show HN: PAST, a secure alternative to JWT
         16    Ink/stitch: an Inkscape extension for machine ...
         17    Texttop - An interactive X Linux desktop rende...
         18             Battle of the Clipper Chip (1994)
         19                   Introducing Preemptible GPUs
         20    Theo de Raadt, 2007: "some [Intel] bugs will b...
         21          Wi-Fi startup Eero lays off 30 employees
         22    Atrium is hiring for 10+ positions (Cofounded ...
```

3. Now, let's go ahead and perform this clustering, using the following function:

```
In [11]: import matplotlib.cm as cm
         import matplotlib.pyplot as plt
         from sklearn.metrics import silhouette_score, silhouette_samples
         %matplotlib inline

         def silhouette_plot(data, labels, metric="euclidean", xticks = True):
             silhouette_avg = silhouette_score(data, labels,
                                                metric=metric)
             sample_silhouette_values = silhouette_samples(data, labels,
                                                            metric=metric)


             y_lower = 10
             for k in np.unique(labels):
                 cluster_values = sample_silhouette_values[labels == k]
                 cluster_values.sort()
                 nk = len(cluster_values)
                 y_upper = y_lower + nk
                 color = cm.Spectral(float(k) / len(np.unique(labels)))
                 plt.fill_betweenx(np.arange(y_lower, y_upper),
                                   0, cluster_values,
                                   facecolor=color, edgecolor=color)
                 plt.text(-0.05, y_lower + 0.5 * nk, str(k))
                 y_lower = y_upper + 10

             plt.axvline(x=silhouette_avg, color="red", linestyle="--")
             if xticks:
                 plt.xticks([-0.1, 0, 0.1, 0.2, 0.3, 0.4, 0.5, 0.6, 0.7, 0.8, 0.9, 1.0])
             plt.yticks([])
             plt.xlabel("Silhouette Score")
             plt.ylabel("Cluster")
             plt.show()

             print("The average silhouette score is", silhouette_avg)
```

4. We will then print out the clusters, using the following parameters:

```
In [12]: headlineclust = SpectralClustering(n_clusters=4, affinity="precomputed")
         hclusters = headlineclust.fit_predict(sims)
         hclusters
```

This results in the following output:

```
Out[9]: array([2, 3, 1, 2, 2, 1, 1, 1, 3, 3, 3, 1, 2, 3, 3, 0, 3, 3, 2, 1, 3, 3,
        1, 3, 3, 3, 2, 3, 1, 3, 3, 3, 0, 3, 3, 1, 3, 3, 3, 3, 1, 2, 1, 1,
        2, 3, 3, 1, 2, 3, 3, 3, 3, 2, 3, 1, 3, 1, 1, 2, 1, 1, 1, 1, 0, 1,
        1, 2, 1, 3, 3, 3, 3, 1, 3, 3, 3, 0, 1, 3, 2, 0, 1, 3, 3, 1, 3, 0,
        3, 2, 1, 1, 1, 1, 3, 3, 3, 2, 2, 3, 1, 2, 2, 0, 1, 2, 3, 1, 3, 3,
        2, 3, 1, 2, 3, 1, 1, 0, 2, 2, 3, 3, 0, 2, 3, 3, 1, 0, 1, 2, 1, 2,
        0, 2, 2, 1, 3, 1, 2, 1, 1, 3, 0, 1, 0, 1, 3, 1, 3, 3, 3, 3, 3, 1,
        3, 2, 3, 2, 3, 2, 3, 3, 2, 2, 3, 3, 3, 3, 3, 3, 3, 3, 2, 1, 3, 3,
        3, 1, 3, 3, 0, 2, 1, 3, 2, 1, 3, 3, 3, 3, 1, 2, 3, 2, 2, 2, 0, 3,
        2, 1, 2, 3, 2, 1, 1, 3, 1, 0, 1, 0, 3, 1, 0, 1, 3, 2, 3, 2, 3, 0,
        3, 3, 1, 3, 1, 3, 1, 0, 3, 2, 0, 3, 0, 3, 2, 0, 1, 0, 3, 3, 1, 1,
        1, 1, 3, 1, 1, 3, 2, 0, 0, 3, 2, 2, 3, 1, 2, 3, 1, 1, 2, 3, 3, 0,
        3, 1, 3, 2, 3, 0, 3, 1, 1, 1, 3, 1, 3, 3, 1, 0, 1, 3, 1, 1, 3, 3,
        2, 3, 3, 3, 2, 1, 0, 1, 1, 3, 3, 3, 1, 3])
```

So, those are the resulting clusters—how did our algorithm do?

5.  Well, let's construct a silhouette plot:

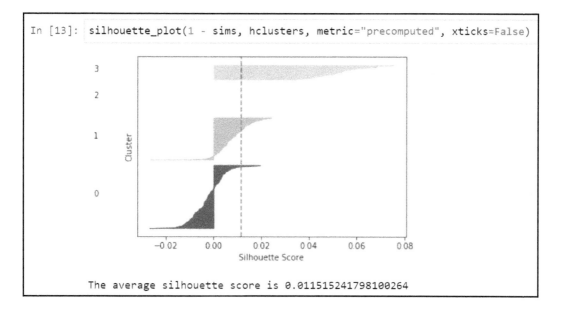

```
In [13]: silhouette_plot(1 - sims, hclusters, metric="precomputed", xticks=False)
```

The average silhouette score is 0.011515241798100264

We have four clusters; the silhouette score is not great, and not all of these clusters are particularly great, but it could be worse. Clusters 0 and 1 are not great. There are points in it that, according to the silhouette score, probably don't belong in clusters 0 and 1. But clusters 2 and 3? They look like reasonable clusters. The silhouette score is pretty low, which is disappointing, but that might be the best we can expect considering that all of these headlines are supposedly very dissimilar.

6.  Now, let's look at some of these clusters. So, we will generate cluster 1:

```
In [16]:  headlines[hclusters==1]

Out[16]:  0
          2         Intel Issues Updates to Protect Systems from S...
          5                 Transpile Java Bytecode to WebAssembly
          6                                     iMac Pro's T2 chip
          7         Productivity in 2017: analyzing 225 million ho...
          11        Xerox Alto zero-day: cracking disk password pr...
          19                            Introducing Preemptible GPUs
          22        Atrium is hiring for 10+ positions (Cofounded ...
          28                        Fighting Fires with Fire Grenades
          35        Reading privileged memory with a side-channel
          40                                  Announcing Rust 1.23
          42        Ask HN: When will Intel start selling chips th...
          43        SiliconSqueak: Adapting processor grain via re...
          47             Learning to Code as a Woman Changed My Life
          55        Ripple Slides After Coinbase Says Not Adding N...
          57        Mitigations landing for new class of timing at...
          58                              Microprocessor Design (2017)
          60                        Why things might have taken so long
          61        Mark Zuckerberg's personal challenge is all ab...
          62        Oceans suffocating as huge dead zones quadrupl...
          63        Scaleway patches infrastructure to mitigate In...
          65        Strengthening Checks on Presidential Nuclear L...
          66        Alan Turing's "Can Computers Think?" Radio Bro...
          68        Hacking WiFi to inject cryptocurrency miner to...
```

We notice that there's not really much tying these headlines together.

7. Let's look at cluster 2:

```
In [15]:  headlines[hclusters==2]

Out[15]:  0
          0          Uber Co-Founder Travis Kalanick Said to Plan S...
          3          Where Pot Entrepreneurs Go When the Banks Say No
          4                        Announcing the OpenWrt/LEDE merge
          12                       The Best Things and Stuff of 2017
          18                      Battle of the Clipper Chip (1994)
          26                                 The Dex File Format
          41         A photographer captures the paths that birds m...
          44         Intel CEO sold all the stock he could after In...
          48         More housing near the Expo Line and other Cali...
          53               The State of JavaScript Frameworks, 2017
          59                      Notes from the Intelpocalypse
          67                       The Attraction of Complexity
          80         New measurement confirms: The ozone is coming ...
          89         Why Rounded Corners Are Easier on the Eyes - U...
          97         Ripple co-founder is now richer than the Googl...
          98         Ethereum breaks new record by reaching $1,000 ...
          101        Ancient Infant's DNA Reveals New Clues to How ...
          102                      The Expensive Art of Living Forever
          105        A gene therapy to treat a rare, inherited form...
          110        The 'app' you can't trash: how SIP is broken i...
          113        Who Took the Legendary Earthrise Photo from Ap...
          118                            The Case for the Subway
```

As an exercise, find and examine clusters 0 and 3.

Again, the algorithm is not using topics explicitly, it's using 3-grams—so, common characters in these headlines. Maybe using 3-grams is not a great way to cluster headlines, but it's pretty clear why it thinks some of these clusters are very similar.

# Summary

That concludes our chapter on clustering. We learned what clustering is, where it is used, and why. We then looked at various clustering algorithms, such as k-means, hierarchical clustering, and spectral clustering. We explored how to compress images using k-means. We also learned how to evaluate clusters using various methods. Finally, we looked at how to cluster datasets using the hierarchical clustering and spectral clustering methods.

In the next chapter, we will learn about dimensionality reduction, which may be considered another form of unsupervised learning.

# Dimensionality Reduction

# 7

The final chapter of this book focuses on dimensionality reduction techniques. We will start with a discussion of what dimensionality reduction is used for. Then, we will look at the first dimensionality reduction technique—principal component analysis. Then, we will talk about singular value decomposition—a linear algebra decomposition of great importance. Finally, we will discuss multidimensional scaling.

The following topics will be covered in this chapter:

- Introducing dimensionality reduction
- Principal component analysis
- Singular value decomposition
- Low-dimensional representation

## Introducing dimensionality reduction

Now, let's start by talking about what we're doing with dimensionality reduction. In this section, I will introduce dimensionality reduction techniques as an unsupervised learning method, and discuss what the objectives of dimensionality reduction are and what it is used for.

Dimensionality reduction is considered an unsupervised learning method, since there is no target variable that we are trying to predict. The other unsupervised learning method we looked at was clustering, which was unsupervised learning's analogy to classification.

Dimensionality reduction is the unsupervised learning analogy to regression. We are trying to discover features, often in Euclidean space, that we do not directly observe in data, yet we believe influence patterns seen in it. Perhaps you may recall the **curse of dimensionality**. This is a phenomenon where distances in higher dimensions tend to be large. This makes learning difficult, since every data point tends to be far away from other data points.

However, the problem could be exaggerated. Data may actually be described well by a space of much lower dimensionality. For example, I've illustrated data in the following diagram that looks as though it's in two-dimensional space, but a one-dimensional space—a line—describes the data fairly well:

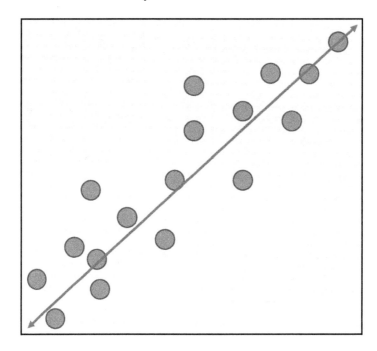

There will be an error resulting from this representation, but this error should be small. The objective of dimensionality reduction is to discover this low-dimensional space.

# Uses of dimensionality reduction

Dimensionality reduction techniques have a number of uses, such as:

- Visualization
- Feature creation
- Simplification

Perhaps the most immediate use is **visualization**. High-dimensional data can be visualized in a two-dimensional space, which humans can understand well, allowing us to spot patterns. We could be using dimensionality reduction to **create features**. This could be by simplifying features, or generating new features entirely when none existed before. With dimensionality reduction, we can try to simplify a dataset. There could be many features, but we can use dimensionality reduction to narrow features down to just a few that can be used for supervised learning. Another use is **compression or simplification**. We might develop a feature set that recreates the original dataset with minimal errors. We will see just about every one of these uses in this chapter. The first dimensionality reduction technique we will see is **principal component analysis** (**PCA**). We'll get started with this in the next section.

# Principal component analysis

Now, let's look at our first approach to dimensionality reduction, using PCA. In this section, we will learn all about PCA. We will see what PCA does, and also show approaches to evaluating the quality of principal components.

We'll start with a dataset. This dataset lies in some dimensional space. In each dimension, the data varies. There's no necessary relationship in this variation. Furthermore, there could be correlations between the coordinates. This is better represented using the following diagram:

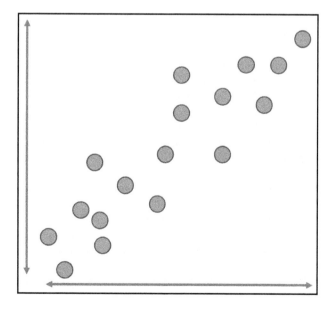

With PCA, we find a new feature space based on linear combinations of the original feature space, with new features, called principal components, as shown in the following diagram:

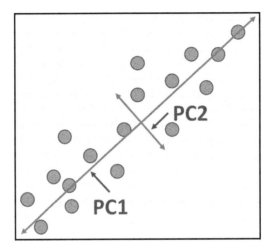

The principal components are all uncorrelated. Additionally, the variance of the dataset with respect to each principal component is decreasing. The first principal component's value captures the direction in which the data varies the most. The second principal component, in the direction which the data varies the most while being uncorrelated with the first principal component, and so on, for each principal component. This means that the first few principal components are likely to capture most of the variability in the dataset, and, in principle, a couple could capture all the interesting variation that could be used for other tasks.

# Demonstration of PCA

In this Notebook, we will see PCA in action. We will do this with the Boston dataset:

1. The first thing we will do is load in the required functions, along with some accompanying objects:

```
In [1]:  from sklearn.datasets import load_boston
         from sklearn.decomposition import PCA
         import matplotlib.pyplot as plt
         %matplotlib inline
```

We will also import the PCA object from sklearn, which we will be using for PCA.

2. Then, we will load in the Boston dataset, as follows:

```
In [2]:   boston_obj = load_boston()
          data = boston_obj.data
          data[:5, :]
```

This results in the following output:

```
Out[2]:  array([[6.3200e-03, 1.8000e+01, 2.3100e+00, 0.0000e+00, 5.3800e-01,
         6.5750e+00, 6.5200e+01, 4.0900e+00, 1.0000e+00, 2.9600e+02,
         1.5300e+01, 3.9690e+02, 4.9800e+00],
        [2.7310e-02, 0.0000e+00, 7.0700e+00, 0.0000e+00, 4.6900e-01,
         6.4210e+00, 7.8900e+01, 4.9671e+00, 2.0000e+00, 2.4200e+02,
         1.7800e+01, 3.9690e+02, 9.1400e+00],
        [2.7290e-02, 0.0000e+00, 7.0700e+00, 0.0000e+00, 4.6900e-01,
         7.1850e+00, 6.1100e+01, 4.9671e+00, 2.0000e+00, 2.4200e+02,
         1.7800e+01, 3.9283e+02, 4.0300e+00],
        [3.2370e-02, 0.0000e+00, 2.1800e+00, 0.0000e+00, 4.5800e-01,
         6.9980e+00, 4.5800e+01, 6.0622e+00, 3.0000e+00, 2.2200e+02,
         1.8700e+01, 3.9463e+02, 2.9400e+00],
        [6.9050e-02, 0.0000e+00, 2.1800e+00, 0.0000e+00, 4.5800e-01,
         7.1470e+00, 5.4200e+01, 6.0622e+00, 3.0000e+00, 2.2200e+02,
         1.8700e+01, 3.9690e+02, 5.3300e+00]])
```

3. Now, let's find the first two principal components of this dataset. The maximum number of principal components is the total number of dimensions that you started with. In this case, we want the end number of dimensions to be 2. We will use the `fit_transform` PCA method. Not only does this find all principal components, it will also transform the dataset so that the features of the new dataset are described in terms of the principal components, as shown here:

```
In [3]:   pca = PCA(n_components=2)
          new_data = pca.fit_transform(data)
          new_data[:5]
```

This results in the following output:

```
Out[3]:  array([[-119.81821283,  -5.56072403],
        [-168.88993091,  10.11419701],
        [-169.31150637,  14.07855395],
        [-190.2305986 ,  18.29993274],
        [-190.13340306,  16.09537059]])
```

So, the first column will be the first principal component and the second column will be the second principal component's value for each of these observations. So, we have gone from a larger-dimensional space to a two-dimensional space.

4. We can plot the values of the data with respect to these two principal components, as follows:

```
In [4]:  plt.scatter(x=new_data[:, 0], y=new_data[:, 1])
         plt.xlabel("Principle Component 1")
         plt.ylabel("Principle Component 2")
         plt.show()
```

This results in the following output:

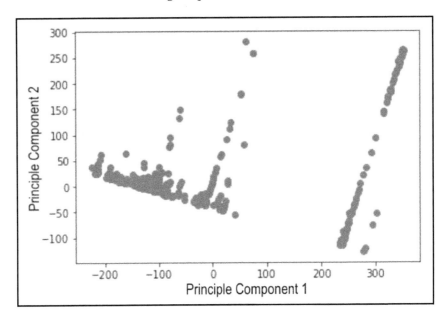

# Choosing the number of components

When we perform PCA, we will want to use fewer principal components than features in the dataset, but the question is—*how many do we need?* For that, we can create a plot where the x-axis represents how many principal components we use, and the y-axis represents how much variance in the dataset is not captured by that number of principal components, as shown here:

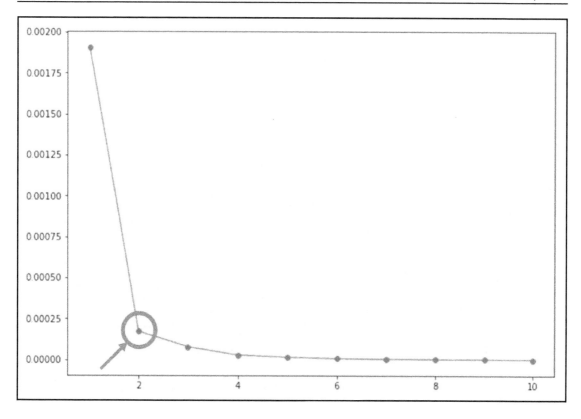

We are looking for an elbow in the plot, where, after using that many principal components, the reduction in unexplained variance starts to diminish.

Now, we will run a function that will create this plot for you. We will do so by using the following function:

```
In [6]:  def explained_var_plot(data, max_components):
             explained_var = PCA(n_components=max_components).fit(data).explained_variance_ratio_
             plt.plot(np.arange(max_components) + 1, 1 - np.cumsum(explained_var), marker='o')
```

So, let's run this function, and look at this plot for our dataset:

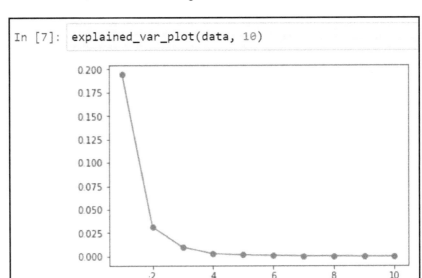

It seems that two principal components is actually a good choice for the Boston dataset. After that, the reduction in unexplained variance as a ratio of the total variance starts to decrease. So, we could actually do a lot of our learning using just the first two principal components, and have essentially captured all of the interesting variation in the dataset. Having discussed PCA, we will now move on to **singular value decomposition (SVD)**—a powerful matrix decomposition technique from linear algebra.

# Singular value decomposition

In this section, we will discuss singular value decomposition, and demonstrate how to use it.

SVD is a matrix decomposition technique from linear algebra that is very powerful. It forms the basis of other powerful methods. For example, PCA is performed after the SVD of the matrix is found first. This is an advanced linear algebra technique, so describing SVD without linear algebra is difficult, but we will look at its intuition.

We start with a collection of unit vectors, each orthogonal to each other. Any matrix, $X$, can be thought of as a mapping from one space to another. The unit vectors we start with will be mapped into unit vectors in a new space. The product of these unit vectors with the matrix of these vectors are unit vectors orthogonal to one another, and are also scaled by values known as the singular values of the matrix. SVD describes the matrix, $X$, by finding the singular values, recording them in a diagonal matrix, $S$—the unit vectors from the original space and the image unit vectors in the output space—and recording them in matrices. Together, these reconstruct the matrix and also give all of the information that's important about the matrix. This can be seen in the following diagram:

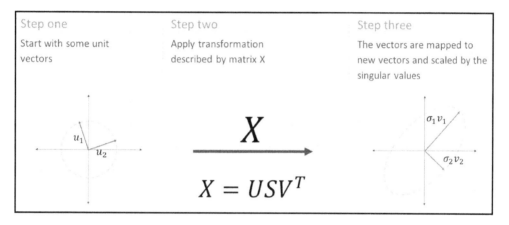

Singular value decomposition is a powerful matrix decomposition technique from linear algebra. We write a matrix, $X$, in terms of $U$, $S$, and the transpose of $V$, and we write it as the product of these three matrices. So, $U$ and $V$ are known as **unitary matrices**. I'm not going to explain what that means; it's not that important right now. $S$, however, is a matrix that isn't necessarily square; it could be an N×N matrix. And the diagonal entries of $S$ are the only potentially non-zero entries of this matrix; all other entries of this matrix are 0. These entries are known as the **singular values**. They are ordered from largest to smallest, and they are all non-negative, so they're either 0 or positive.

The number of nonzero singular values of this matrix is referred to as $r$, and this is not the only way to write the matrix $X$. There is another formulation, called the **compact SVD**, which writes $X$ in terms of $\tilde{U}$, $\tilde{S}$, and $\tilde{v}^T$. $\tilde{U}$ is an M×r matrix and $\tilde{s}$ is r×r. That means that $\tilde{S}$ is a diagonal matrix, and all of its diagonal entries are greater than 0, and $\tilde{v}^T$ is an N×r matrix. So, why do we care about the compact SVD? Well, the compact SVD tells us how we could do what we want to do in this section, which is image compression. We can find a lower-rank approximation to an original data matrix that almost reconstructs the original data matrix, but with less information. That is our objective here.

# SVD for image compression

SVD is used for many more purposes than this. In fact, it turns out that SVD is an instrumental step when finding the PCA, and the two are almost equivalent. But, for now, we will look at how we can use SVD for image compression:

1. So, we are going to import a bunch of functions, such as NumPy, the `linalg` module of NumPy, the `Image` object from `PIL`, and the `pyplot` function from `matplotlib`, as follows:

```
In [1]:   from PIL import Image
          import numpy as np
          import numpy.linalg as ln
          import matplotlib.pyplot as plt
          %matplotlib inline
```

2. So, let's go ahead and look at this image of a frog:

```
In [3]:   frog = np.array(Image.open("frog.png").convert("RGB")) / 255
          plt.imshow(frog)

Out[3]:   <matplotlib.image.AxesImage at 0x28dfed80198>
```

Notice that I've normalized all the RGB entries of this image between 0 and 1.

3. Now, we are going to look at the matrices that contain the red intensities for the image, as follows:

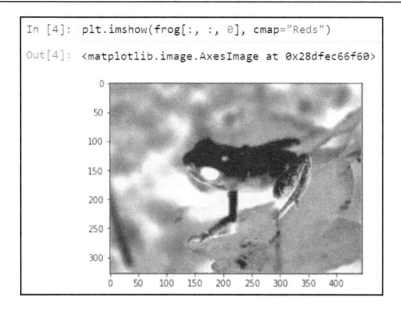

```
In [4]: plt.imshow(frog[:, :, 0], cmap="Reds")

Out[4]: <matplotlib.image.AxesImage at 0x28dfec66f60>
```

Now, you may notice that there are white areas. That means that there isn't much red here.

4. Then, we will look at the green intensities:

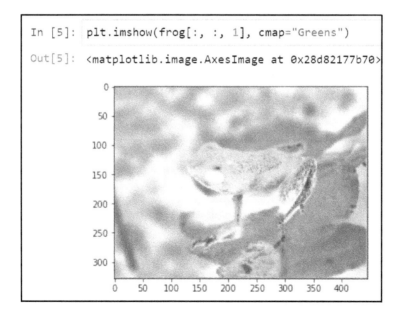

```
In [5]: plt.imshow(frog[:, :, 1], cmap="Greens")

Out[5]: <matplotlib.image.AxesImage at 0x28d82177b70>
```

5. Then, we will look at the blue intensities:

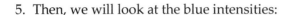

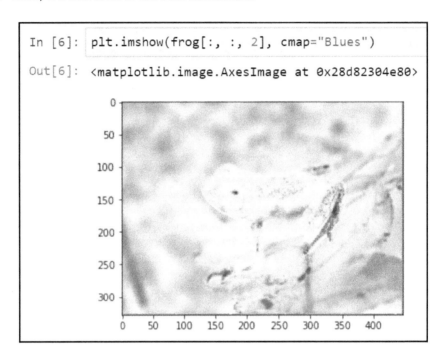

There isn't much green or blue here around the eye, which means that the eye will show up, not as white as these images show, but as black.

Now, we will perform SVD on each of these individual matrices.

6. Now, to give you an idea of what's going on, let's look at the top 5x7 corner of this image, using the following code:

```
In [6]: plt.imshow(frog[:5, :7, 0], cmap='Reds')
```

This results in the following output:

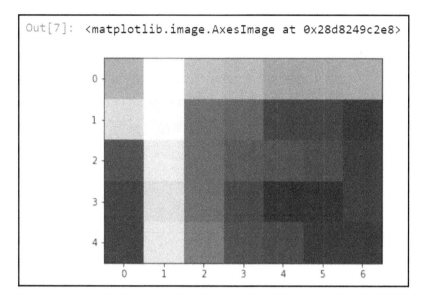

7. Now, we will find the SVD decomposition of the red matrix, shown in the preceding screenshot. We will then display the U matrix, as follows:

```
In [8]:  m, n = 5, 7
         U, S, V = ln.svd(frog[:m, :n, 0])     # The full SVD
         U

Out[8]:  array([[-0.30079621,  0.08769448, -0.70727161, -0.62669344,  0.09409311],
                [-0.43885409, -0.89591289,  0.05756807,  0.02461915,  0.02875761],
                [-0.47834696,  0.21951679, -0.42282951,  0.70478996, -0.21790568],
                [-0.49823305,  0.24445706,  0.45423163, -0.33134133, -0.6130996 ],
                [-0.48977214,  0.28583719,  0.33367891,  0.01154387,  0.75295782]])
```

8. Here is S, the singular values:

```
In [9]:  S     # The singular values

Out[9]:  array([2.83131296, 0.2661903 , 0.03781618, 0.02920216, 0.02417618])
```

So, this is not written as a matrix, but we could turn this into a matrix if we wanted to.

9. This is V.T, which is the transpose of V:

```
In [10]:  V.T    # ln.svd returns the transpose of V as described above

Out[10]:  array([[-0.36782446,  0.89488513, -0.22956794, -0.04021233,  0.06758064,
                  -0.06507665, -0.02766203],
                 [-0.14942511,  0.19213103,  0.68304715,  0.15294601, -0.38274589,
                   0.44862927,  0.32101287],
                 [-0.36329807, -0.20076941, -0.47015602,  0.32647196, -0.66459202,
                   0.14227017, -0.19532581],
                 [-0.40147607, -0.0898807 ,  0.46918391,  0.31797094,  0.05206663,
                  -0.60440097, -0.37614878],
                 [-0.42392097, -0.19481544,  0.01575484, -0.71633357, -0.23936824,
                  -0.29460322,  0.35336631],
                 [-0.42819374, -0.16895182,  0.08346588, -0.29598811,  0.34945942,
                   0.5627993 , -0.50464339],
                 [-0.43145094, -0.21767316, -0.17986147,  0.40811552,  0.47447435,
                   0.07362991,  0.58052801]])
```

The SVD function from ln returns the transpose of *V* that we noticed earlier. So, this is the actual matrix, *V*, as defined. The reason it's doing this is because it's a lot easier to just multiply *USV* rather than $USV^T$.

# Low-rank approximation

Now, we want a low-rank approximation for this original matrix:

1. So, here are the first two columns of U:

```
In [11]:  r = 2
          nU, nS, nV = U[:m, :r], S[:r], V[:r, :n]
          nU

Out[11]:  array([[-0.30079621,  0.08769448],
                 [-0.43885409, -0.89591289],
                 [-0.47834696,  0.21951679],
                 [-0.49823305,  0.24445706],
                 [-0.48977214,  0.28583719]])
```

These are what will actually be used when reconstructing this matrix.

2. Here are the first two singular values:

```
In [12]:  nS

Out[12]:  array([2.83131296, 0.2661903 ])
```

3. Here are the first few columns of *V*:

```
In [13]:  nV.T

Out[13]:  array([[-0.36782446,  0.89488513],
                 [-0.14942511,  0.19213103],
                 [-0.36329807, -0.20076941],
                 [-0.40147607, -0.0898807 ],
                 [-0.42392097, -0.19481544],
                 [-0.42819374, -0.16895182],
                 [-0.43145094, -0.21767316]])
```

4. So, when we want to reconstruct the original matrix but with a lower-rank approximation, we multiply the three matrices we defined previously. We have to write `diag` to create a diagonal matrix, but we will multiply all of these matrices together, as follows:

```
In [13]:  nX = nU.dot(np.diag(nS)).dot(nV)
          nX
```

This is the resulting data matrix:

```
Out[14]:  array([[0.33414672, 0.13174262, 0.3047155 , 0.33981825, 0.35648387,
                  0.36072651, 0.36236319],
                 [0.24361895, 0.13984562, 0.49929009, 0.52028241, 0.57319614,
                  0.57233715, 0.58800357],
                 [0.55045408, 0.21360073, 0.48030112, 0.53848707, 0.56275364,
                  0.57005176, 0.57161621],
                 [0.577105  , 0.22328945, 0.49942328, 0.56049497, 0.58532863,
                  0.59303903, 0.59446342],
                 [0.57815072, 0.22182622, 0.48850882, 0.54988737, 0.5730275 ,
                  0.58092043, 0.58173013]])
```

5.  Here's its shape:

```
In [15]: nX.shape
Out[15]: (5, 7)
```

It's still a 5x7 matrix.

6.  We can, in fact, still create an image, as follows:

```
In [16]: plt.imshow(nX, cmap="Reds")
Out[16]: <matplotlib.image.AxesImage at 0x28d824f7198>
```

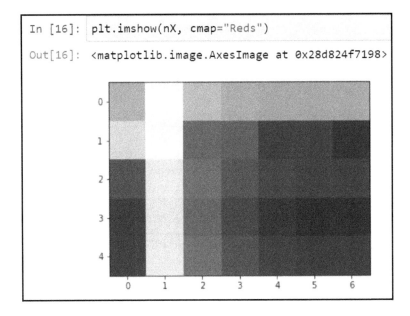

This image actually looks a little bit similar to what we had previously. It's not the same thing though; this is obviously an approximation of the original matrix, not the actual original matrix.

We can improve this approximation by including more singular values, and, in fact, we can make this approximation arbitrarily good the more singular values we choose to include.

## Reconstructing the image using compact SVD

Now, we will apply some functions that create compact SVD and return the matrices used in it, and we also have a function that will do image compression.

The function to find the matrices of the compact SVD is as follows:

```
In [16]:  def approx_compact_svd(a, r):
              m, n = a.shape
              U, S, V = ln.svd(a)
              return (U[:m, :r], S[:r], V.T[:n, :r])
```

The function to perform the actual reconstruction is as follows:

```
In [17]:  def svd_compress_image(img, ranks):
              channels = [img[:, :, 0], img[:, :, 1], img[:, :, 2]]
              new_channels = list()
              for a, r in zip(channels, ranks):
                  U, S, V = approx_compact_svd(a, r)
                  new_channels.append(U.dot(np.diag(S)).dot(V.T))
              return np.array(new_channels).transpose((1, 2, 0))
```

What it will do is find this compact SVD and create a matrix similar to the ones that we created before, and it will return the new matrix. This doesn't actually store the image in a form with less information, but it shows you the image you would see if you did, in fact, store this matrix using only a few singular values and a few relevant lower-dimensional matrices.

So, we will run our functions, and then plot our image with a few parameters. Here is what our frog would look like if we compressed it using just 10 singular values for each channel:

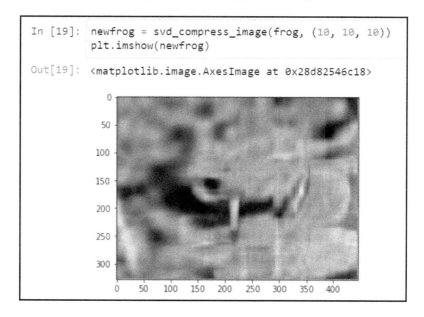

```
In [19]:  newfrog = svd_compress_image(frog, (10, 10, 10))
          plt.imshow(newfrog)

Out[19]:  <matplotlib.image.AxesImage at 0x28d82546c18>
```

You can kind of see a frog here. It's not a great representation, but it is image compression, you can't expect something excellent.

Here is another approximation of this image, where we are using 200 singular values:

```
In [20]:   newfrog2 = svd_compress_image(frog, (200, 200, 200))
           plt.imshow(newfrog2)

Out[20]:   <matplotlib.image.AxesImage at 0x28d825736a0>
```

Again, not great—there are some artifacts here that we don't really like, but it is certainly better than the previous image, and it is actually getting pretty close to the original image. So, we have now learned all about SVD.

# Low-dimensional representation

We have now reached the final section of this book, and in this section, we will be talking about low-dimensional representation. We will see what **multidimensional scaling (MDS)** is, and demonstrate how to perform it.

With MDS, we start with a distance matrix. This could have been computed in any way, using any distance metric we want. Having gotten the distance matrix, we then construct Euclidean coordinates for each point. Perhaps these coordinates representing our data preserve the distances described in the original matrix. If it is not possible, however, we can only hope that the error between the actual and constructed distances is small.

# Example of MDS

MDS creates points that are some specified distance apart from one another. First, I'd like to pose a challenge to you—*can you construct two points that are equidistant from each other while lying on a straight line?*

The answer is obvious—of course you can. Here's a diagram showing how to do this:

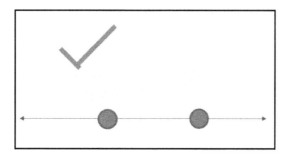

It's an easy task in a one-dimensional space.

Here's another problem—*can you construct three points that are equidistant from each other while lying on a line?*

The answer is no. This is impossible. If you first construct two equidistant points, when you choose a third, it cannot be at the same position as the first, and when you choose the third point one away from the second, it will be two away from the first, as shown here:

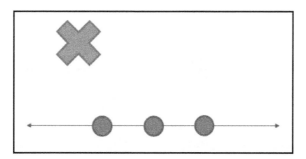

So, the problem has no solution. The best you can hope for is two points that are almost equidistant from each other.

Is there a solution in three-dimensional space, though? Yes, there is—points that together form an equilateral triangle, as shown here:

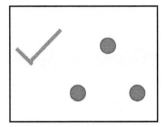

The point of this exercise is to help you realize that there can be distance relationships that cannot be realized in low-dimensional spaces, yet can be realized in higher-dimensional spaces.

# MDS in action

In low-dimensional spaces, we may need to be satisfied with approximations, where distances are close but not quite what we specified. Let's do some MDS with the iris dataset:

1. So, I'm loading in the iris dataset, and I'm also loading in the MDS object for multidimensional scaling:

```
In [1]:   from sklearn.datasets import load_iris
          from sklearn.manifold import MDS
          import matplotlib.pyplot as plt
          %matplotlib inline
```

We're going to be using this to visualize the dataset.

2. You may recall that the iris dataset has four features. You have sepal length, sepal width, petal length, and petal width. Here is the sepal length versus the sepal width of the flowers:

```
In [2]:  iris_obj = load_iris()
         iris_data = iris_obj.data
         species = iris_obj.target

         plt.scatter(iris_data[:, 0], iris_data[:, 1], c=species, cmap=plt.cm.brg)
         plt.xlabel("Sepal Length")
         plt.ylabel("Sepal Width")
         plt.show()
```

This results in the following output:

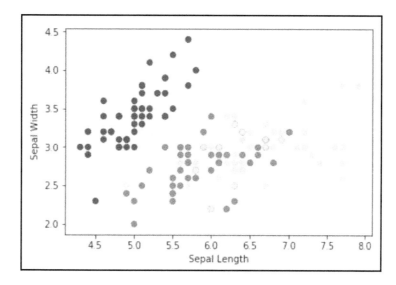

3. Here's the petal length versus the petal width:

```
In [3]:  plt.scatter(iris_data[:, 2], iris_data[:, 3], c=species, cmap=plt.cm.brg)
         plt.xlabel("Petal Length")
         plt.ylabel("Petal Width")
         plt.show()
```

This results in the following output:

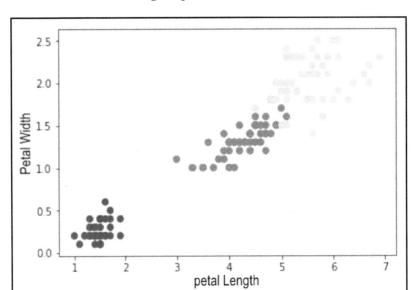

## How MDS comes into the picture

Now, wouldn't it be great if you could visualize all four dimensions at once? The setosa species seems to be pretty different from the versicolor and virginica species, as seen in both plots. So, is there a way for us to visualize all of the distances between these points together without having to visualize sepal length, sepal width, petal length, and petal width?

If we wanted to do that, we could end up with as many as six plots, because we'd have to plot petal length versus petal width, petal length versus sepal length, petal length versus sepal width, and so on for each possible combination, and there are six possible combinations.

So, it would be nice if we could have one plot that visualizes the distance relationships in this dataset, at least approximately, and, in fact, there is. We can use MDS to do this.

In this case, we are going to fit the original dataset, and we are going to tell it that the dissimilarity is Euclidean, which tells it how it's going to compute a distance matrix. Again, I'm using `fit_transform` to not only fit the data to MDS, but also to return a transformation matrix, as follows:

```
In [4]:  iris_mds = MDS(n_components=2, dissimilarity="euclidean")
         iris_2d = iris_mds.fit_transform(iris_data)
         iris_2d[:5, :]
```

This results in the following output:

```
Out[4]:  array([[ 2.63552033, -0.64698985],
                [ 2.72588097, -0.16501118],
                [ 2.89780047, -0.26183482],
                [ 2.77244461, -0.05068756],
                [ 2.68123548, -0.67894703]])
```

The following diagram shows the coordinates that, together, would form a two-dimensional representation of this dataset:

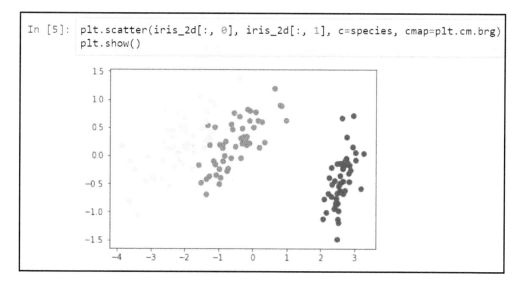

```
In [5]:  plt.scatter(iris_2d[:, 0], iris_2d[:, 1], c=species, cmap=plt.cm.brg)
         plt.show()
```

And, as I sort of hypothesized, the setosa species is very different in this plot from the versicolor and the virginica species. The other two species are different from one another, but they are much closer together, and there is, in fact, a little bit of overlap for some flowers between the two species. This would be information that you'd care about if you were doing clustering. It would tell you that it's easy to find a cluster that isolates the setosa species, but more difficult to cluster the versicolor and virginica species uniquely. Or, if you're talking about learning, it would suggest that it's easier to learn which flowers are setosa, but more difficult to differentiate the versicolor and virginica flowers. So, when you're finding a learning algorithm, this is likely where the error's going to be.

# Constructing distances

One thing that's nice about low-dimensional representations is that we can construct distances using any metric we want, and we can find a representation that we can use.

So, we have the `headlines` dataset, we will use Jaccard similarity to describe headlines and how similar they are, and we can use Jaccard dissimilarity to describe the distance between two headlines. We can also use multidimensional scaling to come up with coordinates so that we can visualize the relationship between the headlines.

We will use the following lines of code:

```
In [7]: headlines = pd.read_csv("HNHeadlines.txt", header=None, index_col=0).iloc[:, 0]
        headline_sets = [set(''.join(u) for u in ngrams(h.lower(), 3)) for h in headlines]
        sims = np.zeros((len(headlines), len(headlines)))
        for i in range(len(headlines)):
            for j in range(i, len(headlines)):
                h1, h2 = headline_sets[i], headline_sets[j]
                js = len(h1.intersection(h2))/len(h1.union(h2))
                sims[i,j] = sims[j,i] = js
```

We then use MDS, as follows:

```
In [8]: headline_mds = MDS(n_components=2, dissimilarity="precomputed")
        headlines_coords = headline_mds.fit_transform(1 - sims)
        headlines_coords[:5, :]
```

This results in the following array:

```
Out[8]:  array([[ 0.57954399, -0.01404295],
                [ 0.37567116, -0.55421608],
                [-0.54387427, -0.01477595],
                [ 0.69126401,  0.06637165],
                [ 0.58300877, -0.19390756]])
```

Now, we can actually come up with a plot to visualize the relationship between the headlines:

```
In [9]:  plt.scatter(x=headlines_coords[:, 0], y=headlines_coords[:, 1])
         plt.show()
```

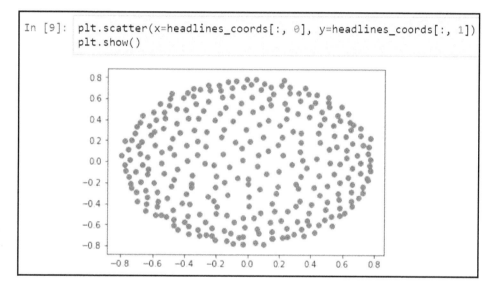

It's not exactly clear here, because of the dimensions of the plot, but this is actually circular, because this plot isn't exactly a square; this looks more oval-shaped. It almost looks like all the points are roughly equidistant from one another. It's like all the points are uniformly distributed over this circle. There may be a little bit of clustering toward the edges, but I believe that's more an artifact of the scaling than an actual property of the dataset.

So, what should we take away from this? Well, to me, this is telling me why we were having some difficulty trying to cluster the dataset. The way we're describing distance between headlines doesn't lend itself very well to clustering; no natural clusters form. So, that means that, when we're clustering the datasets, it'll look like all the clusters are very close to one another, and headlines could easily have fallen into a different cluster. This might suggest that we should be using anything other than 3-grams on Jaccard distance to describe the relationship between our headlines. We might want to look into some other ways to differentiate between them if we want to have meaningful clustering and learning. That concludes this section, and along with that, this book.

# Summary

This brings us to the end of the book. In this chapter, we learned all about dimensionality reduction and its various uses. We learned about PCA and applied it to the Boston dataset. We then learned about SVD and used it to compress an image. Finally, we learned about low-dimensional representation and MDS, and applied it to the `iris` dataset.

We have covered a lot of topics related to statistical modelling in this book, which should help you to analyze data more efficiently. You now have the ability to make sense of huge collections of data more easily than ever before. I hope this book has helped you in your quest to become a statistician or data scientist!

# Other Books You May Enjoy

If you enjoyed this book, you may be interested in these other books by Packt:

**Hands-On Data Analysis with NumPy and Pandas**
Curtis Miller

ISBN: 9781789530797

- Understand how to install and manage Anaconda
- Read, sort, and map data using NumPy and pandas
- Find out how to create and slice data arrays using NumPy
- Discover how to subset your DataFrames using pandas
- Handle missing data in a pandas DataFrame
- Explore hierarchical indexing and plotting with pandas

## Statistical Application Development with R and Python - Second Edition
Prabhanjan Narayanachar Tattar

ISBN: 9781788621199

- Learn the nature of data through software with preliminary concepts right away in R
- Read data from various sources and export the R output to other software
- Perform effective data visualization with the nature of variables and rich alternative options
- Do exploratory data analysis for useful first sight understanding building up to the right attitude towards effective inference
- Learn statistical inference through simulation combining the classical inference and modern computational power
- Delve deep into regression models such as linear and logistic for continuous and discrete regressands for forming the fundamentals of modern statistics
- Introduce yourself to CART – a machine learning tool which is very useful when the data has an intrinsic nonlinearity

# Leave a review - let other readers know what you think

Please share your thoughts on this book with others by leaving a review on the site that you bought it from. If you purchased the book from Amazon, please leave us an honest review on this book's Amazon page. This is vital so that other potential readers can see and use your unbiased opinion to make purchasing decisions, we can understand what our customers think about our products, and our authors can see your feedback on the title that they have worked with Packt to create. It will only take a few minutes of your time, but is valuable to other potential customers, our authors, and Packt. Thank you!

# Index

principal components 250
probability density function (PDF) 42
proportions
  Bayesian hypothesis testing 37
  classical inference 18
  comparing 38, 39, 40
  confidence intervals, computing for 19, 20
  conjugate priors 32, 34, 35
  credible intervals 35, 37
  hypothesis testing 20, 21
  testing 22

# R

R-squared 152
radial basis function (RBF) similarity 240
random forests
  about 112
  hyperparameters, optimizing 114, 115, 116, 117
  multiple outcomes 135
recall 84
recurrent neural networks 192
regression
  demonstrating, neural networks used 201, 202
reinforcement learning 62
ridge regression
  about 164, 166
  right alpha value, finding 167, 168

# S

samples
  testing with 27, 28, 51
scikit-learn (sklearn) 72
SciPy
  using, for Spline interpolation 173, 177
silhouette method 224, 225, 226, 227

similarity score 229
singular value decomposition (SVD)
  about 254, 255
  for image compression 256, 257, 258, 259, 260
  low-rank approximation 260, 261, 262
spectral clustering
  about 238
  Headlines dataset, clustering 241, 242, 244
Spline interpolation
  2D interpolation 177, 180, 183
  about 172, 173
  SciPy, using for 173, 177
supervised learning
  about 62, 206
  goals 68, 69, 70
support vector machine (SVM)
  about 62, 123, 124, 187
  hyperparameters 124
  implementing 125, 126
  training 127, 128, 129
  training, that uses one-versus-one 139, 140

# T

target variable 62

# U

underfitting 71
uninformative prior 33
unsupervised learning 62, 206

# V

variables
  checking, iris dataset used 62, 63, 64, 65, 67, 68

www.ingramcontent.com/pod-product-compliance
Lightning Source LLC
LaVergne TN
LVHW081519050326
832903LV00025B/1547